D1356907

The First Wash of Spring

George Mackay Brown

The First Wash of Spring

Steve Savage
LONDON AND EDINBURGH

Steve Savage Publishers Ltd
The Old Truman Brewery
91 Brick Lane
LONDON
E1 6QL

www.savagepublishers.com

Published in Great Britain by Steve Savage Publishers Ltd 2006

ISBN-10: 1-904246-25-7
ISBN-13: 978-1-904246-25-1

Typeset by Steve Savage Publishers Ltd
Printed and bound by The Cromwell Press Ltd

Contents

6

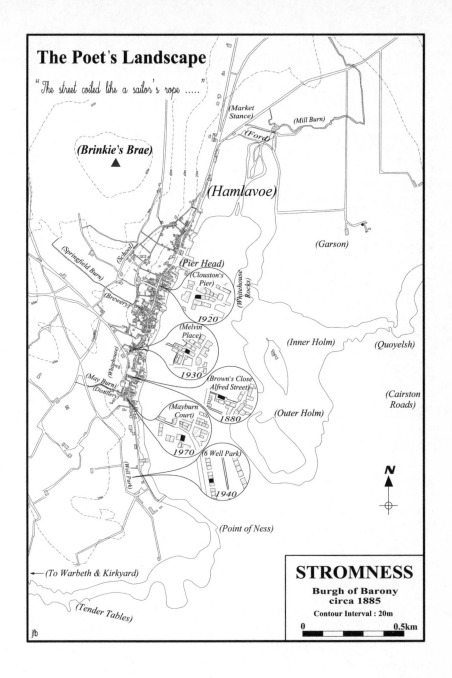

The Poet's Landscape

" The street coiled like a sailor's rope ..... "

(Market Stance)

(Mill Burn)

(Ford)

(Brinkie's Brae)

(Hamlavoe)

(Garson)

(Springfield Burn)

(School)

(Pier Head)

(Clouston's Pier)

(Whitehouse Rocks)

(Brewery)

1920

(Melvin Place)

(Inner Holm)

(Quoyelsh)

1930

(Whitehouse)

(Brown's Close Alfred Street)

(Cairston Roads)

(May Burn)

(Distillery)

(Mayburn Court)

1880

(Outer Holm)

1970

(6 Well Park)

(Well Park)

1940

N

(Point of Ness)

← *(To Warbeth & Kirkyard)*

(Tender Tables)

jfb

STROMNESS

**Burgh of Barony
circa 1885**

Contour Interval : 20m

0   0.5km

Introduction

'These "Letters" (I protested) were never meant to be given the permanence of book covers; far less to be "cuttings in stone" ... they were light reading for quiet townsfolk on a Thursday afternoon ...'

George Mackay Brown's Introduction to *Letters from Hamnavoe* detailed his reservations about reprinting what he considered relatively lightweight, ephemeral articles in the islands' newspaper, *The Orcadian*. So popular did the first collection (1975) and its successor, *Under Brinkie's Brae* (1979) turn out to be, that by the time *Rockpools and Daffodils* was mooted (1992), he was eager to satisfy readers' calls for another volume, substantially thicker than the first two.

The present collection offers 171 essays selected from the writer's weekly columns, starting almost immediately where *Rockpools and Daffodils* left off (December, 1991) and ending with the feature which appeared on 11 April 1996, the last one GMB wrote (on 3 April, well in advance of publication date, as always). It completes a Hamnavoe Quartet of weekly despatches, many significantly longer than those in the earlier gatherings. Unsurprisingly, subject range and quality of writing continue to impress, as favourite themes are revisited, alongside the correspondent's reactions to new developments at home and abroad. While his first three anthologies of extracts contained for the most part models of stimulating compression, the extra space available – and desired – in his last years enabled him to produce extended pieces.

These can be regarded, primarily, as free-standing letters, each with its own theme, action, tensions and structural integrity; each one compact, focused and pointed – high-sounding claims perhaps for work undertaken at the same time week after week, whatever its author's health or mood, and readers will decide how far they are justified. When the pieces are taken cumulatively, however, their overall unity of place and consistently recurring motifs can be seen to inform and reflect GMB's habit of thought and distinctive world-view.

'My country is between Ness Road and the Pier Head' (16 September 1993) does summarise conveniently how the 'Stromness-born-and-bred' writer loved to identify, dwell on and record characters, scenes and events from his early years and from the life described by the previous generation. An excursion into the past would often be suggested by a chance observation from the seaward – and street – facing window, from which the weather was assessed each morning, and at intervals throughout the day. There are many such episodes here.

But GMB's 'country' was also the larger one of wherever people were suffering or being tyrannised. Aware of where and how this was happening, he was prepared to confront and condemn – not in a general way (as he sometimes used to rail against 'Progress') but pointing the finger at specific situations and régimes.

Then there is the increasing number of 'bulletins' about his own health. Described vividly, often with a touch of humour, these ailments clearly did not diminish the appetite for work, for friendship and general well-being traceable throughout the following essays. We learn a good deal more about George Mackay Brown from this volume, it may be suggested, than he was ready to communicate in many of his longer autobiographical compositions.

It is to be hoped that readers will find *The First Wash of Spring* well up to the standard of its predecessors, and that it succeeds in the same aims of communication and entertainment that animated the three earlier volumes.

Thanks are expressed to Dr John Flett Brown, GMB's nephew, for the map which depicts both the Stromness of the writer's parents and locations important to the writer himself.

BRIAN MURRAY
Stromness, November 2006

An Orkney Scrooge

26 December 1991

I think there ought to be an Orkney variant of the marvellous Scrooge story.

How about this?

There was a farmer and he had inherited a big farm and the older he got the more miserable and tight-fisted he became. He didn't altogether trust banks – he liked to see and touch his wealth, and to make the gold coins ring like a bell in his money-bags!

This miserly old bachelor had a farm servant called Jock who lived in a hovel two fields away, and did all the farm work. Jock had a hard-working wife and a lot of bairns. Jock was paid mostly in kind, for the miser couldn't bear to part with money.

Spending a sovereign was almost like tearing his heart out by the roots – it gave him so much pain.

Well, this midwinter the old farmer felt a cold coming on, and he knew the time-honoured way of curing a cold: hot toddy. This meant he would have to walk to the village inn for a bottle of 'Old Orkney' whisky, price two shillings and sixpence. Well, it couldn't be helped. He took a half-crown out of the stone jar on his mantelpiece, and set out through the snow to the village.

On the way he had to pass Jock's peedie[1] croft, and he heard the laughter of Jock's bairns inside, and a verse or two of a Christmas carol, and Jock had been foolish and extravagant enough to have two lamps burning, and an enormous peat-fire on the hearth you could have roasted a sheep at! ... The old man going past thought, 'I'll have a word wi' that fool Jock in the morning.'

When he got to the inn, there were a few of his 'yamils'[2] there, men he had sat with in the island school sixty years before. They were poor men too – fishermen and crofters – but they bade him welcome. The old man asked for a bottle of 'Old Orkney'. Before he knew what was happening half a dozen glasses of whisky were

1 little
2 contemporaries

there on the bar counter beside him: Yuletide drams from his childhood friends.

Well, he wasn't going to pour away such good whisky. He poured them down his throat, one after the other, pocketed his bottle of 'Old Orkney' and set forth into the night.

And, as it happened, into oblivion...

When he sobered up at midnight, he saw to his horror by the light of the stars that he was lying among tombstones in the kirkyard. And he traced with his finger the names of islanders who had passed away through the decades, and one name gave him a pang in the heart – for it was the name of his early sweetheart, that he had thought of marrying for a lyrical month or two – only in the end he had decided that a wife would be too much of an expense...

How he got home that night, he never knew.

But as he passed Jock's door, he knocked and handed in the bottle of malt. And Jock was so astonished he almost dropped it on the flagstones.

Next morning, when Jock turned up – a bit apprehensive, for he thought maybe his master had gone off his head – twenty gold sovereigns were counted into his hand. 'For,' said the old farmer, 'I've been cheating you for twenty years at least...' Then he raxed[1] into the stone jar and counted six shillings into Jock's hand, one for each of the bairns. 'And this crown piece,' said he, 'is for your bonny, cheerful, hard-working wife Bella-Ann.'

After a while he said to Jock, 'Do you think I could come and have a bowl of Bella-Ann's broth for my dinner? And say *A good Yule* to you all at your own fireside...'

And after that he lived for a few winters, a merry old man.

Hogmanay 1891

2 January 1992

Imagine some Stromnessian waking up in the last days of a century ago – 1891.

He would probably wake up in a steep narrow house beside the sea that held another half-dozen or so folk. There would be no wireless beside his bed to listen to the news on. He would hardly know what was happening in the great world outside. He would be aware that he was a part of the far-flung British Empire, ruled over by the apparently ageless Queen Victoria. However poor he might be, he felt a kind of pride in belonging to this 'chosen people'.

The day called Christmas was just past, but that was of small importance. The shops and offices had been open for business all that day. But he remembered the old folk recently dead talking about the marvellous Yuletides of half a century before, that went on – especially in the country districts (Innertoon and Ootertoon and Cairston and Quholm and Kirbister) – for days on end – very solemn but joyous festivals.

There was Hogmanay to look forward to – a fairly recent import from Scotland – and the New Year first-footing. He would have to buy his bottle of 'Old Orkney' or 'Old Man of Hoy' malt whisky from one or other of the dozen taverns along the street. The whisky was distilled in MacPherson Brothers' distillery where Mayburn Court now stands: it cost half a crown a bottle. Of course his wife would have put a strong brew on some weeks beforehand, to cheer the hearts of neighbours. (For I rather think first-footing was an affair of neighbours and close friends rather than the roving troops of the late twentieth century.)

If our Stromnessian of a hundred years ago was a working man, he may not have been able to afford a goose or a roast of beef for the New Year table – unless, as was possible, he had a kind cousin who was a farmer in Ootertoon or Stenness. But he and his wife would have *tried* to have something special. They wouldn't have starved, for there was fish in plenty – but fish was on the table three or four times a week throughout the year...

So, this Stromness man went to his work – maybe at the Ness boat-building yard (Stanger's) – in the last days of 1891; and of course there were snowflakes falling at eight o'clock in the morning and his fellow-townsmen went past him like spectres.

He thought, 'How grand to have the street paved, not like twenty years ago when we were up to our knees in iper[1]'... Coming home tired at 5pm, he thought, 'How grand, to have the street lit with gas lamps, instead of just a random star or two.'

And, after they had had their tea – fried haddocks and bere bannocks – he might have enjoyed reading a book beside the paraffin lamp; but most of the books in the Public Library were of an 'improving' or 'uplifting' character. Besides, it was hard to concentrate with the half-dozen bairns at their loud disputatious fireside games... He thought, wistfully and fleetingly, of slipping out to Billy Clouston's bar or the

Masons' Arms; but last time he had tried that game his wife Merran had met him at the door with a hard fist and a yell!... Besides, it might be a good idea to save his thirst for the first-footing neighbours, each bringing a lump of coal and a piece of shortbread and a bottle.

How wonderful – the twentieth century with all its promise of progress without end was only eight years in the future!

New Year Resolutions

9 January 1992

A man rang me from a well-known Sunday newspaper wanting to know what New Year resolutions I had made, one afternoon last week.

Well, that fairly caught me on the hop, for I have long grown out of making New Year resolutions – knowing the futility of those solemn vows: that are lucky if they are still operant and gleaming with achievement on Twelfth Night.

'I will definitely stop smoking' (a hard one that)... 'I will drink only tea and beer and never spirits' (that one's lucky if it lasts beyond the first of January)... 'I will read such-and-such an author and listen to the tapes of this other neglected composer' (but in such matters it is best, I think, to follow the heart's affections and not the will's)... 'I will try to be nice to such-and-such a person (but in the end the best thing may be not to court the company of the said fellow human being – and, on the rare occasions of meeting, strive to be courteous, at least)...

Such are a few typical resolutions – not necessarily my own.

So we all delude ourselves that we will be bright new people in this new time, not the thralls of boredom and bad habits that we've been too long, in the past.

Alas, for the frailty of the human will, unaided.

So I had to mumble out, over the phone, something like the above to the *Scotland on Sunday* journalist – and that can have been of little use to him – unless he wrote that GMB of Stromness, Orkney has made a resolution to make no resolutions.

But even that isn't quite true. For two summers past I haven't visited that spring of inspiration and beauty and delight, the sea valley of Rackwick in Hoy. I hope I might be able to go there in summer 1992 – to talk to David Hutchison and his dogs Glen and Lady, and to Jack and Dorothy and Lucy Rendall, and to Max Davies[1] if he's there at Bunertoon weaving his music.

1 Peter Maxwell Davies, the composer

Lovely it'll be to cross the burn with the irises and climb up the gentle slope of Greenhill; and to find a way across those enormous spheroids of sea-sculpted stone, and come at last to the sands that sing under your feet ... that could be a good resolution.

Many a time, idly walking through Stromness, it has seemed a good idea to visit some of the piers we haven't stood on since childhood. Or to climb up some of the closes on the Brinkie's Brae side. (Always nowadays one is a bit afraid of intruding on people's privacy. The closes and piers are not quite such public places as they were fifty years ago.)

That could be another resolution.

It must be four or five years since I was last on the top of Brinkie's Brae, which has one of the finest views in Orkney. Last time we tried, there had been such heavy rain in the days preceding, that we sank up to our ankles in mud on the path beyond Grieveship and had to turn back... To get to the summit of Brinkie's Brae might be a joyful resolution for 1992.

Apart from such simple adventures in prospect, I have made no other resolutions – not even to stop beating my wife.

The Day Lengthens

16 January 1992

Now we're past Twelfth Night (Epiphany); and so Christmas ends; except for the Shetlanders with their Up-Helly-Aa on the last Tuesday of January. (I suppose Up-Helly-Aa means, roughly, the end of the Holy-time.)

Santa Claus will be well on his way back to his toy factory, the reindeer making heavy weather of it among the heaped and broken ice-floes.

'As the day lengthens / The cowld strengthens,' the old folk used to say. And they were right. We sit waiting for a snowfall, the children with delight, the old folk with apprehension... Of late years, the magic stuff out of the sky has been scanty – or if it fell as it did two winters ago on 28 February, in sudden abundance, it was gone again like a white dream; as if it could hear, faint and far away, the trumpets of spring faintly blowing.

The day is lengthening, perceptibly. Two afternoons ago, driving to Kirbister at 4.30, there was that faint primrose in the sky beyond the hill Kringlafiold... By about two minutes a day we are hastening towards midsummer and Johnsmas.

Of course there's Robbie Burns day to come later in the month. More of that maybe next week. I wonder if the magic of Burns is as potent for young folk nowadays. I wonder how long the pop lyrics of the late twentieth century will compare with the 'immortal diamond' of 'Mary Morison', 'A Red Red Rose', 'O, Wert Thou in the Cauld Blast'...

In January in my childhood, in Stromness Primary School, the children who lived in Ootertoon and probably The Loons had to be let go early in the afternoon, so they could get home before dark... I sometimes think of those five-year-olds, battling through winter storms along country roads with their schoolbags on their backs. I think most of them had a piece to eat at playtime, and there was a soup kitchen in the Domestic Science Hall (what a grand name!) where some town children as well as country children got something hot to sup at one o'clock.

We town pupils wondered, but only briefly, about the bairns from farms under the Black Craig leaving the classroom early on January afternoons ... I suppose there may still have been a folk memory of the sudden blizzards that smoored[1] folk and flocks and covered them up like the Harray men who died in the snow on the lonely Evie road two centuries ago or longer.

Anyway, for us town bairns in January there was only a brief helter-skelter home to the range with the coal burning in it and the paraffin lamp on the dresser, and the cat licking itself on the rag mat.

Captain Gow Meets Miss Gordon

30 January 1992

Mrs Gordon was to give a reception to the master of the *George*, the fine ship anchored in front of the Holms two days now.

It was not that Mr and Mrs Gordon gave a dinner to all the ships' masters who called at Hamnavoe – that would have been too much – but the master of the *George* had exchanged respects with one or two of the village's leading merchants at the water-front, and – lo and behold! – the man had turned out to be a son of William Gow, lately (until his death) a respectable merchant in the town; the ship-master had gone away to sea, like many another Orkney boy, twelve years before, and nothing had been heard of him since... This was no uncommon thing, though: young men were lost in foreign seas,

1 covered, smothered

or they were carried off with scurvy or typhoid, or it may be that they settled down in Leith or Liverpool or London with a wife and saw no chance of getting back to Orkney again. Write a letter? Few sailors in those days could read or write. The only chance of communicating would be if they saw some ship Orkney-bound in a harbour somewhere, and could get a word with any Orkneyman who happened to be on board.

But this was a bit strange – young John Gow had had as good an education as his father could afford. He had sat in the same classroom as some of the sons of the Orkney gentry – James Fea of Eday, for example... There was no reason why John Gow couldn't have written home to tell his father how fortune was dealing with him on the great oceans of the world.

But let that be, meantime. Over the dinner table in the evening Captain Gow would have many exciting things to impart to them, no doubt.

Mrs Gordon's servants were polishing the silver. A large plump salmon was being prepared in the kitchen, and a joint of best lamb. Mr James Gordon had gone to visit a fellow merchant along the muddy street – for it was deep winter, January, and sleet and flung spindrift during the recent storm had made the street a quagmire – the merchant Mr Gordon was calling on had the best stock in Orkney of French brandies and wines, and Hollands-gin (all lately smuggled).

There was a young daughter of the house, but her parents considered her too fine a girl to soil her hands with kitchen work. Thora Gordon sat in her room and sometimes tinkled on the clavichord and sometimes worked at her embroidery frame. In due course, sooner rather than later, a husband would have to be found for the girl: the hard-working son of some local merchant, or one of the better-off farmers from round about.

There would be no question of marrying her off to a Kirkwall man – at that time relations between Kirkwall and Hamnavoe were not at all harmonious. It all came down to the question of Kirkwall's commercial authority over Stromness. There would be hard inter-town battles to be fought in the law courts soon.

Now, the lamps being lit, everything was ready to receive Captain Gow.

There was a knock at the door.

Host and guest greeted each other cordially.

Mrs Gordon glimpsed for the first time a dark handsome face. She saw at once that he was charming and courteous – and yet there

17

was something about him that she didn't altogether take to: a hidden furtive dangerous desperate quality. How could this be?

Meantime there was a flutter on the stair. Miss Thora was descending in her fine blue satin gown.

When she saw the sailor she gasped in wonderment.

And this is the beginning of the tragic tale of John Gow the pirate and his sweetheart Miss Gordon, in that fatal year of 1726.

'Snowdrops Are Out'

6 February 1992

'Snowdrops are out,' I've heard two or three folk saying this past week... And the January weather has been so mild, it's no wonder the little white shy blossoms have shown themselves, thinking that spring must be here. Alas, we are scarcely past the middle of winter, and there may well be bitter blasts and sharp frosts to come. And then the innocent flowers will wish they had kept their heads low for a few weeks yet.

Ideally, I suppose, the snowdrops should only be appearing when the last snow is wasting in the darkest corners of the garden.

But the winters seem all mixter-maxter[1] these past few years.

Small snow in winter – small sun in summer. That seems to be the general rule. This past decade, there is no firm definition of the seasons.

I think it must be an illusion, that all our childhood winters were thick and dazzling with snow, and our summers brimming over with light and warmth... These are the benign tricks that memory plays. The memory can so entrance and beguile that a great poet like Wordsworth could convince himself, and all those reading his 'Immortality' ode, that everyone's childhood is 'apparelled in celestial light'.

Anyway, good luck to the brave little snowdrops who have shown themselves before the first plucking of Mother Carey's chickens (a phrase rarely heard nowadays, meaning the first snowfall)... It may be – it may just be – that they will get off with it. Two years ago Mother Carey plucked her chickens on the very last day of winter – 28 February – and what wild whirls and swirls of whiteness there were that afternoon... Two days, and the sudden enchantment was gone, almost before the children had time to get the sledges out of the garden sheds. The late snow never lies long.

1 higgledy-piggledy

All winter a bowl of black earth has been lying in the cupboard under the stair, away from the light and the warmth. It contained daffodil bulbs given me on a birthday in October.

Most of the time I forgot about that bowl. Occasionally, in the darkening days, I gave it a passing glance, getting a lump or two of coal or throwing some packaging into the bin: and the bowl was all cold and dark as the grave... I got a slight start of surprise two weeks ago or so, to see little pale shoots breaking surface everywhere – indeed, they must have been an inch high. What was to be done with those small stirrings of life?

I was advised to take the terracotta bowl out of the cupboard into the light of the living-room. So that has been done, after breakfast this morning. The nascent daffodils have pride of place in the centre of the table, among books and candle-ends and papers.

How long will it be, I wonder, till the serene golden heads open, and the house is filled with springtime light? Possibly some time in the middle of February. Those daffodils are protected; they do not have the rash bravery of the little snowdrops that are appearing too soon in so many Orkney gardens.

All the spring flowers are too beautiful for words.

Assault by Media

13 February 1992

From morning to night you get assaulted on radio, TV and newspapers about all the hideous things that are happening in the world – bombings in Ulster, famine in Ethiopia, civil war in Somalia, Kurds perishing in the mountains, killing avalanches in Turkey, unemployment worldwide... The thought came to me yesterday, 'Now, if we'd been living in Orkney a century ago, we'd know nothing of all this. A few middle-class folk who got *The Scotsman* a week late might read it in the headlines but their eyes would glance lightly across it...' Is it better to know how things truly are in the world, or to remain cocooned (as our grandfathers were) in their own little world? They had problems enough in that little world to worry about, without taking in every cataclysm from China to Peru.

It isn't an easy thing to decide.

I imagine the average Orcadian of a century ago, however poor he might be – and assuredly he was much poorer materially than the average Orcadian today – didn't worry at all about the great world outside. Instead, he was a great chauvinist. The British race were the new chosen people. 'Land of Hope and Glory' was the great anthem, written by a third-rate poet called A. C. Benson:

> Land of hope and glory, Mother of the Free,
> How shall we extol thee, who are born of thee?
> Wider still and wider shall thy bounds be set;
> God who made thee mighty, make thee mightier yet!...

So a Hamnavoe worker might hum to himself, well pleased with the world, on a Monday morning, although he had hardly a sixpence in his pocket for a pint of beer in Billy Clouston's bar at the day's end.

Wider still and wider? Well, it seemed there might be some trouble sooner or later with the Boers in South Africa... And yes, the Yanks had ungratefully turned their backs on us a hundred years earlier – but look what had befallen them, a terrible civil war that had been the death of hundreds of thousands!... The Indians had mutinied in mid-century, but we had soon settled their hash... Not much trouble with the old enemy France lately – the Prussians (who were our blood-cousins after all) had recently taught them a good sharp lesson... and weren't we spreading our enlightenment among the Chinese and the Eskimos?

We, a generation later, were never taught racial superiority at school, but there it was, in every classroom, a world map liberally splashed with the red of the British Empire. And our innocent little eyes looked, and grew large in wonderment.

Now at least we know that we who inhabit the earth are all akin to one another, and must ultimately share in one another's sorrows and joys.

Watching the TV news, it is the world sorrows that are flung at us in generous dollops week after week. Either this way of presenting world events makes people at last indifferent and they grow a carapace; or else sensitive people feel that they are existing precariously at the edge of some black hole of bottomless suffering, that must eventually engulf everything.

I suppose it is difficult to convey that wonderful things are happening hourly and daily all over the world too; compassion, bravery, kindness, altruism, goodness – that (we must hope) more than outweigh the horror and the wickedness. But readers of *The Sun* don't want to read that.

The Unheard Anthem

20 February 1992

Not every Academy pupil knows that there is a school song, and not in tepid run-of-the-mill English either, but in *Latin*.

I was reminded of the anthem last night when my ex-classmate Ian MacInnes (who in the end was of course headmaster of Stromness Academy) phoned to ask if I remembered any of the words.

They are probably printed somewhere, and lying gathering cobwebs in some cupboard or drawer in Stromness.

Anyway, Ian remembered lines from the second verse, of which only a word or two had lodged in my mind. But I remember distinctly the opening verse:

> *Nobis est amicus pontus,*
> *Tecta nobis Boreas.*
> *Habitamus Orcadenses,*
> *Insulas pulcherrimas.*
> Chorus   *Floreat Stromnessia,*
> *Floreat in saecula!*

A rough translation might be:

> Our friend is the sea,
> Our home is the north.
> We live in the Orkneys,
> Most beautiful islands.
> May Stromness flourish,
> May it flourish in the future!

It is not a very old song going back to the beginning of Stromness Academy (or Stromness Secondary School, as it was until 1937 or so). I think possibly it was composed to celebrate the completion of the refurbished school about that time. It was a great opening, performed by an ex-pupil, Professor Drever of the Psychology Department of Edinburgh University... It lingers in my mind that Professor Drever opened the school with a golden key – but that might only be memory gilding the scene.

Anyway, there we stood, hundreds of pupils, while this awesome ceremony went forward for our benefit (though at the time we didn't see much good coming out of it, personally speaking).

There one day stood our Latin master, Mr William Ritchie, writing those strange verses on the blackboard, that we would be expected to learn by heart. Mr Ritchie had composed the words of the new school anthem.

I'm afraid I was rather in trouble that morning, because I laughed at the strange verse (more out of wonderment than mischief) and Mr Ritchie was anything but pleased with me.

However, we duly learned the school song by heart, and whenever there was a school prizegiving (I think) or any other official ceremony, there we belted it forth for all it was worth.

One noteworthy thing about the tune is that it had been composed by Beethoven, and was in fact the choral movement (the 'Ode to Joy') of the Ninth Symphony.

I'm not surprised that *'Floreat Stromnessia!'* is no longer sung in Stromness Academy, which is no longer at Brinkie's Brae but at Garson; for Latin is no longer taught there. No longer do the Gallic *Commentaries* come rolling off youthful tongues, *'Omnia Gallia in tres partes divisa est'*... or Virgil's magnificent opening *'Arma virumque cano'*...

Escape from Westminster

27 February 1992

One of the good things about going to bed was that you could listen to a radio programme and so get wafted pleasantly into sleep. (I rarely shift the wavelength from Radio 4, lest I get lost in the jungle of wavelengths.)

For months past, all I've been hearing at night is 'Today in Parliament'. Even at its best, this is one of the most boring programmes conceivable – worse than boring, because so many people have been disturbed by the zoo and barnyard noises emanating from this 'Mother of Parliaments' when debates are going on.

For many weeks past, with an election certain some time this spring, the prolonged electioneering has been unbearable.

In the old days, a General Election would be announced three weeks or so beforehand, and the general melée thereafter was to be expected, but it was short and sharp and soon over... We could in fact be sure of one night of pure entertainment when the results came pouring in from over 600 constituencies, and the 'swingometer' shifted this way and that, and the party pundits gravely debated the way the tide was setting – some of them exulting, some of them putting a brave face on it... In those days, in exchange for three weeks of electioneering, you could be sure of that one thrilling night till 3am, either in front of the TV or listening to the radio in bed.

But in 1992, I wonder how many folk will be so fed up of it all, month after month, that they'll hardly bother to vote...

A week ago or so, I decided that I could take no more of 'Today in Parliament' in the half-hour before midnight, so I began to span the dial on different wavelengths. There were pop-singers making demented noises, which was on the whole rather worse than the MPs in Westminster. Another twirl of the knob, and it was a militant feminist; that was worse still.

The air-waves seemed to be full of goblins and monsters.

Never despair, though. Another little flick, and a gentle civilised voice said we would be having some music by a Czech composer... I didn't know the music but it sounded good to me; and on that gentle tide I drifted sleepwards.

So, I thought, it *is* possible to escape from Westminster.

Sometimes in the afternoon, after the morning's work, and as befitting a senior citizen, I go to bed for an hour in the afternoon.

Quite often, there are entertaining programmes – a play, or 'Kaleidoscope' in the afternoon. Complacently, I switched the bedside radio on, and to my horror the announcer said we were to have 'Today in Parliament', live...

Nothing doing. Silence was infinitely to be preferred. If one listened hard enough, there was through the window an almighty chorus in the Farafield tree not far away. Even in the depths of winter, those hundreds of songsters are thronging the air with their carillons... And then suddenly they are up and away, like a drift of smoke.

I think it was probably a bad idea when MPs decided they were good enough to be on radio and TV.

Swung Gently through the Years

5 March 1992

Some folk – generations of them – have been sitting in this rocking-chair for well over a century, I should think.

Where countless thumbs have rested over the decades, the round wooden arm-bar is worn smooth on the right side, but the left side doesn't show so much wear. Obviously, when one is agitated or happy or merely ticking over, it is the right thumb that caresses the woodwork, in sympathy with the motions of mind or mood.

I don't know where the rocking-chair originated. I've been told, it's in the American style. All I know for sure is that a quarter of a century ago a cousin of mine left Stromness for London and she gave me the rocker.

It wasn't in the best of shapes then, but kind friends from time to time have polished it and covered it in what one journalist called 'cardinal purple'. And so I swung gently on it through the years, reading books, listening to tapes, talking to friends, drinking cups of tea (mugs of home-brewed ale it used to be, until about ten years ago).

The rocking-chair is a very delicate structure. You can hear it creaking gently when you lower yourself into it. I try to head off my six-foot-high, sixteen-stone friends from it, in case the whole structure flies asunder. But it has borne such rugby-forward physiques, up to now.

Children, of course, make for the rocker as soon as they enter the room, and they send it galloping like a thoroughbred in the Grand National. But the rocker seems to enjoy children and their carry-ons.

A few weeks ago disaster struck. Well, not disaster – a minor inconvenience; but shocking all the same.

I was sitting on my rocker when the whole right arm gave way – there it was, swinging out like a broken bridge.

I thought, dolefully, 'This is the end of my rocking-chair. It's breaking up. It will go to light the fire on a few mornings next week... What'll I do for my hour of rest after that?' ... I was very melancholy about it, I can tell you.

But then my friend Surinder came, and he said there was nothing seriously wrong – the dowel had come out of its socket, all it needed was some glue to hold it. So my friend Renée came along with some special glue, and the dislocated arm of the rocker was quickly set, and it has held firm ever since.

And that old rocking-chair will still be riding folk into meditation or gentle slumber or enjoyment of books and music till far on in the twenty-first century, maybe.

Sometimes, when I am feeling happy, I sing a wonderful blues song from the thirties: 'Old rocking-chair's gonna get me...' The sentiment is melancholy, but the music is full of joy.

Signs of Spring

12 March 1992

Everybody has different definitions of the seasons – the quarterings of the year.

Yesterday I recognised with a quickening of the blood that it was the first of March – spring!

Oh, I know we'll have two or three wintry blasts between now and mid-May, but all the same I think, with the last day of February, 'That's an end of winter!'... And as you get older, to have broken through into another springtime is a triumph.

The snowdrops have been around for weeks, and the first crocuses are showing, and it won't be long till daffodil time.

In fact, 'those flowers made of light' are brightening many a boreal house as I write.

I was given a bowl of daffodil bulbs for my birthday in October, and instructed to keep them in the dark, in the cupboard under the stairs.

I quite forgot about them in the depths of winter.

But one morning, when I went to get firewood in the cupboard, there were a few pale shoots poking out. Another few days, and they were higher and greener, and more of them.

So then I was told to bring them into the warmth of the living-room, and water them more often.

They responded at once, like a fountain of greenness, rising higher every morning. And there they were, the future flowers, like furled yellow umbrellas.

The first daffodil opened, with a soundless shout of joy.

Then they came out like stars, jostling and leaping, one after the other.

They came with such a rush, in tha\t heavy surge of greenery, that presently the blossoms were leaning at all angles, as if they were quite intoxicated with the new light coming to them from all three windows.

It was time to bind them with a piece of string – though a silk cord would have more befitted such splendour ... but after a few days, even that cincture wasn't enough to hold them, and they had to be bound up again, almost under their glorious chins.

And still there are buds to open. The song of the daffodils isn't over yet.

Of course, those house daffodils have been mollycoddled compared to the wild daffodils of the Orkney ditches.

We'll have to wait for a week or two yet before they stitch the fields and hills and moors with their golden lace.

It has been worth enduring winter for, to see that wind-and-sun-and-rain-blessed beauty.

Sea Haven amid Storms

19 March 1992

The storm has howled all night about the Hamnavoe houses.

What can it be like, on the Pentland Firth this morning? Two friends are leaving for Italy. Two friends are arriving from Ayr.

The light outside the curtained bedroom window glooms and glows alternately, in cold sunbursts and as the clouds go over.

As I listened to Radio Orkney, John Fergusson mentioned that there was a snow shower over Kirkwall.

It seems colder this morning – even in bed – than in the depths of winter... The poor daffodils in the ditches, struggling to come out! – The bravest of the early flowers, they 'take the winds of March with beauty'.

One thing has made memorable this spring in Stromness – the publication of Keith Allardyce and Bryce Wilson's *Sea Haven*.

It is a fine collection of photographs, and the accompanying text is deeply interesting and well written.

Stromnessians are very pleased with the book already. Locally it is bound to sell widely, and the summertime tourists will be delighted to have it.

Sea Haven is possibly the best book produced yet by The Orkney Press. It is not at all expensive, at £17.95. A bottle of malt whisky might cost you that, and be polished off by a few friends before midnight. Whereas *Sea Haven* will be handed down through generations of Stromnessians, with increasing delight and curiosity.

Over breakfast there was a cold fleeting brightness through the kitchen window.

The fan heater has boosted the temperature from 50° to 70°.

A pot of tea, wholemeal toast and an egg – what better way to begin the day?

I have just glanced through the window again – an ominous grey pall, and Orphir across the Clestrain Roads hidden by a cloud. When the wild westerly blows that cloud away, I expect we'll be seeing Orphir streaked with white.

My Hopedale friends will be halfway across the Pentland Firth, as I write this. My Distillery Close friends will be on their train, somewhere on a storm-swept Highland moor.

Well, I'm glad I don't even have to venture into Stromness today. It's fireside weather ...

Sometimes – very rarely – I juggle with the radio knob. How pleasant, on two or three mornings recently, to hear a warm pleasant rich Orkney voice – I'm not entirely sure about radio titles, but I suppose Ruby Rendall is a 'disc jockey'. Very good she is at it too – the best I've heard.

Long may she enchant the ears of Scotland – hers is the music of the Orkney accent at its best.

So now we're in for another kind of rough stormy weather – political – since the Prime Minister[1] announced the election date yesterday afternoon. As if we hadn't had enough of it already.

The SNP went into action quickly. There, on Stromness doorsteps last night, in pouring rain, stood the candidate, Frances McKie, handing out leaflets.

Thanks to the ex-pupils of Stromness Academy who sent me the Latin text of '*Floreat Stromnessia!*'... I also had a nice letter from our former Latin master, who wrote the words – William F. Ritchie, who now lives in Arbroath.

Stamp of a Private Man

26 March 1992

I see they are honouring the poet Tennyson with an issue of postage stamps on the centenary of his death.

I think Tennyson may be the third poet to be celebrated in this way. One of the very first illustrated stamps was for Burns. Then, two years ago, Hardy appeared.

The picture of Tennyson on the 24p stamp must be approximately as he looked when they gave him and W. E. Gladstone the Freedom of Kirkwall in the 1880s. The Poet Laureate and the great Liberal statesman had dropped by at Kirkwall from their yacht, the *Pembroke Castle*, on a holiday cruise to Kristiansand in Norway.

It couldn't have been much fun for Tennyson, who was a private man and of a melancholy disposition, to have his holiday cruise interrupted by the city fathers come to heap honours on him. He had arrived at that stage in life when honours mean little. He might have thought, with his own Lady of Shalott, 'I am half sick of shadows'... What he was wanting was a little rest, a change of scenery, the communion of the ocean. And here they were, coming to put this new unexpected wearisome burden on him.

No wonder the aged poet made such a gloomy forbidding impression on the citizens of Kirkwall, gathered along the way between the pier and the United Presbyterian Church – the largest building in town, as far as seating capacity went. One thinks of him striding along, his great cloak wrapped about him, looking neither right nor left. 'Tell them,' he said, 'that I won't make a speech – not a word or a syllable'...

His friend Mr Gladstone was only too willing to oblige. He spoke, in long rolling periods, for Tennyson and himself. And doubtless the citizens were enthralled.

I hadn't meant to go on so long about the freedom of Kirkwall – The statesman and the poet never stood under the shadow of Brinkie's Brae; there was no time; the *Pembroke Castle* had to set out across the North Sea.

Yet often, when I used to walk along the West Shore road, the lines of Tennyson came into my mind –

> But such a tide as moving seems asleep,
>   Too full for sound and foam,
> When that which drew from out the boundless deep
>   Turns again home...

Tennyson would have loved the brim of ocean between the Kame of Hoy and the Black Craig.

His marvellous poems are still among our happiest school memories – 'The Lady of Shalott', 'Morte d'Arthur', 'The Lotos Eaters', 'The Palace of Art', 'The Brook'...

He kept his silence. Unlike Sir Walter Scott, he left behind no scurrilous verses about the islands.

Unheeded Equinox

2 April 1992

The spring equinox came and went last weekend, and nobody paid any attention. It always seems to me to be a wonderful time, when the scales of light and darkness are held in perfect balance all over the world... But whereas we in the northern hemisphere are moving now into summer, in Australia and Argentina they are on the long road into winter.

So March 21 passed without celebration last Saturday. The excitement in Stromness came from the arrival of the new *St Ola*. I have just glimpsed it once in passing – it looked so huge, tied up at the North Pier. And yesterday I saw the huge bulk of her gliding past, through my window.

This makes four *St Olas*, in my time. Only the oldest Stromnessians remember the first *St Ola*, a small narrow black vessel that must have been very sturdy to cross the Pentland in all weathers. It was about 1950 that she sailed away for the last time after sixty years' service. We older Stromnessians had a good deal of affection for her – she seemed almost as much a part of Stromness as the Holms or Brinkie's Brae.

A great sport of boys, on summer afternoons, was to row out into 'the *Ola*'s waves'. There for half a minute or so our little flattie reared and plunged rather frighteningly. I for one was always glad when we got into calm water again.

I think it was always fairly late in the afternoon when the first *Ola* returned from Scrabster. You could hear the beat of her engines approaching; then at the mouth of the harbour she vented two blasts on her siren. It was somehow very reassuring – in Stromness, all was well for another day.

May the big new *Ola* soon be as affectionately regarded by Stromnessians. In these times of swift turnover, we cannot expect her to last for sixty years.

❀

Listening idly to the radio yesterday afternoon, I heard that there is a demand for British summer time to continue all through the year. Also – if I heard right – that there might be 'Double summer time' in the light months, as happened during the Second World War.

I suppose an argument could have been advanced for it then – though what exactly it was, I'm not sure – but why the clocks should stand an hour ahead of Greenwich mean time, I don't understand at all... When summer time was introduced, I can imagine the farmers all over Orkney shaking their heads gravely at this interference with 'God's time'... To the natural rhythm their farm work was attuned, and the cows and horses and sheep knew nothing of this artificial time. It was introduced, I think, for the convenience of munition workers during the First World War, so that they could see to make shells and warships for an hour longer each day. There was maybe a smitchkin of sense in that, but to prolong it into peacetime, even up to the present (the clocks go forward this weekend as I write) seems meaningless.

It shows maybe how the convenience of city dwellers must always override the values and rhythms of the comparative few who work on the land and the sea.

However, we must face it – nobody in Orkney seems to mind any longer. Just as, last Saturday, the marvellous equinox-time passed without one murmur of wonderment or thankfulness.

The First St Magnus Day

16 April 1992

Today, April the sixteenth, is St Magnus Day.

In these 'enlightened times', St Magnus Day means nothing. For our ancestors, it was a day of feast and rejoicing (even though it involved a very dark plot and a cold-blooded murder).

Did Earl Magnus know he was sailing to his death that Easter Day, on Egilsay? Nine centuries ago, particular attention was paid to omens. Sailing to Egilsay – from Shetland, recent researchers may show – a wave rose out of a calm sea, and drenched Magnus and his men.

Once the two peace ships of Magnus got to Egilsay, it wasn't long before they knew they had walked into a trap. For his cousin Earl Hakon arrived with a fleet of eight ships, and Hakon's men weren't singing psalms when they waded ashore and spread out over the island.

I imagine the Egilsay folk retired indoors and barred and shuttered their houses.

A man is walking alone under the first star, among the rockpools of Egilsay.

On the other side of the island, Earl Hakon's men are enjoying a good supper of beef and fish, bread and ale. But their lord, Earl Hakon, eats little.

He can't join in the songs and laughter. He is almost as lonely as his cousin Earl Magnus.

Lifolf the cook has a busy time of it. The revellers are still wanting their plates and ale horns filled at midnight.

Meantime, the Egilsay priest, looking into his church to see that all is well, notices a solitary figure up near the altar. The priest can't tell, by the light of his lantern, who or what the kneeling man is. Between midnight and dawn is the coldest time. The priest closes the door and leaves the church.

It is now April 16th, Easter Monday.

The sleep of the island is soon broken.

Earl Hakon's men are searching everywhere for Earl Magnus. They hear he has been seen walking on the tidemark the previous sunset. 'Come up,' they shout. 'Come out of the cave, coward! Show yourself'... They are a bold swaggering crew, having broken their fasts with beer and left-overs.

Nowhere – Magnus is nowhere to be seen in Egilsay...

Then they know that he is in the sanctuary of the church, where no man may be touched or harmed or taken.

So they take their taunts to the open church door. And there he is indeed, inside.

And he rises to meet them.

'What's all the brawling and noise about?' Earl Magnus says; and even those rioters whom even their lord, Earl Hakon, couldn't control that morning, are struck by the cheerfulness of his voice and bearing.

'No need for all this rowdiness,' says Earl Magnus. 'We're all here in Egilsay for a peace conference. Is Hakon there?

'Tell Hakon, I'll be out at once for the peace meeting.'

By now he is in the door of the church. He looks to where the strong man, Earl Hakon Paulson his cousin, is standing at the edge of the crowd of armed men. And Hakon turns away; he dare not look him in the eye.

Everyone in Orkney – at least it is to be hoped so, for nowadays the great legends of the world are being forgotten – knows the rest of the story. The loaded negotiations there, in the barren centre of the island – the decision that only by the death of Magnus can peace come to Orkney – the refusal of Ofeig the standard-bearer to do the deed – the summoning of Lifolf, the harmless cook, away from his fire and stew-pots to be the executioner. The cheerfulness of the condemned man, 'he was blithe as though he were bidden to a feast'

– Magnus's blessing on his unwilling weeping executioner – Earl Hakon's ride to Paplay in Holm to tell (weeping himself, that strong man) the news to Earl Magnus's mother.

What did they think, the Egilsay folk, when the sound and the fury had died away and they could open their doors at last?

Before seed-time that spring, the news was known in the fishing hamlet of Hamnavoe.

Another year or two, and the story was known and celebrated all over Western Europe.

Who Discovered America?

30 April 1992

I see that the latest first-class stamp commemorates Christopher Columbus and the 'landfall in the Americas 1492'.

At the weekend a letter came from the Faroe Islands, with a stamp celebrating Leif Ericsson's voyage from Greenland to America 500 years before Columbus.

This Norse discovery of America is documented in two brief sagas, that came out in a single Penguin book some years ago, translated and edited by Magnus Magnusson and Hermann Pálsson.

There's little doubt that Leif Ericsson's ships made landfall somewhere on the east coast of America – just where is a matter of continuing debate. Here and there archaeologists have discovered foundations and artefacts strongly suggesting a Norse settlement, usually pretty far northwards in Labrador. On the other hand, the first Greenland explorers called the country Vinland, because of the abundance of wild grapes; and that suggests a more southern landfall.

Our kinsmen attempted a settlement, but were unable to establish themselves because of the hostility of the 'skraelings', their name for the native Red Indians.

A few centuries later, Greenland itself had to be abandoned because of the worsening climate.

But the sagamen had that piece of history well documented.

I wonder if, quite soon, Ireland will produce a postage stamp depicting the oxhide boat of Saint Brendan and his crew of monks.

Many claim that Brendan may have reached America 500 years earlier even than Leif Ericsson.

There are medieval accounts of the famous voyage of Brendan. The abbot Brendan, in his monastery in the west of Ireland, had heard accounts of 'the earthly paradise' under the rim of the great ocean westwards, where there is neither age nor sickness nor sorrow. So he had his ship built and sailed out with his crew.

In those days scribes weren't too particular about literal accuracy – the dullness of fact was lost in the wonderment of life and being. So it is by no means certain that Brendan actually got as far as America – though not so long ago, a replica of his ship made the journey (but it was fitted out with all kinds of navigational aids, and no doubt those young fit twentieth-century sailors didn't have to worry about where their next meal was coming from).

So, the voyage of Brendan reads more like a piece of pure surrealism than a cold factual account. Monsters and angels and miracles met them at every turn. Yet it seems certain that they made landfall in Iceland – there is a convincing description of the volcanoes... I think, too, in Faroe (and perhaps Shetland) there are voes and havens named after Brendan... He may even have sheltered in an Orkney bay: even Hamnavoe...

Brendan did come at last to the Earthly Paradise, and tasted its delights. But he returned to his monastery in the end.

Even if it is conceded that the abbot St Brendan beat Leif Ericsson and Christopher Columbus to it, in the discovery of America, it should not be forgotten that there were Americans there already. The Red Indians, it is claimed, crossed over the Bering Strait from Asia long before, and also their cousins, the moon-faced smiling Inuit people. So they were the true discoverers.

So, there might even be another stamp in the offing, from Alaska or Siberia.

Daffodils on the Retreat

7 May 1992

Now the daffodils, having endured the tempests of late March and most of April, are on the retreat at last.

They put beauty on the inclement days, swaying and dancing joyously in the cold northerlies and easterlies. Are the daffodils happy in their season, as Wordsworth thought? Or is it that they merely strike a natural joy from us, after the dreariness of winter?

I thought, 'How brave the daffodils are!' – because one weekend the bulbs and green shoots were drowned in snow, so cold and sudden and sinister it seemed nothing so delicate could survive that white smothering... The deep snow melted, almost as quickly as it had come, and there they were, all sheathed and ready to throw their blossoms on the wind of spring... It isn't really bravery – the daffodils can't help behaving the way they do. But to our human perception it is bravery, and the courage communicates itself to us ... there must be this web of sympathy that holds all nature together, men and mice and daffodils.

My room was splashed with daffodil light, three jars full, for weeks. A few days ago, the fresh petals began to wilt, then turned sere and papery. Yesterday morning they had to be thrown out ... lacking them, the house is a duller place.

The amount of rain that has fallen!

There used to be a custom in Stromness that the yard was dug and the seed tatties planted on the April holiday. Not this spring. The earth is still a churned-up mess. No sooner did it seem that a windy day would dry out the ground – and gardeners went out to the garden sheds to look out their spades – than another hours-long spate of rain would fall – and the sopping earth lay untroubled for another day or two. 'Late tatties this year,' say the gardeners.

Some days this week we have felt the kindling of spring in the air; the climbing sun sought out dark corners unvisited since September... But always, those immense black rainclouds were cruising here and there, settling blue-black over Hoy and Orphir.

One fine sunny afternoon I was walking home, when I met Sandy Tait hurrying home from his walk. 'Look at that raincloud over Hoy Sound,' he said.

There it was, a grey immense advancing shadow.

Hardly had Sandy Tait and I parted, than the cloud dropped buckets and pails and pitchers over me; while all around, towards Stenness and the Scapa Flow islands, the sun was shining.

That rain fell so tumultuously that, walking home, I actually began to enjoy it. There's something about being in the black throbbing heart of a raincloud.

As soon as I reached Mayburn, the sun came out again...

Today, as I write, is the last day of April. We've known gentler sweeter Aprils in past years – but still, watching on TV the awful things happening in Afghanistan, Yugoslavia, Ethiopia, Ulster – any month that brings daffodils, lambs, rain, and blackbirds is sweet indeed.

Spring at Last

21 May 1992

Suddenly, a few days ago, the weatherman on TV spoke about a heatwave approaching from the south.

This was news so astonishing and rare to us, after the bleakest coldest wettest spring I remember, that we northerners couldn't quite take it in. It was impossible; that kind of weather didn't exist any more. Who wants temperatures in the 80°s anyway, such as the southern English were about to be lapped in?

We have come to be a bit sceptical about national weather forecasts, in any case. There sits a black cloud over Orkney on the TV screen – and behold, we get a pleasant sun-splashed day... Or, more rarely, there's a coy little white trefoil with rays of sun at the corner, and next day it rains on and off... Shetland seems to have the black cloud all the time; which I'm sure, from my own experience of Shetland, can't be entirely true.

Anyway, by the first week in May the gardeners could wait no longer to plant their sprouting seed tatties, though the ground was sopping wet. So very wet it was, indeed, that Stromness Golf Course was unplayable for a time, and the kye[1] were kept indoors, with fodder running low. We thought, 'This can't go on. Tomorrow spring *will* come'... I looked through the window one afternoon in May, to see a flurry of flakes swirling past the window, followed soon by the small artillery of hailstones!

An unheard-of spring! The daffodils – as I've said before, more than once – danced brave and joyous through all that dreichness[2]. Suddenly a few days ago, daisies rushed out like stars, and there were the dandelions, too, like little suns... Thrushes and blackbirds sang through the wind and rain.

Yesterday, said the TV weatherman, spring was to come at last.

1 cows
2 dreariness, bleakness

It didn't seem much like fine weather to me, when I drew back the curtains at 8.30am. The sky was grey, and an hour later a smirr[1] had put a dampness on the street... But then, slowly, the unheard-of began to happen. There was a gleam of sunlight, then the gold was everywhere, a generous splurging. After all the greyness of March and April, we were surprised once more by the rich blues of sea and sky... A cow began to appear in fields here and there.

A covering had to be removed from the wintertime bed. Time too to discard the quilted waistcoat called a 'body warmer' that has been a comfort all winter. No need to put a match to the fire till early afternoon.

Depend on it, we'll see one or two storms and rainy days and glowers of cloud between now and Johnsmas. But spring hasn't forgotten us, after all. It is here, faithful as always, in all its 'juice and all this joy', as the poet of eternal springtime, Gerard Manley Hopkins, said... At least, until the hole in the ozone layer and 'the greenhouse effect' and global warming banish all four of our cherished seasons forever.

But surely humanity, which has endured so much and adapted itself to so many vicissitudes, won't behave now, in the late twentieth century, like the Gadarene swine.

Melvin Place, 1928–34

28 May 1992

I visited Melvin Place in Stromness yesterday evening, for virtually the first time since 1934. For six years, from 1928 to 1934, my family lived at 3 Melvin Place; we had 'flitted' there from Victoria Street (Clouston's Pier).

Melvin Place, a beautiful little complex of houses, is very much the same, structurally, as it was half a century ago, but of course there are variations.

The gardens and closes seem to be smaller than they were in my childhood. Just opposite 'our house' is a house known as the Doocot, where an old couple called Joe Renton and his wife lived. Joe Renton was a brother of the John Renton who was a castaway in the Solomon Islands in the mid-nineteenth century. The Rentons' father had been a tailor and lived in the tall house immediately above.

At 1 Melvin Place lived William Rendall, the printer, whose little firm (where *The Orcadian* Stromness office now is) produced books

1 drizzle

like John Firth's *Reminiscences of an Orkney Parish* and Goodfellow's *Two Old Pulpit Worthies of Orkney*.

On the little branch-close leading on to Hellihole Road lived the Robertson family. Mr Robertson was engineer on the *Ola*.

Higher up, the close narrows and leads between dark houses to a garden at the top where my mother hung up her washing to dry on a Monday. The garden belonged to Mr Rendall, and was full of bluebells, and teeming grass, and had two trees. I remember the garden and the trees because one day, at the age of seven or eight, consequent on some telling-off or misdemeanour at home, I decided to run away. So I hid myself in one of the trees, hoping to be persuaded with apologies or consolation. But nothing happened. No one came. The world, I concluded, was a heartless place... After an hour or two, I crept off home... In the end, everything was all right.

Further up still, right under a little crag that old folk called 'the Hammars', was a group of plots for growing vegetables. There my mother had the loan of a tattie plot from Mrs Robertson. From there you had a good view of the Town Hall (now the Youth Hostel) and the Braes where Captain Swanney of the *Pole Star* lived with his wife and five sons. Just across the road was the Temperance Hall where the Salvation Army met... Sometimes a solemn procession followed the hearse up Hellihole Road to the kirkyard. Mr Couper of Quildon drove the splendid dark horse-drawn hearse: the mourners followed. In those days a funeral procession had to walk all the way to the kirkyard, in all weathers, at Warbeth two miles away.

We sometimes played football and even cricket in the little field above the Temperance Hall.

There were three sweetie shops within easy distance of Melvin Place – Mrs Hutchison's beside the Lifeboat Station, and Miss Black's at the foot of Hellihole, and Henry Carroll's in Alfred Street. There we spent our precious Saturday pennies.

And in summer boys caught sillocks[1] and crabs off Gray's Pier – not possible any more because it is a built-up area, Gray's Noust...

And sometimes the rockets went up, and then all the folk of the South End gathered at Gray's Pier to see the launching of the lifeboat *JJKSW*... Down she went, and hit the water in a bursting flower of foam!

It was a great area, Melvin Place... Every Saturday we changed our library books at Peter Esson's Library just across the way. I liked best school stories by a writer called Harold Avery.

1 coalfish, kind of coley

Faded Glory of Football

11 June 1992

When we were boys in Stromness in the 1930s, we lived mainly for one thing – football. Real footballs were hard to come by, so we made do more often than not with little rubber balls that cost only a few pence. In those days it was safe enough to kick a ball about the street, for there can have been no more than a dozen cars in the whole of Stromness.

But then when we saw the two policemen coming – for they went along the street regular as clockwork several times a day – we pocketed the ball and ran up a close.

The only danger was that the ball might break a window – then you had to be off in double-quick time.

We kicked anything we saw, an empty syrup tin or an empty chocolate box.

Of course every playtime we played in the school field, North End against South End.

The greatest joy of the week was to go to the Market Green to see Stromness Athletic playing against Hotspurs, Thorfinn or Rovers from Kirkwall. (In those days, Hotspurs was the most formidable Kirkwall team.) And as for Stromness, it was crammed full of heroes, Hugo Munro, Attie Campbell, 'Yokko' Johnston, George Clouston, W. Groundwater... that team of the thirties achieved greater glories than any other Stromness eleven before or since.

We knew, of course, all about the legendary teams in the South – Rangers, Celtic, Hearts, Aberdeen. Sometimes there were wireless commentaries on their epic encounters, on a Saturday afternoon; but wireless reception in those days was so erratic that we had only the vaguest idea of the ebb and flow of play... One of the great tragedies of childhood was the death on the field of battle of the great Celtic goalkeeper, John Thomson, going down to save a certain goal against the great enemy, Rangers.

One never quite forgets the enthusiasm of childhood, but how the early glory has faded! I sometimes watch a game on TV, and there's a great deal of boredom in it, even when famous teams are playing and players that cost two or three million pounds to enrol.

The other night there was a touch of the old magic, when Brazil completely outclassed the English team... And, a night or two later,

I watched a truly magnificent game out of the archives of twenty-five years ago – the European Cup Final of 1967, Celtic v Inter Milan. There was the finest vintage football, and though I'd seen it before half a dozen times, and knew the victorious outcome, the excitement of watching it, in black and white, was as great as ever... It was almost as good as Stromness v Hotspurs in 1934 or so.

Cats

18 June 1992

'What a lot of cats there are in Stromness!' the visitors say. And I suppose there are, and always have been. In any fishing town, there must be cats. The water-rats in the score of piers and slipways – how better to control them than with an alert and agile troop of cats?

So it's true – cats were everywhere, asleep under boats and flowing along garden walls, eyeing with great speculation the half-dozen milkcarts at morning and evening, aware of the floodtides bringing in the little boats overflowing with skate and haddocks.

The first cat I remember at home was a striped black and grey cat called Trixie, who was always having kittens. She was glad to eat any scraps tossed to her, not like the pampered messieurs and mesdames of today. Trixie, who never had a vet in her life (nor I think did any other Stromness cat) inhabited the environs of Melvin Place, till she died in the fullness of years.

The next one, at Well Park, was called Becca, and she was patched tawny and black, and was a very affectionate cat, and had plenty of kittens. (I unwittingly killed one of her little black kittens one summer morning, swinging a golf club in the back green – but Becca didn't hold it against me...) How intently she must have listened to the mice stravaiging[1] inside the cavity walls, and eyed the sparrows and the starlings. But I never remember Becca catching a mouse or a bird. She was a gentle cat, and only growled fiercely if you came near her when she was eating 'lights' – the smell of lights reduced her from being a friendly pussy to a savage snarling predator.

Then there was Tiger at Hopedale, who (his owner said) dug his grave with his teeth; for Tiger would visit all the neighbourhood houses and have five or six breakfasts before dragging himself home, groaning with surfeit, along Ness Road.

1 roaming

There is, of course, also Gypsy, born in Birsay, reared in South Ronaldsay, in her radiant black prime in Dundas Street, Stromness, and still alive in serene age in Deerness. (Gypsy stayed with me for a fortnight recently, and, being highly intelligent, remembered my house well – though the concrete balcony of Mayburn was a poor substitute for the wide green field at Deerness, swarming with voles and mice.) In fact, she rarely left the rocking-chair or the bed or the mat in front of the fire... Whether Gypsy lost her voice in childhood, I don't know, but she never 'meows'. If you scratch her head, though, or open a tin of liver Whiskas, she throbs through and through with songs of delight – then curls to sleep the afternoon out, in the rocker. And I, evicted from my favourite chair, have to find somewhere else in the room to read or listen to a tape.

Last week, there was the young cat Mona, stalking butterflies so lithely and beautifully in the Melvin Place garden of my childhood, where Trixie used to do the same green dances.

Summer Solstice

25 June 1992

In two days' time it will be the summer solstice, a wonderful time in Orkney and all the lands of the north.

The light grows so suddenly, after the equinox on March 21, that the full wave is upon us almost before we are aware. Among other delightful things, how wonderful to sit up near midnight, in what Shetlanders call 'the simmer dim', without drawing curtains.

Outside, as one puts down the book before bedtime, there is only a slight infusion of shadows.

After those three weeks of marvellous weather in late May and early June, the weather has turned grey again. On a clear midnight, that furnace glow never leaves the north; the sun is not that far under the horizon.

Visitors have been dropping by. This weekend there will be a few more, over the St Magnus Festival – and I see my diary is fairly full for the rest of June and for July. (For old crabbit[1] recluses like me, the weight of humanity can sometimes be too much – yet I suppose we should be glad that people talk to us at all.)

A night or two ago I sat in the Braes balcony, having beer with an old university friend, Ian MacArthur, who comes originally from

1 crabbed

Stornoway but is now a retired teacher in Forres. The trout fishing hadn't been all that good, but he was enjoying his Orkney visit... We watched the triangles of sail leaning towards the Clestrain shore, and the *Ola* coming in and the *Sunniva* going out, and then a strange craft like a medieval longship drifting in...

We suddenly remembered that it was 'Bloomsday', June 16 – the day on which all the events happen in Dublin, in James Joyce's novel *Ulysses*, in the year 1904. And there we were, drinking a new Irish stout called Murphy's, rich creamy stuff, the like of which the old Orkneymen used to call 'maet and drink'.

Two pints of Murphy's, and the midsummer evening acquired even more enchantment.

Yesterday, June 18, was, if I'm not mistaken, the anniversary of Waterloo. It would be interesting to know if there were any Orkneymen in that terrible battle – it's certain there had been some at Trafalgar ten years earlier.

But one of those war veterans, from the Peninsula if not from Waterloo, was the Irish soldier Phin who opened the little tavern in Firth parish where the Pomona Inn now is, and a village grew up about Phin's 'Toddy-hole', as it was called, and in the end he bequeathed his name to Finstown.

This is the season when it behoves folk to step warily in the first shadows, for the peedie folk, the trows[1], are abroad – and especially they are on the look-out for fiddlers (music is their greatest joy). Didn't they cajole a fiddler, two or three centuries ago, to their chamber under the Knowe, to give them a tune, and wasn't it fifty years or so before he appeared in the world of men again, though it seemed to him he had only been under the hill a half-hour or so?

So the musicians at the Festival, which begins today, better have a care.

Books for All Time

2 July 1992

As you get older, the world of literature seems to shrink. Fewer and fewer new writers seem to cast the spell that once Eric Linklater, E. M. Foster, Thomas Hardy, W. B. Yeats, and Thomas Mann did.

There must, of course, be marvellous new writers sprouting everywhere – only one's bedimmed instincts can't see them.

1 trolls

Two weeks ago or so a friend recommended a book called *Songlines* by a writer new to me called Bruce Chatwin, and it was about the Aborigines of North Australia and their marvellous understanding of and sympathy with the earth and the elements, and how in the 'dreamtime' the ancestors of man sing the world into existence.

Songlines is a wonderful book, the rare kind that opens a door in the mind and the imagination – so that the reader, though he doesn't understand everything on the page, at least has the illusion that he is glimpsing a hitherto unapprehended truth.

The white Australians – some of them – don't come out of it all that well.

I must hasten along to the Pier Arts Centre to see the exhibition 'Songlines' – Aboriginal art, which forms an important part of the book.

Subsequently I have read a novel about farming on the Welsh–English border, by the same author: *On the Black Hill*. Good stuff too, but not so exciting as *Songlines*.

I'm grateful that I can still be impressed by new books and new writers.

Or else one can discover again a thrilling book from youth.

One of the few books I enjoyed at school was actually a book of French short stories from the nineteenth century called *Lettres de Mon Moulin*, by Alphonse Daudet.

I suppose no two places in Europe could be so removed as Provence in southern France and Orkney. And few greater obstacles to enjoyment than a foreign text that schoolchildren had to translate; or else...

But, aged sixteen or seventeen, to read that French book was pure delight, and the language enhanced rather than deterred.

The wonder of those short stories: '*La Mule du Pape*', '*La Chèvre de Monsieur Seguin*', etc! The first words of the first story, when the writer Daudet leaves Paris to live in his disused mill, enchanted me more than half a century ago: 'How astonished the rabbits were...'

I think perhaps when I began to write stories myself, the smouldering embers of *Letters from My Mill* (the English title) were waiting there, all those years, to be blown into flame.

So, it was marvellous to come on the Penguin translation a few nights ago, and to rediscover those treasures from adolescence.

A good thing too, that the mind grows tired of the coloured shadows of TV, and knows that certain books – new and old – are there for all time.

Famous Stromnessians

16 July 1992

Do we really know where Bessie Millie's hovel is? I wish somebody would take me there, to the possible site, some fine day. There's a fine photo of Keith Allardyce's in *Sea Haven* that shows a ruckle[1] of stones near the top of Brinkie's Brae – that seems to be a possibility.

There are no title deeds, I'm sure: not for poor Bessie Millie.

All we know is that Sir Walter Scott climbed a series of 'dirty and precipitous lanes' to reach the place – and he with his lame foot. And he wasn't exactly impressed by the hut or the ancient sybil who lived there. But, that day in 1814, he stored all of it up to use in his novel *The Pirate*.

Bessie, he said, was nearly a hundred. But there were no birth certificates then either, and country folk set little store by exact computations. So Sir Walter's estimate of Bessie's age was likely impressionistic. She might have been nearer seventy – a hard poverty-stricken life two centuries ago might grind the features closer to the skull prematurely.

Having written the above, I must apologise at once to the shade of Scott. He had after all, done his groundwork before he climbed up to the shack among the high granite. He had been told that Bessie Millie remembered, as a young girl, seeing John Gow the pirate in Stromness – that must have been in the winter of 1725–26. In that case, Bessie in 1815 must have been nearing her century.

It is intriguing to speculate what the peedie lass looked like when the stylish young skipper – and a local boy too, reared over there on Garson shore – passed along the street, to call maybe at the house of Mr James Gordon, a leading Stromness merchant. There were rumours all over Hamnavoe of an affair between the master of the *George* and Mr Gordon's daughter.

Bessie Millie may have been a bonny enough lass then and old enough perhaps for her heart to be kindled by the handsome sailor.

Another Stromnessian who would have seen Gow during those few hectic days when he was a local hero, was Alexander Graham, a young merchant, not so affluent or highly regarded as Mr James Gordon.

1 loose pile

What did Graham think of the 'local hero' as he passed along the unpaved street? He must have been a shrewd judge of character. It is possible that, getting reports from this quarter and that of the thievings and fights of Gow's crew, Alexander Graham had his suspicions. But what were his opinions worth, when James Gordon, that important man, had opened his house to William Gow, the merchant's son who had gotten on so well on the trade-routes of the world?

Might not all three – Millie, Gow, Graham – have met by chance at a street corner, at the foot of Chalmersquoy, say (the modern Dundas Street / Graham Place)?

'Good morning, sir,' says Gow ingratiatingly. 'I think you're Mr Graham, are you not?'... And Alexander Graham turns without a word into Mistress Beaton's ale-house... And young Bessie Millie, her eyes shining like stars, says, 'A good voyage to you, Captain Gow, and a fair wind all the way...'

I must have another look at Keith's beautiful photograph.

Surprising Weather

23 July 1992

Our weather, as always, continues to astonish everybody but the Orcadians.

It rained so much on Monday this week that the windows that have been sliding up and down so easily since May came in, are glued fast again... Lovely it has been, after a long winter of stale air indoors, to fling open the windows in the morning, first thing, and let the sweet airs flow through all the house. And, with them, the noises of birds and sea and the South End ladies talking in the shop door below.

There was one series of small berserker yells one afternoon a fortnight ago! It was the children released from school for seven weeks.

The busiest phone in Stromness by far is the public box in the Museum corner. It seems to ring almost non-stop from tea-time to supper-time. Always there seem to be tourists expecting calls.

Through the open window, too, can be heard the series of little waves on the beach below Mayburn as the *Ola* and the *Sunniva* come and go.

So pleasant it is, to have currents of air in summer flowing through the house, with all the sounds of Hamnavoe.

Of course, in a few hours the pleasant airs can turn bitterly cold; then it's time to close the windows and blow up the fire.

This morning we woke to a world steeped in early morning gold. Everybody should have been out enjoying it, really. But once you have got into a fixed routine, like me, you ignore the blue sky and sit at the desk over the manuscript. They say it is inbred Calvinism that places duty before spontaneous natural happiness – pen on paper rather than taking a walk out to Ness or down a pier, or sitting drowsed with sun in a sheltered garden.

Peter and Betty, my friends who are staying with me, came in from a long walk to Warbeth and said there was a lacing of high white cloud moving in from the west. We knew that such signs betokened rain.

But the weather was still fine when, after lunch, we set out in the car, by way of Miffia (from which half of Orkney can be seen – from the Flotta flare to Kirkwall Bay glimpsed through the Firth gap) and Skaill (where the meadowsweet wafted enchanting scents into the car) to the Marwick shore. There the strands of silky white cloud thickened to webs of grey, and a gurly[1] sky was coming in from the west, beyond Hoy.

However, we enjoyed that famous walk along the sea banks to the restored boat shelter, as lovely a small cove as can be seen anywhere, with the little stone sets to receive the non-existent boats. But yes, in one of the shelters a boat waited. How many lobsters, how many baskets of cod, have been landed here, over many centuries?

The light was greying fast as we drove home by Twatt and Skeabrae and Voy.

The rain hasn't come yet, but it will fall, surely, tonight.

Tomorrow, maybe, in wind and sun, the boards in my windows will shrink a little, and open once more for all the summer to flow through.

Astonishingly, the expected rain didn't come. So, the natives as well as the tourists can be surprised by our weather...

A Warbeth Wander

30 July 1992

One fine afternoon last week we thought we might visit Warbeth.

It was a beautiful day – the *Ola* was going out fast on the ebb – a few rabbits hopped about in a field – another field was dense with yellow charlock. Hoy Sound glittered with a thousand points of light.

1 stormy, threatening (of weather)

Warbeth beach is one of the places Stromnessians visit with pleasure all their lives. So much childhood happiness was experienced there. Something of the wonderment lingers on into age. Warbeth at last is more than a place – it is a symbol.

Before we went to Warbeth we wandered into the kirkyard, into the very oldest of the three God-acres: the most interesting, in my opinion.

I suppose there are people who are frightened of kirkyards – who would rather go anywhere than among those labyrinths of the quiet dead.

From childhood on, the kirkyard at Warbeth has fascinated me – ever since some local man, probably my father, said that there are more Stromness folk lying here than there are living in the town at present. And so there must be – many thousands of them, reaching back for centuries.

The earliest tombstones date from mid-eighteenth century. But Stromnessians must have been buried here for hundreds of years before that.

Maybe 250 years ago or so people began to yearn to be remembered somehow; an inscription engraved on stone would do. And there must have been one or two good engravers in Hamnavoe about that time, because the names they carved so deep are quite as legible as the day the tombstone-maker took his mallet and chisel to the dark grey slab. (Is the hard stone limestone?)

Many of the later Victorian engravures are worn and withered and hardly legible. Besides, winter storms have blown the tops of many headstones down, or even flattened them completely.

We oughtn't to forget that it was only the wealthier Stromnessians who had memorial stones put up for them. So, many of them are for ships' masters and merchants, and for the scores of their children whose flames flickered briefly and went out. For the poor – and they were the majority – it was only the opening and closing of the wave of earth, made by the gravedigger's spade. Their memory lingered on in a few minds, growing ever fainter: then those anonymous ones were part of the great silent company.

And yet – the mind can't help insisting – nothing is ever completely lost... Here and there in Stromness, after hundreds of years, abides a glance or the lifting of a foot or an intonation of the voice, that must have been vivid once about the piers and close-ends of Hamnavoe.

There was one tombstone that always intrigued us, as children. It was set up for a girl called Ellen Dunne who died, aged seventeen, in the mid-nineteenth century.

> Stop for a moment, youthful passer-by,
> On this memento cast a serious eye.
> Though now the rose of youth may flush your cheek,
> And youthful vigour, health and strength bespeak,
> Yet think how soon, like me, you may become,
> In youth's fair prime, the tenant of the tomb.

How was it that this melancholy legend did not in the least depress us? It seemed, rather, to shed a tranquillity and a frail beauty, like faded rose-leaves. (There is a rose carved on top of the stone.)

Hail and farewell, poor Ellen Dunne – and may you have found some happiness in your all too brief sojourn on this earth.

At Warbeth, half an hour later, the tide was full, and the banks above were lyrical with curly-doddies[1], sea-pinks, ox-eye daisies.

But there was only a scattering of people – whereas, sixty years ago, Stromness children would have been there building sandcastles and bathing and sifting the rockpools for whelks.

Ah well, it was the middle of Shopping Week, and they had other things to do.

The Artists of 1948

6 August 1992

Talk about Orcadian hospitality! – I keep some visitors (tourists) away with a little yellow square of paper Sellotaped to the door: 'Working till 1pm'.

Well, I have to earn my bread and butter in peace.

One afternoon a stranger called who gave his name as Paul Farmiloe and said he was a nephew of John Farmiloe.

Paul was due to 'dive' in Scapa Flow in an hour's time.

Well, the news of his uncle took me back to 1948, the summer of that year, when three artists (Ian MacInnes, John Farmiloe, and George Scott) resided in Alfred Terrace when they weren't painting the houses, closes, piers, sea and cliffs around Stromness.

1 clover

Everybody knows Ian MacInnes, and many remember George Scott. John Farmiloe wasn't a stranger to Orkney either; he had been a 'camouflage officer' here during the war.

All three were then students at Gray's School of Art, Aberdeen.

The summer of '48 was, I think, quite good – not quite so sun-filled as that *annus mirabilis*, 1947, but part of the same cycle of brightness and warmth.

Away they would go, all three painters, every day to some chosen place, and would return hours later carrying a box of paints, brushes, etc in one hand while from the other dangled a painting that was still drying in the wind.

All through the summer the stack of paintings grew, up the stairs in Alfred Terrace.

Somewhere or other the artists picked up frames for the growing hoard of canvases.

Well, the summer was warm and painting all day at the Black Craig, or down Copland's Pier or at the top of Khyber Pass, makes artists thirsty... I forget about the level of the cuisine at the artists' quarter – I was a frequent guest that summer – but one evening a bank-teller called Bob MacMurtie arrived with a bunch of mackerel fresh out of the sea. What a feast there was that night! I think it was the first time I had tasted mackerel, for nobody ate them in Orkney in my childhood; mackerel was a taboo fish. There were no table or chairs, but it was a delicious supper.

That summer, Stromness had gone 'wet' again, after a quarter-century of publessness. There was only one bar, at Stromness Hotel, unless you counted the cocktail bar in the same establishment (but only the better class, and women, went there).

So many a night the three artists and friends sat in that very austere narrow bar and drank pints of draught beer at one shilling and threepence a pint (approximately 6p in modern currency). There was a good deal of laughter, song, and anecdote, till Bill Langskaill the barman shouted 'Time!' at nine o'clock. (Yes, the pubs in Orkney closed at that hour, then.)

One morning I woke up not in my own bed at Well Park but lying on the floor in the artists' studio at Alfred Terrace. I am still rather confused as to what happened between 9pm and 9am on that morning. My head banged like a drum, my throat was dry as the Sahara.

Well, such things happen in the dear delightful days of youth...

A Summer Cold

13 August 1992

There's not much you can do with a summer cold, it seems.

Where does it come from, in the first place?

There's the enchanting meadowsweet blowing, acres on acres, by the roadside, and the larks singing near sunset. and healthy winds blowing off the sparkling sea and over the shoulders of the ripe hills. And all that excitement of shows and regattas in the air, and Shopping Week in Stromness and St Magnus Fair still to come at Kirkwall, at the Kirk Green there.

And *Ola* and *Sunniva* coming in laden with tourists, and the tourists laden with bird-books, binoculars, maps and different languages.

Where in all that crowded summertime is there room for a summer cold to insert itself, like a dirty knife in a pat of bright sun-smelling Orkney butter?

But it happens.

There you are, one day, enjoying the loveliness of late July, when the nose begins to drip like a tap. That's nothing! – A grain of pollen must have got blown up the nostril when you were looking the wrong way.

The very next day, you're speaking in a rough bass voice, as if the throat had been sandpapered by a couple of trows in the night.

Then you know from past experience that there might be a bit of trouble.

Your fears are fully justified on the third or the fourth morning; for all the bronchial tubes are 'quarking' and making beastly black noises as if it was a tree laden with crows, rank upon rank of them – all making the lovely summer ominous and ugly.

Ah well, best to just be patient and let the nuisance pass – as it always does, sooner or later, generally with medical help.

And you're lucky if roast beef and good new tatties don't taste like blotting paper on a cobweb salad. (In my case that didn't happen, my only guest Betty Grant is such a good cook, and so are all the other friends I choose so well and so cunningly ... cold or no cold, I ate the steaks and the casseroles, the plaice and the roast chicken with all the old relish.)

Surely no summer cold could stand up to such fare – such delicious healthy in-season fare; not to speak of the delightful

French, German, or Californian wines we occasionally washed it down with. The summer cold hesitated, and seemed to be on the way out. But then the monster changed its mind, and struck again, foully, for the second time.

So last Friday I found myself fighting for breath, and my pulse going like a young wild colt through a meadow of curly-doddies and marsh marigolds.

That's why I'm writing this from hospital in Kirkwall on Sunday afternoon; with my bed table laden with black grapes and white grapes, peaches and bananas and kiwi fruit, and bottles and boxes of juice, and a bottle of German wine from my friends Michael and Simone Kraustopf who've just been to visit me and are starting out for home on this evening's *Ola*.

Twin Pillars of Scottish Poetry

20 August 1992

The poet Hugh MacDiarmid never was in Orkney, except maybe passing through on his way to Whalsay in Shetland in the thirties.

And in fact I never heard his name spoken till Mr Paterson our English master read us a MacDiarmid poem in the classroom – I expect to let us teenagers know that poetry hadn't stopped with Tennyson. It was the well-known lyric in Scots, 'Auld Noah was at hame wi' them aa, / The lion and the lamb...'

We liked it a lot.

A few years later there was a great kerfuffle in the Scots literary scene. The Orkney poet Edwin Muir had written a book called *Scott and Scotland* in which he advocated that Scottish writers ought henceforth to forget about Scots and write in English.

That put the cat among the pigeons!

Hugh MacDiarmid and Edwin Muir had been quite good friends up to then – I think the poet from Langholm in the Borders had even dedicated one of his early lyrics in Scots to the poet from Wyre.

But Edwin's essay was the end of that friendship. Henceforward he was in MacDiarmid's index of enemies – and he went for Muir like a terrier (whom he resembled somewhat) that had been disturbed at his bone. Over and over again...

50

Muir didn't retaliate: what he had written, he had written – there was nothing more to be said. In his fine autobiography *The Story and the Fable*, MacDiarmid isn't mentioned once.

I believe they did meet once in the 1950s, in a radio discussion – and then they were quite civil to each other.

But those two were the twin pillars of Scottish poetry in the mid-twentieth century. MacDiarmid and Muir produced the really great verse that is sure to last, each in his different way.

There are celebrations for MacDiarmid this August, because it is his centenary.

Muir's centenary passed in 1987, without much fuss – with a quiet man like Edwin the media find it difficult to cope. About MacDiarmid there are a hundred controversial trails to follow, political and literary. To show how complex a man he was – he was both a Communist and a Scottish Nationalist: when hordes were leaving the Communist Party at the time of Hungary in 1956, he (having been expelled from it) hastened to rejoin it.

That was, in part, the kind of man he was.

He was, in addition – apart from the violence of his generally bad prose – a man of great personal charm and kindness; which I can vouch for, having experienced it in Edinburgh in the fifties and sixties.

And the best of his poetry is magnificent. You have only to read the opening and close of his masterpiece 'A Drunk Man Looks at The Thistle'. It is like a great ship under a full spread of sail. Too many of his other long poems float about in the ocean like sterile icebergs.

Let us hope the poet from Wyre and the poet from Langholm are having fine dialogues now in the gardens of Elysium.

Children in the Slump

17 September 1992

Recession is one of the words on everybody's lips nowadays.

There was a kind of naive belief in the seventies and eighties that we were on the high-road to prosperity without end.

Experience – if we are old enough – ought to teach us that economic forces tend to move in cycles; or in ebbs and flows, to use a metaphor more familiar to Orcadians.

There was a deep recession (only in those days they called it a slump) in the thirties, when we senior citizens were children. Only we were so carefree and contented then that we never worried about such things ... probably some of the old folk blamed Ramsay MacDonald, or the 'Wall Street Crash', or cheap Japanese imports. So unstable was Europe that France seemed to have a new government every fortnight or so. A few thought highly of Mussolini who was making the trains in Italy run on time. Some spoke with admiration of Stalin and the vast collective farms in the Ukraine. Occasionally in the *Daily Express* there would be a brief paragraph about a Herr Hitler. (The only thing I read in the *Daily Express* was Rupert the Bear.)

But then, the slump hit us twelve-year-olds. Henceforth, we were suddenly told, there were to be no free jotters – we had to supply our own jotters... This was a very serious matter. Jotters from Rae's shop cost twopence each, the price of *The Wizard* or one of those new delights of confectionery, a Mars bar.

Fortunately, Rae's jotters had about a hundred pages and if you wrote in them small enough they might last you most of a term.

At the same time, teachers wore worried looks, because their pay (I think) had been docked.

Also, a sizeable number of Stromness men worked at Metal Industries (I think that was the name of the firm) that was still raising the German High Seas fleet from the floor of Scapa Flow. There seemed to be perpetual anxiety among those workers as they came ashore for the weekend. People would meet them and say, 'Have you got your books yet?' (meaning, had they lost their jobs?). And sure enough, every weekend a few more were on the dole.

These were just a few passing impressions we boys had. Nothing really mattered to us except that Stromness Athletic should beat Kirkwall Hotspurs at their next epic encounter (for Hotspurs were the big Kirkwall team in those days). Nothing mattered but that *The Wizard* came on the *Ola* every Tuesday afternoon, for us to buy at Rae's. Nothing mattered but that every week ended with the glorious freedom of Saturday (and Friday evening had a special kind of enchantment).

Attempts were made to channel our energies into the Life Boys[1]; for adults thought that somehow the wild anarchic freedom of boys ought to be turned to useful disciplined ends. Most of us joined the Life Boys, but I doubt if many of us really enjoyed it, in the Old Kirk hall (now part of the Community Centre) every Friday evening.

Dynasties might fall and Mr Baldwin might replace Mr Ramsay MacDonald and the little man with the drooping forelock and the

1 junior section of the Boys' Brigade

toothbrush moustache might become Chancellor of Germany – it was all one to us, so long as we had a football to kick in a park somewhere.

Stamp Collecting

24 September 1992

You never hear of boys collecting stamps nowadays. It used to be a favourite pastime.

'Foreign stamps' we called them, though we would take British stamps too, of course.

The British stamps were a very dull lot, compared to the wide variety of British stamps nowadays. In fact, I think there is a bit too much proliferation, and some of the stamps recently have been on the frivolous side.

Orkney collectors were favoured in respect of colonial stamps, because so many Orcadians were settled in Australia, Canada, New Zealand, South Africa, and they kept writing letters home. So we plagued folk with second cousins in those distant places splashed red on the map, 'Have you got any foreign stamps?' ('Foreign' was, to us, anywhere overseas.)

Well, in no time we got ourselves albums, and to begin with we made the horrible mistake of pasting the stamps flush on the album with 'Gloy' paste... Quite soon it was pointed out to us that a serious stamp-collector never did that, he mounted them carefully on adhesive hinges. Furthermore he never touched the precious squares with his fingers, but lifted the stamps on tweezers... But I think we never reached the sophisticated stage of tweezers.

So there we sat, in houses all over Hamnavoe, under the paraffin lamp on the kitchen table, sorting out little heaps of stamps: French, Austrian, Norwegian, Canadian, Italian, Spanish, Japanese ... I think we ordered the stamps from advertisements in *The Wizard* – if we sent this firm in London a shilling postal order (a fortune!) back would come a cellophane envelope full of stamps.

We had read all about the rare stamps – the 'penny blacks', the first true postage stamps of the 1840s, and a very rare stamp from some place in the Caribbean that was worth thousands! 'What!' we asked ourselves: 'A fortune for one little scrap of paper?' ... but we never found a penny black in the assortments we were sent.

There were plenty of mint German stamps – too many – there was a load of them in every packet we received. Most of them were for one million marks, but later this rose to two million marks, and at last the two million was overprinted in black by three million.

How came it that the Germans were so rich, we wanted to know? It was pointed out to us that those amazingly-priced stamps, as common as confetti, came from the time of the great German inflation of the mid-1920s, when, we were told, German workers wheeled their wages home in wheelbarrows.

So, with our albums and stamps, we passed some winter evenings, when we weren't reading *The Hotspur* or playing Ludo or, on fine moonlit nights, playing Leave-O outside.

Or sledging in the bounteous snowfalls of those days.

But suddenly spring was here – the stamp album was pushed into some closet – it was time for football once more, and sillock-fishing from Gray's Pier.

Autumn Insects

1 October 1992

The midgies are having a long season of it this autumn.

Usually they confine their activities to a couple of weeks or so in August. Then the first pre-equinoctial gale drives them away. The 1992 midgies are a tough long-lived lot. Stromnessians would go out into their gardens on a quiet afternoon in mid-September and get driven in by the monstrous little multitudes. One trembles to think of how it was in such favourite midgies' places as Rackwick and Mull...

Even yesterday, two days after the equinox, while we were sitting on the Pier Head seat, there was one at least of the little demons munching at the side of my face. But they don't have quite the ferocity of a month ago... The question is, where do they go for the rest of the year?

We Orcadians used to congratulate ourselves that we had no wasps. Somehow or other, they have found their way across the Pentland Firth – attracted maybe by our famous heather honey or the rhubarb jam the ladies make so deliciously for the WRI competitions...

For, just about the same time that the midgie bit me yesterday, at the Pier Head, there with a sinister drone this wasp came hovering around. He was dismissed with a wave of the arm and an uncomplimentary remark, and that seemed to do the trick... Still, now we must admit wasps into the list of our Orkney fauna.

I happened to look through the kitchen window yesterday, and there was another reminder of autumn – a big bluebottle on the thither side of the pane wanting to get in. He was so patient, he must have sat there for half an hour or so. No doubt, this being September, he'll find his way in somehow, and a few of his pals with him...

It's always on September evenings when you're reading a book in the evening, beside the Anglepoise lamp, that one of those crazy bluebottles hurls himself at the hot bulb, two or three times, and then retires with singed wings. But not for long. Just when you're resuming where you left off in mid-paragraph, there he comes zooming out of nowhere again, and wildly importunes the 60-watt bulb. I think he might have been an alcoholic when he was a man, that bluebottle, and is now given to yellow light as he was crazy for the 'wee yellow men' (whisky) once upon a time...

This splurging, with regular retreats to cure his burning hangover, goes on for half an hour maybe... Either you switch off the light, close the book, and go to bed – or else you search in the kitchen cupboard for the can of insect spray. But I'm always a bit reluctant to do that – because we might be bluebottles ourselves in some future transmigration or another; and wouldn't relish the idea of being gassed to death.

But where have the moths gone this summer? And there has been no sign of earwigs, that swarmed so triumphantly through the long-ago summer of 1947.

Pre-Radar Sea Fog

8 October 1992

The fourth day of fog now, as I write this, after that spell of peerless bright late September weather.

Yesterday the wind got up from the south-east, and we thought the fog would get blown away. But it didn't happen. So there was no mail again, apart from a few local items.

And still, this morning, after another night of wind, the wet sea-haar is with us – and, it seems, the entire east coast of Scotland is fringed with this cold greyness.

The boats with their radar come and go. The skippers can see, like bats, in the densest weather.

It wasn't always like that.

The favourite time for fogs used to be in high summer, and then all ships kept to their ports. But one of the vagaries of a sea-haar is that it can descend suddenly: one minute a ship is sailing through glittering seas, the next she is blind and bewildered – and nobody from captain to cabin-boy knew when the swathings would be removed.

Something of the kind happened in my boyhood, and to the most familiar of our ships, the *Ola* – that slim black swan that plied the Pentland Firth for sixty years.

I don't know, sixty years on, how accurate my memory is, but I seem to remember our elders speaking about this very remarkable thing. There lay the *Ola*, in the entrance to Hoy Sound, caught in the webs of fog. It was high summer, and there would have been tourists on board, but there was no way of navigating between Graemsay and Ness, into the safety of Hamnavoe.

How long this strange situation went on I don't know. Memory – that distorts everything – suggests that it was a day and a night, maybe longer, before the sun of high summer at last broke through the mist like a sword and allowed the *Ola* to get through.

Our young minds were amazed at the phenomenon. The tourists, we were told, who had hoped to be comfortably ensconced in the Stromness Hotel or Robb's Temperance Hotel (where the Ferry Inn is now) or in one of the decent boarding houses, had to pay something like a shilling for a cup of tea and a biscuit. (A shilling, for the enlightenment of the younger generation, is 5p now.) What a small fortune for a cup of tea and biscuit!

That's how things went, in those days. Maybe the tourists of sixty years ago enjoyed their sojourn, lost in the grey air and the grey sea, but with the sound of breakers against the Black Craig and the boom and echo from under the Kame, and gulls circling clamorously out of the blindness ... I don't suppose we shall ever know what those early tourists thought.

But the sun, when at last it appeared, would have been richer than gold to them... Ten more minutes, and they were at the sun-smitten pier at Stromness, with Jimmy Harvey the harbour master to greet them, and a score at least of curious townsfolk.

Childhood's Meals

15 October 1992

Orcadians over the years have come gradually to adopt the 'meal names' from further south: Breakfast – Lunch – Tea – Dinner (or Supper).

I think it can't have begun during the war: because then the four meal-times, if there were as many as four, tended to have a grey similarity.

I think the influx of people from the south might have had something to do with it. More likely it is watching the way people eat in stylish houses on TV.

'Dinner' continues to be the central meal of the day. But in my childhood dinner-time was 1pm, and a typical dinner might consist of Scotch broth, beef and tatties and cabbage (or fish and tatties, boiled) and a pudding of Creamola or rice and prunes... All of which I detested very much in childhood, though my mother was a good enough cook.

All that stable fare was for adults – only about the age of fifteen or so I began to enjoy them – but never Creamola or rice! (and sago was hideous beyond words!).

Breakfast is universal and timeless. Porridge was common, though I never enjoyed it much in childhood, either. It was a wonderful day when Kellogg's corn flakes first appeared on the table. Rolls warm from the bakehouse, with fresh farm butter, were a joy too. You ran off to the school cramming the last delicious mouthful in...

Tea-time was five o'clock. Wonderful things could happen then. Ham-and-eggs might appear or – most delicious of all – a juicy kipper. There were no cakes on the tea-table except on Sunday.

Supper appeared about 8pm. Then you speared a slice of bread with a fork and held it before the glowing ribs of the range... If there were any tatties left over from dinner-time, they were cut up and fried. There was generally cocoa to drink. But if there happened to be no cocoa, then milk was warmed in a pan – a very disagreeable drink, especially when a skin appeared on the surface and adhered to your lips.

Such were the main meals. But every day seemed to be an endless quest for sweeties, chocolate, sherbet, liquorice. I suppose they gave us the energy to play football: we would kick anything, an empty tin can if there was no ball available. The street was hideous occasionally with an empty Lyle's syrup tin as we lashed out at it with our boots. (And that was another delicious item of diet, Lyle's syrup – though we would take treacle too...) Oddly enough, I never cared for such things as rhubarb jam or marmalade till later. And cheese I wouldn't let pass my lips in those days.

Tea was just drinkable, but never coffee (which was rare anyhow). Gowans' lemonade was like nectar. After a strenuous game of football, water from the street tap was hard to beat...

How grown men could suffer the taste of beer, far less that fire-water (whisky) was beyond my innocence to comprehend, round about New Year.

A great treat was the Sunday School social in the UP Kirk on a winter evening, when after such games as 'The Jolly Miller' and 'The Farmer takes a Wife' we were sent home with a paper bag crammed to overturning with cakes, buns and shortbread – all the left-overs from the feast...

Signs of Winter

22 October 1992

I wonder if we'll be having a real winter this year?

There are promising signs. All this week of mid-October the wind has lain in the north, and it has been bitterly cold, and sudden dark showers have alternated with bursts of cold sunlight...

You can tell winter rain from summer rain, for every drop has a core of ice, and it rattles like small artillery against the windows.

So then, what about 'the peedie summer'?... Maybe we had it ten days ago, when there were a few mild bright days. Maybe the peedie summer is still to come – it is keeping its treasures till the end of October. And after that, the real winter begins.

Anyway, I've had to dig out of the cupboard the quilted winter jacket ... Any day now – if this bitter 'blashy'[1] weather goes on – I'll have to look for the 'thermals' that are supposed to keep old folk like me warm, according to the latest scientific principles.

Also, I have four new storage heaters in the house since August, and one of them has been on for the past week.

1 wet and blowy

But of course it's impossible to say – this may be only a cold snap in a mild autumn. Next week may be benign and tranquil again. It is still only autumn, after all: 'season of mists and mellow fruitfulness'.

And the past five winters have been so mild that we may be caught up in a cycle of mild winters that could go on for a decade yet. (Let nobody so much as whisper 'greenhouse effect', for the mere thought of such a man-made global catastrophe is enough to keep a person off sleep at nights.)

The truth is, I suppose, that in one lifetime it's difficult to note and evaluate those great cosmic moods that make for a sequence of bitter winters and bleak summers... But I remember the old men talking about the farmers driving horses and carts across the frozen Lochs of Stenness and Harray...

Meantime, today, there are wild dramatics going on in the sky. Great swathes of blue are swept away, time after time, by purplish-black ramparts of cloud. The house darkens – volleys of sleet and hail assault the north-facing windows... The fire leaps high in the grate. The fan heater in the corner of the kitchen purrs like a huge cat... Maybe three last leaves are clinging to the big tree in Farafield garden.

I suppose people who visit Orkney from more equable climes are amazed at the weather-wise way we Orcadians greet each other on the street: 'An aaful day'... 'Is this no' a bonny morning?'... 'We'll pay for this yet' (if it is a bonny morning: but only the pessimists among us say that).

So important is the weather to us northerners.

I suppose, truly, we ought to be glad we have weather at all. The men who have been to the moon say that, there, there is no stir of healthful wind, no snowflake on the back of the hand, no leaf budding or fading, no mists or mellow fruitfulness.

Breakfast with a Guest

19 November 1992

Occasionally, somebody stays overnight, and then there is the question of breakfast in the morning.

Breakfast has to be in the small kitchen, where everything is easily fetched from the cupboard, and the fan heater quickly warms the air.

There is one problem. The kitchen table is loaded with the tools of the writer's trade: pens, pencils, letter-rack, rubbers, letter-openers, stapler, notebooks, envelopes, writing paper, Sellotape, address labels, etc.

This weekend my good friend from Oxford is staying. We agreed last night that breakfast would be at 8.30.

How would it be possible to have breakfast for two in the small space remaining on the kitchen table? (For one person, myself, there is no problem.)

Downstairs, at 8.25am, there was only one drastic solution – to sweep the table clear of all writing material, including the table-lamp (fortunately it was a bright cold morning), and that left two square feet more space to manoeuvre in.

Not boundless space, but enough – just – for two cups, two plates, the butter and honey and marmalade, the egg-cups and salt cellar, sugar bowl and milk jug.

In fact everything went quite well. The eggs were real free-range; the marmalade had been made in midwinter up at Quildon; a cousin in the Highlands had sent me a pot of local honey for my birthday.

The eggs had been timed well, in spite of the rush and fluster. The toast came crisp and brown from the toaster (wholemeal toast, too). My guest enjoyed his Orkney-made oatcakes, as always.

Normally my breakfasts are eaten in a monastic silence. It is a welcome change when Hugo Brunner comes, because the eating and drinking is counterpointed by agreeable talk about books, publishing, and anything whatever pertaining to Orkney and its people. (Hugo has been visiting Orkney for twenty years or so, usually twice a year, and often at Festival time.) It is Hugo who lured me to England four summers ago, to 'the dreaming spires' of Oxford; when Gunnie and I packed so much into eight wonderful days. We were actually there when Seamus Heaney was elected Professor of Poetry at Oxford, and I attended the beautiful centenary Mass for the poet Gerard Manley Hopkins.

Anyway, breakfast is successfully over, as I write this. Hugo has gone along the street, a simple matter that he always manages to make into a delightful action-packed ceremony.

I realise that this week I have been very remiss in letter-writing, and 'Under Brinkie's Brae' is two days late in the writing. So here goes.

The mass of writing implements and material are back in their usual places. The table-lamp is casting a little blond circle of light (unnecessary in fact; the late autumn sun is so bright outside).

No need to clear the decks again for lunch. We are to have smoked Shetland haddocks, clapshot, and lager in a cottage down a pier.

History of a Column

26 November 1992

A parcel came with a thump through the door yesterday morning.

How hard it is to get into parcels nowadays, with all those swathings of thick green tape!... Not like the old days, when you took scissors to string only. Of course there were always some who didn't like to waste string, so they might spend twenty minutes or so patiently undoing the knots; and there at the end of it, was another neatly-tied coil of string to add to the dozen or so other bits of string in a drawer: 'just in case'... It was no consumer society in my youth – nothing was wasted that might be put to conceivable use some time in the future ... in consequence, many a house was stuffed with the 'just-in-case' bric-a-brac of two decades or so... Until a new generation came and made a bonfire of the lot.

The same with the brown paper that parcels were wrapped in. All the sheets were kept and folded and laid by – to send next Christmas with that knitted jersey to cousin Jimmo in Canada, to keep him warm among the blizzards; or to send a round crumbly cheese to Maggie in Edinburgh or Manchester, to remind her of home...

Not much chance of saving brown paper nowadays – that green sticky stuff rips the strongest paper to shreds.

Then of course the boxes round which the paper was wrapped, they were generally saved too, until the cupboard under the stairs was piled high with cardboard boxes, that 'might come in handy'... Those boxes were for the bonfire too, in the end...

After the above long preamble – almost as wearisome as getting into the contents of the parcel – at last in my parcel there were six copies of *Rockpools and Daffodils* from the publisher in Edinburgh, Gordon Wright.

In case you are wondering what *Rockpools and Daffodils* might be, I suppose it is only common decency to tell the readers of this column that the book is a selection of twelve years of 'Under Brinkie's Brae', the task of collecting and editing being done with great skill and patience over the winter and spring by my friend and neighbour, Brian Murray.

This writing of a weekly column goes back a long way. It began in *The Orkney Herald* with a little weekly essay called 'What the Pier Head is Saying'.

When the *Herald* ceased publication, 'What the Pier Head is Saying' moved to *The Orcadian* under another title, 'Letter from Hamnavoe'. Then the stream seemed to run dry after a few years, and when the weekly column surfaced again, it had changed its name to 'Under Brinkie's Brae'.

Gordon Wright made books out of of both sets, *Letters from Hamnavoe* and *Under Brinkie's Brae*.

It's twelve years since the book *Under Brinkie's Brae* was published... What to call this new book? – '*Under Brinkie's Brae 2*' didn't seem a good title.

After much rummaging among possibilities, we finally agreed on *Rockpools and Daffodils*... May there be a little sea silver and earth gold between the covers.

Desert Island Poems

3 December 1992

'What's the use of poetry?' the practical people are always saying... For unless you can eat something or drink it or wear it or use it to fly away to Majorca or buy new curtains for winter, what's the point of it?

Poetry does have its uses, after all. Two and a half years ago I spent some time in that wonderful place, Foresterhill Hospital in Aberdeen... After an operation, there were several nights in a row when I hardly slept at all. We all know what a desert that is to traverse, when we can't sleep. How heavy and wearisome the burden of the night is!

I was lucky, for there were several oases in my desert. I remembered the poems learned at school, especially the long ones like 'The Hound of Heaven', 'Lycidas', the 'Intimations of Immortality'. Also the great Shakespeare speeches, 'To be or not to be', 'Friends, Romans, countrymen', 'If it were done when 'tis done'...

So the burden was lightened, night after night.

I often wonder, on the pattern of 'Desert Island Discs', what flimsy leaflet with eight poems in it I would choose, until the rescue ship arrived.

Starting with two Orkneymen, I would want Edwin Muir's great poem 'The Transfiguration' and Robert Rendall's 'Celestial Kinsmen'.

Still in Scotland, I wouldn't like to be without the marvellous closing section of MacDiarmid's 'A Drunk Man'. And what is perhaps, the greatest of the Border Ballads, 'A Lyke-Wake Dirge', ('This nicht, this ae nicht'...).

Nothing nowadays seems as fresh and lovely as some of the medieval lyrics, like 'He came alle so stille'... In the last century or two, especially, the grime and dust of industrialism has spread, even into the arts.

There is Thomas Hardy's wonderful elegy for himself, 'When the Present has latched its postern'...

What about the great treasure hoard of the Romantics? Out of them all I would choose Keats' 'Ode on a Grecian Urn'.

The riches of our poetry are so great that the difficulty is to know what marvels to leave out of that flimsy desert island pamphlet... How careful I'd have to be to preserve it from the erosions of salt and sun and devouring insects!

There ought to be a Shakespeare sonnet: 'When to the sessions of sweet silent thought'... and a Miltonic chorus, the magnificent 'Come, come; no time for lamentation now', from 'Samson Agonistes'.

I wouldn't want to be without a Hopkins sonnet: 'The world is charged with the grandeur of God', which sees to the clean roots of things under all the grime and the dirt...

There would be days and nights when one would despair of ever getting away from the pitiless sun and the shark-infested sea. Or one might feel out of sorts. Then a great consolation would be Donne's 'Hymne to God my God, in my sicknesse...' Then the exiled one would know that all places are the same place really.

I think enumerating the above, maybe I have got the printer to stitch an extra poem into the pamphlet, and I have got away with nine instead of the stipulated eight. No one will begrudge that; since I would want to be washed ashore with a box of a thousand poems at least – book after book.

Far-Travelled 'O.O.'

10 December 1992

Little did he think, the man who was filling bottles from a whisky barrel at Stromness Distillery eighty or ninety years ago, that one of those same bottles would be auctioned by Christie's in Glasgow and be knocked down for £1,045.

At the White Horse Inn, North End Road, the landlord Maggie Marwick was selling the same whisky for half a crown a bottle, and three-and-six for the special blend; though it was said there was no difference, they came out of the same barrel... Only, the grander folk of Stromness thought they were getting a superior blend.

Also – I was told by the ancients when I was a boy – when you bought a bottle of whisky from The White Horse, you were given a brimming noggin free. (Half a crown was 12½ new pence.)

I wonder how many bottles of 'Old Orkney' malt there are left in the world?

£1,045 sounds like a great price for a bottle of whisky. But as the Persian poet Omar Khayyám said: 'I often wonder what the Vintners buy / One half so precious as the Goods they sell...'

Mayburn Court stands where Stromness Distillery used to be. Can you wonder that, from time to time, a faint far-off whiff of 'Old Orkney' drifts, through the houses, like a benign ghost?

To return to the distillery worker who has been filling bottles from that great vat in the year 1915. He maybe filled two or three hundred before yoking time in the late afternoon.

It's said, the fumes of John Barleycorn can make you merry, without a drop passing your lips.

Home he goes, happily, to his tea in his house at the South End. His wife knows ower-weel when he's been at the bottling; the normally silent man talks and talks all through the ham-and-egg tea and half-way through the evening, until at last he nods asleep in the straw chair beside the fire.

Then the neighbour women can come in and exchange the news of the neighbourhood: for the whisky-bottler is snoring soundly with a blissful look on his face.

This evening, earlier, he has been telling his wife and bairns about the 300 bottles he filled in that great distillery in the golden triangle between Billy Clouston's Inn and the Police Station and the Town Hall.

'Don't think for a moment, woman,' he has said, 'that the bottles will be drunk only in Stromness and Orkney, of course they won't. A case or two will be sent as far as Aberdeen or Edinburgh. They ken good whisky in the hotels there. I wouldna be surprised if a case got as far as London. Now I think aboot it, there must be Orkney men in New York that'll drink "Old Orkney" only – nothing but

"Old Orkney" for them. Imagine that if you can, woman – one of the bottles I filled this morning might be standing in a month's time on the gantry of a great bar in New York!...'

But if somebody had told him that another of his bottles would find its way to Japan, eighty years later, and would cost £1,045 – he would think he had maybe stood among the fumes a bit too long that day.

My Christmas Card

24 December 1992

Now, on December 17 as I write this, the Christmas cards have been coming in thick and fast.

The problem is, every year, what to do with them all? At present I have crammed them into a plastic bag. But soon they'll have to be brought out into the open.

We used to be able to stand the cards on the mantelpiece and the sideboard, but that's not on (as they say). For if someone opens the door to come in, down flutter the cards like a dozen white birds... Then for a few years they were strung along the walls – Nativity scenes and log fires and robins-in-the-snow and stage coaches and Santa Claus navigating among stars and smoking chimneys; and that seemed to be a good idea, except that I'm handless – as the old folk say – at rigging-jobs like that.

So for the past few Christmases a friend has lent me a wide shallow basket, and there the cards lie, to be picked up and read by visitors. The basket keeps them all in one place. The living-room doesn't have a Christmassy feel to it; but that can be remedied by lighting a few candles on St Lucy day and St Thomas day (Tammasmas, as Orcadians called it until about a hundred years ago) – the winter solstice, the shortest day.

The stillness and purity of candlelight in midwinter, round about sunset – that is a very beautiful thing.

Once again my friend, the artist and publisher, Simon Fraser of Nairn, has designed a Christmas card for us both – Simon's drawing, my poem. The theme is *Maeshowe, Midwinter*. There is a lissom lady on the drawing, and people wonder what she has to do with Maeshowe, that place constructed with magnificent artistry and mathematics to allow the setting sun on December 21 to enter and touch the tomb of the dead – as daring an intuition of resurrection as the Stone Age mind was capable of...

I thought perhaps the girl might be Ingibiorg, who is praised in one of the Maeshowe runes: INGIBIORG IS THE LOVELIEST OF THE WOMEN. So carved a young crusader, wintering in Orkney to go on pilgrimage with Earl Rognvald Kolson to Jerusalem and Rome in 1150 – a greeting and a farewell to his girl back in Norway.

Also, on this card of ours, there are little scatterings of bright tinsel... Again, recipients might want to know what they are, at Maeshowe on the winter solstice... I thought about this for a while, and remembered there was a rune to the effect that nearby a great treasure is hidden.

One morning when my friend Brian Murray was lighting the fire, he himself suggested the Ingibiorg rune and the great treasure rune; and so I was confirmed in my reading of the symbols.

It just remains for Simon Fraser to confirm all this. Then there will be no doubt about it.

A good Christmas and New Year to all readers of 'Under Brinkie's Brae'.

The New Year Song

31 December 1992

In some barn in the parish they would have met in the afternoon of New Year's Day, about sunset – many of the young men. In secret it seemed, but the whole parish knew about it, and looked forward to what was to come, with some excitement.

In a dozen farms and crofts they were expecting the singing of the New Year Song, which was a kind of blessing on every house and steading. So the tables were loaded with meat and cheese, bannocks and oatbread and butter, and the vat in the corner seethed with ale that probably would have been put down in the first days of winter.

And peats were piled high in the hearth, till the hearth flames gave more light than the little lamps.

Meantime the young men in the barn sorted themselves out. There was a fiddler. Those with good voices were told to sing when the time came, loud and clear.

They had had well-salted fish for their dinner, and so every man of them had a good thirst.

One man was chosen to be the 'cerryan horse'. He carried an empty sack. He was the travelling clown, or fool. Before midnight he would be well kicked and punched by his buddies – but not too hard – and as compensation he always got in every house more food and drink than the others. The sack was to hold the surplus food from the farm tables.

At last the leader of the group gave a sign. The sun was under the horizon, but the glow still lingered in the south-west.

The leader carried a lantern. The midwinter night, if there was no moon, would be very dark.

In the first farm, all the household were assembled – the grave farmer and his apple-cheeked wife, the sons and daughters and maybe a grandchild, the farm labourer and the two servant lasses. This was an ancient farm with a Norse name: the family had lived here, generation by generation, for centuries.

Through the frosty evening air they heard at last the footsteps and the voices of the dozen young men. The door was thrown open to them: they entered with starlight and cold airs from the Atlantic.

At once, over the threshold, they began the song that is the greatest poetry that Orkney has ever produced:

> Good be to this buirdly bigging[1]!
>   We're a' St Mary's men.
> Fae the steeth-stane[2] tae the rigging.
>   'Fore wur Lady...

They stopped after the third verse or so. There were things to be done. The bold band of itinerants and bearers of the New Year blessing went round greeting all the inhabitants, from the oldest to the youngest. The daughters and the farm lasses were kissed till their faces glowed, and the woman of the house was gravely saluted with a kiss too.

Then a few more verses were sung:

> May a' your hens rin in a reel,
>   We're a' St Mary's men.
> An' every ane twal[3] at her heel,
>   'Fore wur Lady...

1 sturdy building
2 foundation-stone, anchor-stone
3 twelve

Then it was time to stand round the table and eat and drink. The young men were hungry and thirsty. They didn't eat and drink too much: there were several more farms and crofts to visit before midnight .... any food left over was put in the sack carried by the 'cerryan horse'. Then the bearer of the sack was given a few blows and kicks – but merely token punishment.

The fiddler flashed bow upon strings. There might be a few steps of a reel.

Then the rest of the wonderful ballad was sung, well over a score of verses.

> This is the seventh night o' Yule,
> We're a' St Mary's men...

At last the first-footers left the house, under the wide arches of the stars, for the next house.

A long evening of merriment was in prospect for the whole parish; but every household felt that they had an immemorial blessing put upon it.

The Poet and Opinions

7 January 1993

Tomorrow, as I write this, is the last day of 1992.

Outside, hoar-frost covers the grass, and I'll have to be careful going down the slippery concrete Mayburn steps.

Not a cloud in the sky for days, the isles and the waters still as if a cold angel was spreading wings over Orkney. (Very poetical: but extraordinary winter weather like this, five or six days of it, is enough to shake any mind out of its greyness.) And the gash of dawn over the Orphir hills, and the mist-rose serenity of sunset over Hoy, and the noontides quiet and cold as crystal... It's a splendid bounty to be given at the year's end.

I almost forgot: the new moon. There it was, high up in the south-west, on Sunday evening, and a brilliant star beside it.

Winter can be a very beautiful time. But as the pessimists say, 'We'll pay for this!'... We optimists say, to restore the balance, 'It's been paid for beforehand...'

I sometimes think it is wrong, or at least inadvisable, to re-read a book that one has enjoyed some years before.

Yesterday, December 29, being the feast-day of St Thomas Becket of Canterbury, I took down T. S. Eliot's play on the subject, *Murder in the Cathedral*, and much of the enchantment had evaporated.

There are one or two wonderful speeches by Thomas himself, and the speeches to the theatre audience by the four murderers, who (though medieval) were of the shooting-and-hunting squire type, were very funny.

But the play as a whole left me cold. There is a chorus of the women of Canterbury, ordinary housewives, and they would never have used such bizarre and eccentric images to describe their situation – and the language was stretched to screaming point and beyond... I think the grief of ordinary housewives under communal stress must be quite otherwise.

All the above remarks are in no way to diminish the great admiration I have for T. S. Eliot.

I doubt if there are as good poets writing in English now.

Certainly not the poet who is currently most spoken about, on account of his *Selected Letters* that has recently been published. Philip Larkin wrote a handful of very fine poems that came out of his own time and circumstances, but he seemed unable to rise high enough to take a world view, or to transcend the mood of the late twentieth century in England. What he did achieve – 'Whitsun Weddings', 'Church Going' – is extraordinarily good.

Then why did they have to go and publish his letters, so soon after his death in 1985? Letters are very intimate communications, meant for the recipient and no one else. At least a half-century should pass before they see the light; whereas many people still alive are certain to be hurt by things in them.

For me, I was slightly shaken that a man of such hidebound reactionary opinions could have written poetry at all.

But then, one is constantly being surprised, and a good thing too. Away with stereotypes. Ezra Pound the American poet broadcast for Mussolini, during the war. T. S. Eliot was a high-Anglican and a royalist. Wordsworth after his revolutionary youth – he wrote his great verse then – lived on to become a stuffy old Victorian gent...

The poet is forever soaring above the opinionated man (though both inhabit the same framework of blood and bone and think-box)...

A Happy New Year to all readers of 'Under Brinkie's Brae'.

Happy Winters of Old

14 January 1993

What are they planning for us, the snow giants of the north, this midwinter?

They decide suddenly. 'Let them have it,' they say. And then a black blizzard is suddenly about us – and down come the power lines, and inside an hour Orkney is a mini-Siberia. (This happened one Saturday afternoon some fifteen winters ago. Even the dead had to be sledged to the kirkyards.)

Since that fearful onslaught, the snow giants have been too lazy, or indifferent... Three years ago there was an eccentric outburst on the last day of February – a white thick dazzlement that melted as soon as it fell, and left the snowdrops.

Let's hope it's only laziness or indifference, up there with the snow giants in North Greenland or Spitzbergen, and not something more sinister, like global warming or the greenhouse effect, that's pared their teeth or their claws, or curbed their ferocious gleefulness.

For, however we dislike snow and blizzards, to be walking mouth deep in a tepid ever-rising sea is too hideous to think about.

Think of the water washing among the roofs of Stromness...

(I am writing this in a minor sick-bed, having caught one of those winter bugs – and so every thought is touched with gloom and foreboding, a little.)

It is suddenly cheering to think – for the first time since childhood – of the first flurry of snow, and the stars snapping frosty fingers in the sky.

It was Twelfth Night yesterday; the Three Kings are off east, going home, with their empty camel saddles; and the lesser stars flash about their going.

In northern lands, haggises are being stuffed and ale brewed for Burns Suppers, in case the Snow Giants decide to join in the revels... Country children are dreaming of snowmen with coal for eyes in the school yard – or, better still, of holidays from school if the roads are too deep for the buses to get through.

Grannies are knitting mufflers and bonnets and gloves as fast as their needles can clack, while outside the snow drifts down soft and grey as their frail grey hair.

And the blackbirds throb on the telegraph-wires, little blocks of ebony.

Happy winters of old, may they come again, and often.

Long may the Arctic Snow Giants decide to have games with us, this winter and that.

(Having written the above, I can lie a bit more easy in my bed of flu – and even in old age extend a frail welcome to the first snowflakes, if they do come.)

The Fiddler of Fara

21 January 1993

There was once a fiddler in the island of Fara who had been a good fiddler in his youth, but now his hands were all knotted up with rheumatics, and he was bidden no more to play in alehouses or harvest homes.

Two younger fiddlers were summoned each January now to the Burns Supper.

So old Jimmo felt like an outcast, with no road in front of him except the road to his long home (that is, the kirkyard).

He sat at his blink of fire and saw the full moon through his window. It was a night of pure enchantment.

The island tracks would soon be full of Burns celebrants, going to the barn at the Ha with their whisky bottles and bits of tartan sewn in their bonnets. And a score of bonny lasses too.

And there would be ham and cold hen, clapshot and haggis and home-brewed ale.

And the two young fiddlers would be tuning their fiddles – new fiddles with fresh varnish shining.

Old Jimmo thought there would be no harm in him putting in an appearance, but he would leave his worn-out fiddle at home.

It was a fine, cloudless winter evening. The moon shone new-minted in the loch and in every turning shore wave. There were a thousand stars.

There was not a soul on the road to the Ha. And the barn, when Jimmo got to it, was silent, though in a bleeze of light.

And there, at the long tables, sat the strangest company Jimmo had ever thought to see this side of the grave. Head by head they turned to old Jimmo as he walked uncertainly to the warm kiln, and introduced themselves. 'Black Pat,' said one. 'Sweyn Asleifson,' said another. 'Lord William Sinclair'... 'John Gow, pirate'... 'Lord Odivere' ... 'The Earl Bothwell' ... 'The laird of Hether Blether'...

And there were a score of dark handsome ladies. All smiled a welcome to the poor old man, who had never had such generous greeting in all his long life no, not since he was a famous fiddler in the first flush and zest of youth.

'We have eaten and drunk well,' said Black Pat who had been executed for high treason in Edinburgh two centuries earlier. 'Now it is come to dancing-time.'

So the tables were cleared.

Old Jimmo was going to say he had left his old bruck[1] of a fiddle at home when he realised he was clutching a fine old Norwegian fiddle in one hand and a bow like a shaft of light in the other.

A silver cup with red wine in it was passed to Jimmo. He wet his mouth; he reddened it more than once. Blood flowed joyously through his veins, like fifty winters ago.

Never in the island of Fara had there been such music and dancing. It went on and on. They heard across the still waters the cathedral kirk bell striking midnight. And the high revelry went on and on.

It struck Jimmo that the music and dancing were much older than Burns.

Jimmo felt a bit tired, just as the January sun was flushing the south-east.

He sat down. The fiddle quivered in his hand like an ecstatic bird, that had made a long daring migration.

One by one the famous guests took their leave. Each as he went pressed a silver coin into Jimmo's hand.

At last Jimmo was done.

'Time I was makan[2] homeward too,' said Jimmo.

Outside, he could hardly believe what he saw! The island was like a great white enchanted whale with smoke coming from a dozen half-buried crofts.

There was no one to be seen. All Fara, and the other islands too, were snowbound.

Every step Jimmo made, his boots sank two feet in the drifts.

At the smithy door, there stood Andrew the smith. And, 'Mercy, boy,' said Andrew. 'Thoo're the only man in Fara that's been oot since the blizzards yestre'en in the efternoon. What's taken thee oot, boy?'

Jimmo said he was on his way home from the grandest Burns Supper there had ever been in Fara, with the highest noblest guests.

1 broken pieces
2 making (my way)

'But Jimmo,' cried Andrew, 'there was no Burns Supper. The Supper was cancelled – nobody could get oot for the blizzard yestere'en.'

'I have good silver to prove it,' said Jimmo, but when he searched for the leather poke, all that was there was a dozen grey hailstones, that melted.

And the Norwegian fiddle he was carrying, it had fallen from his shoulder into that white bedazzlement; or else it was changed to that rook on the branch of the kirkyard tree.

'Anyway,' said Jimmo, 'it was a good enough night, thanks to the vanished grandeur of Orkney...'

The Winter Bug

28 January 1993

The first thing that happens when this winter bug gets into you – as it did between Christmas and Hogmanay – is that you get a slight rawness in the throat. Sudden it falls as dew on a grass-blade.

Then you rapidly begin to lose interest in things – in food, in reading, in the stark magnificence of winter.

The little roughness in the throat spreads rapidly into head and bronchial tubes. Coughing becomes the main activity of your life – coughing and a general malevolence and misery.

I think: 'I can always write a little...' Not creatively, but the feel of the pen in the fingers is somehow reassuring, a lifeline.

Every morning, I write a kind of diary – nothing like Pepys or Boswell – a dull factual record that even bores myself on re-reading... I was shocked to see how badly the letters were formed, and the writing clotted and all over the place – a right mess!

Also I had to write a small cheque – a wretched mess I made of it, and I even forgot to sign the thing.

A bowl of broth – some orange juice. Nothing else. The appetite had closed down hatches.

What it is, to sit day-long in the rocker, indifferent whether you look at the flames in the hearth or the nonsensical shadows on TV! Books! – why waste energy on them? All your energy is required to cough up vile thick stuff out of the lungs, and to plunge deeper and deeper into misery.

Of course doctors and good friends hurried to help. (The way ahead was not helped by the fact that BBC people were coming to interview me in a few days' time... A torpor of anxiety weighed like a cloud.)

At last it was thought advisable to shove me into hospital for a few days. There I breathed healing vapours three or four times a day through burbling, fizzing masks, and seemed to be bombarded with hailstorms of tablets and pills ... all the nurses were kind and considerate; and so busy...

I was lucky that in the little three-bed ward I was neighboured on one side by Albert Thomson, ex-custodian of St Magnus and an expert on the building, and on the other side by Ned Spence of Brodgar, trout expert and boatman. Neither of them, I'm thankful to say, wanted to watch the TV on the opposite wall. (I feel strongly that, for the general well-being and recovery of patients, TV in hospitals ought to be banned, except in common-rooms... Subjected to constant ITV for a few days, I feel sure I'd be driven mad... We had no TV. It was a good silence.)

Outside, storms howled and snow fell thickly...

Now here I am in a friend's house in Stromness, very well looked after, beginning to feel at last much better.

The dreadful gales from the west have gone on for days. This morning the sky is all blue and silver, and the faltering electricity fully restored.

It's time I was thinking of Mayburn Court and the tasks to be done there.

The Door of the Oval Room

4 February 1993

I lay on the couch one day last week and watched the inauguration of President Clinton.

That young man won't be having his troubles to seek in the next four years... Yet thousands of American politicians would give anything to be in his shoes.

People commented on President Bush's geniality on the steps of the Capitol. I am sure it was the light of relief in his eyes: to wake up every morning with that heavy burden rolled away for ever – what joy!

The first President I really remember was Franklin D. Roosevelt. He was in office for so long, it was difficult to think of America without him. The news of his sudden death brought brief joy to Hitler in his Berlin bunker in April 1945.

And who on earth was the little guy who succeeded him? Harry S. Truman. Nobody knew anything about him. He was sure to be booted out in the 1948 election. A famous handsome Republican, Governor Dewey, I think, opposed him. Harry S. Truman won against all the odds. The public opinion polls had been wrong – not for the first time. There was something tough and terrier-like about HST.

How does it happen that American presidential elections always fascinate Orcadians, in our remote islands? It isn't as if anyone of Orcadian descent ever aspired to the White House... Northern Ireland is the place that has supplied so many Presidents for some reason.

If you preside over a victorious war, the door of the Oval Room is yours for the asking. So General Eisenhower was elected for two terms – though he was opposed by a clever able charismatic man, Adlai Stevenson, on both occasions. Adlai never stood a chance, though he would probably have been a much greater President.

Then the legend of John F. Kennedy began. America was young again, and full of hope. In the end a crazy man looked through his telescopic lens high up in a Dallas book-store, and that was the end of the dream... Yet already a dreadful thing was happening to America; with all her massively-deployed technical skills, she was losing the war in Viet-Nam. (Edwin Muir has a very fine poem, 'The Combat', about that kind of thing.) President Johnson inherited that mess, and pulled out in time. Johnson looked like a tough cowboy. A term and a half of it, and the rough rider had had enough.

Then Nixon came out of the shadows, and taped all his private talk, possibly as an aide-mémoire when the time came to write his memoirs. Surely he would have had time to destroy those tapes? It is a mystery. In the end it was too late. He had to go.

There ensued the grey reigns of Presidents Ford and Carter, Reagan and Bush. We've seen their careers daily on TV.

Far behind, the Stromness schoolboy reading the *Daily Express* by the light of a paraffin lamp in 1933 or 1934, and wondering what on earth President Roosevelt was going to do about all those poor men queuing at the soup kitchens (some of those singing 'Brother can you spare a dime' had been well off a few years back...).

President Clinton, may you have some of the foresight and luck and imagination of that illustrious predecessor...

A Stone Age Pub Crawl

11 February 1993

Did I read about it, or did I dream that one or other of our ancient monuments is to get a drink licence?

Five thousand years ago, there were three young Sandwick men who thought they might as well go for a drink to Skara Brae. It was sheep-shearing time: they had had a long day of it.

So off Prem and Prad and Poke set from the hill Kierfiold to the village.

When they got to Skara Brae they found that the village was busy. The fishermen were in with a good catch and the women were cleaning haddocks down at the rock pools, and the salty-throated fishermen were kicking the stone door of The Limpet Arms, demanding a drink.

At last the landlord, who had been brewing all day and was a bit awkward and tired, let the fishermen in.

Prem and Prad and Poke thought it best to seek another tavern. The hill-men and the boat-men never got on at the best of times.

The landlord of the Hole o' Rowe was just sliding back the stone bar across his stone door. He was a very merry man called Malik. 'Come on in, lads!' cried he. 'I always like to see the shepherds. No trouble with the shepherds. Now, what would you be wanting to drink?' Prem and Prad and Poke thought for a while, then they ordered three stone mugs of tangle ale... It was a rough drink but it quenched their thirst... The landlord wrote down their debt on a square stone: he would be paid with a sheep's head on the next killing day.

'Let's move on,' said Prem to Prad and Poke. 'No more tangle ale for me.'

A great noise of singing and laughter was coming from The Limpet Arms. The thirsty fishermen were getting into their stride.

The three shepherds went into the Partan, that was kept by a fierce old lady called Ona. Ona kept only root beer, on her stone gantry. Prem ordered three mugs. The root beer tasted of ditches and bogs but the three shepherds downed it in a few gulps. 'You're drinking too fast,' said the landlady. 'Watch yourself. I want no trouble in here, mind.'

She marked them down for sheep's liver and lights on the next killing day.

'Coorse stuff,' said Prad to Poke as they left the Partan. The noise inside The Limpet Arms was louder than ever, and here and there it had an edge to it.

'What about The Hether Blether?' said Prem. 'Good stuff, the heather ale they sell there... It's a bit dearer, of course.'

By the time they had downed their mugs of heather ale, they began to think that no men anywhere in Orkney could be so happy as their three selves. They laughed. They sang a song or two. They even mentioned going to The Limpet Arms. So they heaved themselves from the stone bench to their feet.

'Aren't you forgetting something?' said the wily keeper of The Hether Blether. They promised him three legs of lamb, come killing time.

'It mightn't be a good idea,' said Prad, 'going to The Limpet Arms' ... sounds of raised voices and splintering stone issued from that tavern.

The three shepherds were too happy to fight.

Instead, they lurched merrily rather than walked into The Selkie, where all the wise old men went to tell stories and discuss deep matters. Only mead was sold in The Selkie. The landlord lost no time in telling Prem and Prad and Poke that they would not be served. Shepherds from the hill were too poor to afford the ale with honey in it, called mead.

Prem promised most solemnly that The Selkie would have two of the best fleeces now the shearing was done. Stone mugs of foaming heather ale were set before them.

The old village men – aged about thirty-five or forty – smiled from every corner. A few shook their heads.

Prem and Prad and Poke remembered nothing after that until they woke up next morning in their bothy. Prem had a black eye. Prad had lost two teeth, Poke said he was sure his nose was broken.

They concluded that they must have gone to The Limpet Arms in the end, to have a word with the fishermen.

Changing Taste in Song

25 February 1993

Last Monday evening I was talking to fifteen-year-old Magnus Dixon about TV programmes due later that night.

Magnus said there was a programme about Michael Jackson that would be watched by maybe millions.

'Who's Michael Jackson?' said I.

Magnus was absolutely astonished that I didn't know who Michael Jackson was – far more so, it seemed to me, than if I had been ignorant of the existence of Mr Major or President Clinton.

I said I knew hardly any pop stars' names, after The Beatles. I was, I said, only beginning now to catch up with The Beatles.

When the hideous din of new pop music comes pounding out of the TV, I switch off at once. I've done that for the last twenty-five years.

So how would I know who this Michael Jackson is, or the young lady called Madonna?

The scene is so much changed since, in the mid-thirties, we switched on the first battery in the house, and listened to Henry Hall and the BBC Dance Orchestra, with their signature tune 'Here's to the next time'... There were, besides Henry Hall, Joe Loss and Billy Cotton and many other bands ... Those orchestras had a few new numbers every week that we could hum going to school. The 'lyrics' were generally a bit weak, but we didn't worry too much about that: 'Red Sails in the Sunset'... 'Home, James and Don't Spare the Horses'... 'I'm Going Home for Christmas'... 'The Yellow Rose of Texas'... 'The Isle of Capri'... 'South of the Border, Down Mexico Way'...

I don't remember the names of any of the singers except a lady called Elsa Lanchester. Whoever they were, they weren't adored like the pop heroes of today. They just sang their little group of songs each week, and we looked forward to hearing a new number or two the following week – but there were none of those howling mobs of teenagers prostrating themselves before inarticulate savage rhythms.... The first indication that anything like that was coming was when the youthful Frank Sinatra in America began to attract the 'bobbysoxers'.

Going further back still, I don't of course remember Edwardian music hall lyrics, but my father had a large collection of them that he would sing round about New Year – 'It was Only a Beautiful Picture in a Beautiful Golden Frame'... 'I'll Stick to the Ship, Lads'... 'A Tiny Seed of Love'... 'Mind the Paint'... 'While London Sleeps'... 'A Bird in a Gilded Cage'...

I think the tough teenagers of today could never have come to terms with those songs, which tended on the whole to be sentimental. The 'Beautiful Picture' drew tears down the cheeks of aging spinsters and hard businessmen... The songs of the turn of the century would have been a long time getting to Orkney at all. I think they were maybe sung at Orkney street-corners by unemployed wounded soldiers after the war. Sheet music would have been slowly sifting into the islands. The first 78rpm gramophone records were arriving. Then the wireless sets.

The new age was breeding, even as long ago as the turn of the century... But the local singers of popular songs never dreamed that Michael Jackson or Madonna were on the way.

'Hail, Brave Ship!'

4 March 1993

For one birthday present last October I was given a ship in a bottle – and not any old ship either, but the *St Ola* – and not one of the three post-1950 *Olas* either, but the original *Ola* that plied the Pentland Firth between 1890 and 1950.

She was a small narrow black steamer that could only take about three cars, but all the mail crossed on her, and the comparatively few tourists of those days.

She seemed as much a part of Stromness as Brinkie's Brae or The Holms.

I first crossed on her about 1927, at the age of five, with my mother and brother, and I don't remember a thing about it. I think I was sick, but a merciful amnesia has wiped that misery from the mind. We were going to stay for a week or two with my Gaelic-speaking grandpa and grandma at Braal in Strathy, Sutherland. All I can remember of that holiday was the desolation of the landscape, the kindness of my grandma, the sea-monster called 'the rone' that lived in the crags below (I suppose 'the rone' might have been a device to keep us away from that dangerous place) – and the fact that I fell in the burn nearby. Also my grandfather read aloud from the Bible, probably in Gaelic...

I hadn't imagined that such a lonely place could be. Stromness was like an ant-hill compared to Strathy.

On the way to Scrabster, to catch *Ola I* going home, my mother took us to see the train at Thurso for the first time. This was meant to be a great treat. But my brother and I said we had seen far better trains in books...

There was something wonderfully reassuring about the *Ola* as she left the old wooden Warehouse Pier every morning, and returned every afternoon about 4pm. There were the two familiar blasts as she rounded Ness. Then, in the summer holidays, we boys rowed out to meet her and enjoy the bow wave; up and down the flattie went, several times. We all let on to enjoy the *Ola*'s waves tremendously, but in truth I was always pleased enough to be in calm water again.

No radar in those days. There was a dramatic day or two in the early thirties when the *Ola* was fog-bound somewhere off Hoy Sound. Those summer fogs made a swift sinister descent and rolled away as suddenly, but sometimes only after a day or two.

My father and the other postmen were there to meet the *Ola* at the Warehouse Pier, to wheel the bags of mail to the Post Office for sorting and delivery – letters delivered in the late afternoon, parcels the following morning.

There on the street, one by one, the crew of the *Ola* went home, each with a little box or satchel under his arm (possibly it held his sandwiches and Thermos flask).

So now I have *St Ola I* sailing the Pentland Firth forever, on top of my bookcase, in its crystal case; which looks to me to have been an empty whisky bottle.

Hail, brave ship! – I wonder are you still sailing among Aegean islands, with some Greek or Albanian name. If she's still on the go, she'll be 103 years old.

From Cruisie to Anglepoise

18 March 1993

Suddenly, reading a book late at night, there is darkness... The 60-watt bulb in the Anglepoise lamp has died the death, without any preliminary sign of ailing – with what Thomas Hardy called 'an eyelid's soundless blink' the lamp is extinguished.

Fortunately, most responsible citizens have a small supply of spare bulbs, and it's no trouble to fit a new one.

I'm trying to remember how we fared in the days before electricity, pre-1947. (I was actually present at the switching on of electricity, officially, in Banks's café in Alfred Street: but it was a very quiet affair, and I was present in my capacity as Stromness correspondent of *The Orkney Herald*.)

We had, of course, gas. You had to have a plentiful supply of pennies (the big old round heavy ones) to put in the gas meter.

Gas light was diffused through a mantle, which was very fragile and had to be renewed fairly often. But then one might get some warning. The mantle might begin to look ragged, and in the end collapse in a silent shower of fragments, soft and white as snowflakes... Time to fix a new mantle – it was stiffened with wax and the wax had to be burned off with a lighted match, first of all.

Another step back in time, and we are in the age of the paraffin lamp.

There it stood on the dresser or in the middle of the table, crowning the winter with its soft radiance. There we did our homework or played games of Ludo or read *The Wizard*... The paraffin lamp needed more attention than electricity or gas. The wick had to be trimmed from time to time with a red-hot poker. The bowl had to be filled with paraffin.

The paraffin was kept in a gallon can in the closet. Forby the lamp, paraffin was used to help light the fire in the morning. A dollop of paraffin was poured over the paper and sticks – then with a swoosh a towering flame poured up the lum, and the housework could begin.

Before the paraffin lamp? Now we venture into unknown territory. My father liked to collect old things and so there were a few cruisie[1] lamps in the house... What a meagre glow-worm flame they must have given – impossible for our great-great-grandfathers to have read by them. More light came from the peat fires, probably, than from those glimmerings on the wall.

No wonder the old legends flowered from the lips on winter nights, for many generations. No wonder it was a good era for fiddlers. Both spoken stories and music might well have sounded magical by those muted lights.

And further back than the cruisie lamp even. How did they pass the long winter nights in Skara Brae? I expect, once the sun went down, they went to their stone beds.

'Unwillingly to School'

25 March 1993

Another rainy morning, after a rain-swept, wind-swept day yesterday.

If I had looked through the window earlier, I'd have seen 'the scholars' struggling to school with their anoraks or other rain-

1 open, boat-shaped lamp with a rush wick

cheaters on – a long distance out to the Garson shore. We thought it long enough on March mornings to the Academy on the side of Brinkie's Brae, rain or sun.

And very often, alas, we were late, stumbling up the Boys' Lane, or along the road behind 'the Owld Kirk'... There, at the school gate, we were often met by the headmaster, Mr Learmonth, and he had some pretty hard words for us Southenders, or Well Parkers; for there were frequently half-a-dozen of us peching[1] up the brae...

But we didn't have all that far to go, after all. Pupils had to come in from Outertown, two or three miles to the West. It can't have been any fun at all, trekking along that exposed road on stormy winter mornings, past Dale and The Castle and Oglaby, and round by the back of St Peter's Manse.

In the Primary, the Outertown pupils were let off early on the shortest afternoons in winter, when 'the grimmlings'[2] came on at three o'clock.

The Outertown pupils seemed to have no problem being there in the morning when Mr Wilson (janitor) rang the bell... But the Southenders, we never seemed to time things properly.

What a rush and bustle there was in the morning! I think we must have lain abed till 8.30 or so. Did we have time to wash our faces, even? (Maybe we had done that the night before, just to get it out of the way.) ... Cornflakes and milk spooned in, one of Porteous's rolls thickly buttered with Citadel butter, the cramming of textbooks and jotters into a school-bag coming apart at the seams, then the hastening along Ness Road, joined by other late-comers, from the Double Houses and the Lighthouse Buildings... The misery was compounded by the knowledge of home-lessons inadequately done or not done at all. (What healthy boy bothers with Latin or Algebra when there's a ball to kick and a field to play football on, on an early summer evening?)

On we struggled, along Alfred Street and Dundas Street till we came to Khyber Pass. That was halfway to the school. Would we make it on time?

At Khyber Pass the slow climb begins, and takes you along Franklin Road to within sight of the Academy (which had only recently been known as the Secondary School) ... And somewhere along the last ascent, the 'North Col', the tocsin of doom sounded. The janitor was ringing the bell. We were late.

82

A few brave souls ran on faster. A few slowed down; for what was the point, our fate was sealed... Ten chances to one, Mr Learmonth was there to meet us, at the stern gate.

I remember being alone, and late, one winter morning of deep frost. I slithered about at the top of the Kirk Road. The last reverberations of the bell were in my ignorant unwashed ears. I slithered and fell and rose on the glassy surface. Such misery! And then, to crown it all, my school-bag burst, and books and jotters were strewn all over that wintry scene...

And still the old ones kept saying, 'Your school-days are your best days'...

Winter Reading

1 April 1993

Real winter-in-spring weather, with seemingly endless gales howling from west and northwest, and dropping flurries of flakes or lashing the windows with sleet.

The only signs of spring are the occasional sunbursts, the brave daffodils, and the lengthening light. From next Sunday on – as I write – we'll be having an extra hour of light.

A sign of age is that I no longer feel inclined to venture out in this weather, among those wolf-packs of cold wind. Ten years ago I'd have enjoyed battling with the gale and enjoying the flung sun and sleet.

The fireside becomes a better and better friend; that and a book in the rocking-chair.

I've been ashamed for a few years past of neglecting the Victorian novelists. A fortnight ago I began to read *Middlemarch* by George Eliot. In those days when they had no radio or TV and few newspapers, writers were expected to write long novels and readers wanted it that way. Also they had time to unravel long intricate sentences: I find I have to read many sentences of *Middlemarch* twice to get the gist. But it's worthwhile, in the end. The characters unfold slowly, like flowers opening.

And Dickens – I think we may have been put off Dickens at school, as we were put off Scott. *David Copperfield* and *The Talisman* – they are not among the happier memories of school reading.

The other night I began to read Dickens's *Bleak House*, which begins with the famous picture of the London fog, especially as it swirls round the Court of Chancery. Plenty of sentimentality, in the midst of mud, fog, and misery. But then suddenly begins a gallery of droll characters – Mrs Jellaby, Mr Jarndyce, Harold Skimpole – comical puppets exquisitely contrived.

I look forward to a few entertaining evenings.

I did; until my faithful Anglepoise lamp, after much blinking and darkening, went out. I have to read by an unsatisfactory substitute, until the Anglepoise is repaired. Or if it can't be repaired, a new one will have to be bought.

A cunning exquisitely-contrived invention, the Anglepoise lamp.

I wonder what Dickens would have said about it...

Crazy March Days

8 April 1993

March came in like a lamb, and went out like a lamb yesterday, in a blaze of sun. But in between, a whole pride of lions went raging about Orkney!

There may have been stormier Marches, but I don't remember one that racketed about our roofs so savagely, and broke the daffodil stems, and mingled rain and wind for days together in long-drawn misery.

There were magnificent episodes. I could stand some mornings at my window and watch the great waves thundering into the Museum noust. The tide rose – the wind shrieked louder – the driven waves were torn to shreds against Mr Burgon's pier, and magnificent cascades of spray were flung, time and again, athwart Tommy White's house and the Museum and the noust between. I could have stood and watched for an hour, but there was work to be done – and besides, the seaward-facing east window was slowly becoming more and more opaque with the drifted salt. (Even if the window had been as clear as crystal, it would have been difficult, in all that grey turmoil, to see Orphir across the Bay of Clestrain.)

Only the folk who had to be out were blown about the streets: a wretched getting of messages[1] and going to and from work.

And there, in the madhouse of a harbour, serene as queens, floated the three swans that have been gracing our waterfronts for the past weeks. They seemed to be quite impervious to the storms, drifting calmly from pier to pier... No doubt, apart from their serenity, they are clever swans, and they know (almost literally) which side their bread is buttered on, for the housewives of

84   1 shopping errands

Stromness throw them several snacks a day, and they live royally, I'm sure, compared to some loch-bound swans.

It wouldn't have been safe for me, on those crazy March days, to go and feed the swans, or I might have ended, like Lycidas, in the tormented sea.

Instead, I break my crusts for the small birds on the balcony at Mayburn Court. After the bread is scattered, they hold back for a time until they know the coast is clear. Then there are quick darts and whirrings past the window, and I know that the sparrows have come to dine.

The gulls try to come and drive the little birds away. But the railing prevents them, time after time. There's no room for the gulls to make a swoop and a descent and a landing. The crusts and crumbs are there – the small birds are having a great time of it – the gulls beat their wings impotently above.

It somehow does the spirits good to stand at the window and watch this David and Goliath act....

Yesterday, after all the prolonged rages and rants, March put on blue and gold to make its bow.

'Not before time,' we muttered; expecting – oh, foolishness! – that the real Spring would come with April.

April fools, we. For we woke this morning to wind howling about the chimney-pots, and rain lashing the windows.

Hope springs eternal. Perhaps tomorrow, or the day after, it will be tattie-planting day.

Sun after Storm

29 April 1993

At last, a morning of sun. May it last all the day through. For we need some sun, after the bleakest April I remember. After the wild winter tempests that went on and on, from before the time the *Braer* oil tanker went ashore in Shetland (and I with the greyness of flu on me ...).

'Never mind,' we consoled one another towards the end of February. 'March will be bright and windy.' The 'windy' part was an understatement, and we forgot almost what the sun looked like.

'The equinox will bring an improvement,' we assured the folk we met on the grey gusty street ... the equinox and after gathered its brows together.

'April,' we said out of the depths of gloom, 'is always a happy lyrical dancing month...' If there was any dancing in April it was the dance of the rain on the street, and the dark toss and whirl of the east wind – a very bad airt[1] for Stromness, the very worst: bringer of bronchitis and rheumatics.

We were just about to write April off as a dismal failure – not a laughing lass but a sullen young virago – when I drew the bedroom curtain back this morning and saw the fold of spring light over the South End gardens.

We forget easily – we are quick to forgive – at least as far as weather is concerned. (Would that we could forgive our fellow human beings so cleanly and generously!) So, thank you, April: as I write this you have another nine days to dower us with your dews, young light and freshness... But we have to be realistic – it won't all be like the April you see depicted on calendars, and celebrated by Chaucer and Shakespeare and Keats.

We will get a soaking or two before the sweets of May. We'll get flung about the street by an over-boisterous wind, this afternoon or that.

I think our unanimous bad report about the winter just past stems from the fact that we have had five or six mild winters in a row. You might say the winters have been almost as mild as the summers, and but for the changing light we wouldn't have known one from the other... Some of the children have hardly known what snow is, it came and vanished so quickly, a day-long dream of whiteness.

So, this hardly-endurable winter past was perhaps a reversion to the winters that used to be. Except for the snow, that was a sudden disappearing gleam in early January... What's happened to the snow, the winter delight of children, the overnight falling enchantment that lasted for weeks, with sledging, snowmen, snow-fights, and days off school?

We all hope, in our hearts of hearts, it has got nothing to do with global warming.

So, I'd better get out this morning while the sun shines. I need, among other messages, to get some money. Nowadays in Stromness, to get money you stand before a 'hole-in-the-wall' and slide a plastic card through a slit, and press certain buttons, and out comes the sum required, neatly stacked.

Our grandparents would have thought it magic, like TV and aeroplanes, and I imagine some of them would have shaken their heads.

1 direction, compass-point

Science v Faith

6 May 1993

The erosions of old age! It isn't only that the Atlantic gnaws away at the western seaboard of Orkney, perpetually, but the ocean of eternity is beating evermore at our frail mortal structures.

One day a fortnight ago a sudden pain clamped itself to my right foot, like a vice, and tightened.

Ah well, I'd had it before, several times in the past, and after a few days it had gone as suddenly as it had arrived. It folded its tents like the Arab, and as silently stole away...

But it seemed that this time it had planned on a longer stay. For one thing, it shifted to the left foot and there it began to ply its blacksmith work with great thoroughness: forge and anvil, and the red-hot blades piercing to the bone.

To walk about inside the house was an effort. To go into the town called for a bit more heroism than I possess by nature.

The blacksmith would suddenly decide to do a bit of night-time working, about 3 or 4am. There, in bed, the forge was blown up and hammer beat on anvil, and the left foot was subjected to the outrage.

They say, nearly everybody in Orkney gets rheumatism at one time or another – so one ought not to complain.

There are aspirins and other painkillers. There are roomier shoes for sale, for the swollen feet to be more comfortable in.

Many of the older Orcadians resorted to primitive remedies. My father was tormented for years by arthritis in feet and hands. So he'd send us for sea water. The sea you scoop into a bucket from the harbour was no good. It had to be a bucket of the Hoy Sound water, taken from round by Ness Point.

I don't think it helped him very much, but maybe the folk-memory passing down generations is a kind of salve.

I'm sure, in medieval times and long afterwards, nearly every community in the western world had a 'holy well', the waters of which cured many troubles. Orkney was full of them. Faith, it seemed, could get rid of many a grievous ailment.

Near the farm of Brownstown in Innertown, there is a well that a year or two back had fallen into ruin. Now, I'm glad to see that the stonework around it has been repaired. I rather think the laughable name 'Hellihole' meant originally, the brae leading to this well.

Well, its cures were still believed in, in the early 1930s. I remember being sent to 'the mineral well' – as it was called – with a pail to get water from this well. I think it was for my mother's asthma, or hay fever, from which she suffered cruelly in the summer months.

Again, I don't know whether the Brownstown water worked or not. But my mother was by no means the only Stromness person who went there for cures.

A Stromness hotel manager, just after the war, sent some of that well water for analysis. Back came the scientist's report: it was just ordinary water.

That sunk Stromness's hopes of ever being a spa town.

But what scientific measure can be applied to faith?

A Little Tale

13 May 1993

I used to think, long ago in childhood, that there was – or ought to have been – a King in Orkney, with a court and an army, a national anthem and a navy; and he ruled in peace over a contented people.

But then a descendant and successor, also a king, decided that Orkney was too small a place to contain his burgeoning population.

So he decided that the time had come for a little expansion. He would need a bigger army and navy. So the taxes had to be increased a bit, which caused some grousing and grumbling.

This king – let's call him King Mansie IV – had a swift way with grousers and grumblers. The worst ones were exiled to Suleskerry, their hangers-on were sent to labour in the shipyards where the new navy was building, with only bread and water for sustenance.

So far, so good.

King Mansie sent envoys to the Caithness King that he should forthwith make over the island of Stroma to Orkney, together with all the Stroma folk, their lands and holdings and revenues.

The Caithness King objected, of course. That Pentland Firth island had always been part of Caithness. Patiently he pointed this out to the Orkney envoys. The Orkney envoy and his men stalked down to their boat at Scrabster and sailed home.

Two days later Stroma was occupied by armed men from Orkney.

King Mansie said to his commander-in-chief, 'You ain't seen nothing yet.' Next spring the envoy was sent north to make a proposal to King Ollie X in Shetland. 'Fair Isle belongs to Orkney. That's as plain as can be. Why don't you hand it over without any fuss, your majesty?'...

King Ollie, a peaceable man normally, was so enraged he threw his silver-rimmed ale-horn at the arrogant envoy – who returned forthwith to Orkney with a discoloured eye.

'An outrage,' declared King Mansie, and the following week his ships came out of the sunrise against Fair Isle, and the commander-in-chief read a proclamation on the shore that henceforward Fair Isle was an integral part of Orkney.

'Where next?' said King Mansie ... North Rona seemed too far away to claim. Anyway, what could he ever do with a few wild birds and their eggs, and a few scraggy sheep?

But he would have to claim and attack some place, otherwise his powerful commander-in-chief might get ideas of usurpation. (They didn't much like each other, King and commander.) He conceived certain wild ideas about claiming territory in Faroe or Iceland.

One day a stranger appeared in court and said to King Mansie, 'Your Majesty, the people of Hether Blether in the west are very discontented with the tyrant who rules over them, King Selkie the Second. They would give you a great welcome. One shake, and King Selkie would fall like an over-ripe apple.'

So King Mansie led the way to Hether Blether with his army and navy. The sea fogs beyond Rousay swallowed them; they were never seen again...

After that, the Orkney folk began to have a really happy time.

They chopped up King Mansie's throne to make a fire on the shore. Round it they danced all night, to the music of the king's fiddler.

I thought it might be a good idea to welcome in May, and Festival time, with a little tale.

Fine Weather Surprise

27 May 1993

The fine weather comes so suddenly, we get taken unawares.

Even the elderly, like me, though we've had plenty of experience, are surprised.

Yesterday morning (Tuesday, May 18) for example, I could see through the window what a bright morning it was, though the mild south wind was smiting the harbour water to merry dancing furrows.

After breakfast I sat in my rocker. A fine new-lit fire was making merry on the hearth, and the storage heater in the corner was giving out waves of warmth. And I had on what we used to call a waistcoat in olden times, though nowadays they're called body-warmers.

Having done a little tidying-up work with words on a page, I thought of other needful tasks to fill in the morning, and found myself very much disinclined. (This is unusual – I usually enjoy my work.)

The sun was shining in full magnificence in the early afternoon, when I had to go out for lunch.

At this time of year, in wind and sun, the light is wonderful in Orkney. I ought to have been walking cheerfully through constellations of daisies and dandelions like little shaggy suns, but my feet were dragging, and I had to stop every now and then on the brae to get my breath. The peedie May Burn was making flute songs as I trudged up the brae on leaden feet. It was then I realised that early summer had taken me by surprise. The 'bodywarmer' and cord jacket were as heavy as a suit of armour... On the ridge above, the south wind came boisterous and warm... I was glad to lean against a dyke and watch the *Ola* coming in fast through Hoy Sound...

Year after year we are caught in this dilemma: summer is hastening to greet us, and yet winter is loath to go; you never know when it might come back for a few more words of farewell ... so the old adage is best kept in mind, 'Ne'er cast a cloot till May be oot'... Otherwise winter might turn once again for a final stab, and leave pneumonia or pleurisy as a parting gift.

It isn't quite so bright today, and it's overcast. I've switched the heater off, though there is a steady glow in the hearth... The great question is, do I get rid of that waistcoat or not?

Later that afternoon, there was a solitary swan on Skaill Loch.

The storms of winter had piled a barrier of great stones above the shore of the bay.

The sail of a yacht, drifting south, caught the light.

There were a few walkers on the sand at the Bay of Skaill.

A tourist bus stood waiting for some Skara Brae visitors.

I took several deep breaths of Skaill air: the wind was delicious, like wine.

Marigolds in throngs beside the loch, and rich clusters of primroses on the banks above.

Coming back by way of Brodgar, a few fishermen were standing thigh-deep in Harray Loch.

If the Brodgar stones were – among other things – a calendar, there they stood, rejoicing in one more spring of their five thousand.

Beauty of Unsung Plants

3 June 1993

'Nothing is so beautiful as spring' wrote the poet Hopkins a century ago, and he never said a truer word. Then of course he launched into a display of verbal pyrotechnics that is magnificent; but that is not so important as that all the sweetness and freshness and goodness of this time of year are gathered into the fourteen lines of a sonnet...

I think I have never seen so many daisies as this spring. Walking up the May Burn to the Back Road, there are swarms and constellations and galaxies of daisies everywhere – each one singing its own silent *gloria*.

In the wet places, the marigolds have spread their brightness, and primroses (what we called mayflowers sixty years ago) are thick in the ditches and especially on the banks above the Loch of Skaill.

Now the daffodils have completely gone. There were still a few brave ones in the garden outside my kitchen window last week, lingering as if they were loath to leave 'the high midsummer pomps'... But they sang their silent *glorias* well all through the storms of March and early April, and it was time for them to go.

Nobody ever celebrates grass, which is regarded as a bit of a nuisance by gardeners with lawnmowers. Lawnmowers used to rattle merrily in my childhood – many a time I have pushed the stuttering inept blunt thing through a back garden at Well Park – but now they are almost silent and lethal and efficient, and when they have done their work millions of grassblades lie dead on the shaven lawns... But I have been looking at the springing new uncut grass this May, and it lies lovely and rich in the light; and how it welcomes the rain, and is thronged and hung with jewels afterwards. I give the grass this iota of praise, though one afternoon recently I walked down the May Burn after a shower, and the wet grass had soaked through my thick shoes that I thought invulnerable!... It was, in a way, a pleasure – and I had another pair of shoes to change into.

So, grass tends to be looked down on as too common. Even the poets have ignored it, except the seventeenth-century Andrew Marvell in his great lyric 'The Garden'... 'Stumbling on melons, as I pass, / Ensnared with flowers, I fall on grass'... Some people might think that a blemish on the verse, but Marvell knew where praise was owing...

And the dandelions – they don't last long. A week or so ago, I saw that their brief span was drawing to a close. The 'clocks' were beginning, those globes of seed waiting for the first small gust to scatter them for the long entombment till next spring. 'Dandelions – a pest!' cry the gardeners, more enraged by them than by the ever-swinging waves of grass. But they are beautiful too, like shaggy little lions. And folk who know how can make delightful wine out of them.

Children, we used to pluck the hollow stems and wonder at the milk along the rim. Spread on the back of the hand, it left a dark stain.

We ought to be glad that a whole long summer of wild flowers stretches ahead.

Husky Saunders

10 June 1993

There seem to have been a few half-Orcadian half-Canadian Indian boys in Stromness towards the end of last century.

I remember my father speaking about them.

Those boys were sent to Orkney by their fathers – hunters and traders at Ungava with the Hudson Bay Company – to be educated.

Among them was a seven-year-old boy called William Saunders. He stayed with his grandparents in a cottage near Login's Well – now demolished. The grandfather was a blacksmith at Stanger's shipyard (now Stenigar).

Strange it must have been for a small boy whose ancestors on the distaff side had lived for centuries among the immense forests and rivers of north-west Canada, to find himself in a small stone town with hardly a tree in sight, and only a few seals to remind him of the beavers, reindeer, walrus, wolves of his homeland...

But it seems that William Saunders settled down well enough. In true Orcadian fashion they gave him a nickname, 'Husky'.

The headmaster of Stromness Public School in 1886 was Mr D. F. Reith, a name to cause elderly men – such as Tom White the tailor of Alfred Terrace – to blanch when they mentioned him, the times I sat in Tom White's house to listen to his stories... Mr Reith was something of a disciplinarian, it seems.

Maybe a hard man was needed to weld all the little schools of Stromness into a single unit, after the Education Act of 1872.

Anyway, Husky Saunders sat under Mr D. F. Reith. School must have seemed a kind of prison to him after the boundless spaces of Ungava. However it is recorded that Husky passed his examinations.

Sometimes stranger boys are given the cold shoulder – at least for a time – by their yamils. But Husky Saunders was accepted almost at once, it seems. He was such a daring active imaginative boy that he soon became 'the leader of the gang'. There is no record of what exploits the gang got up to. But whoever has been a boy in Stromness about the age of ten will have no difficulty in remembering. Did Husky and his friends row out beyond the black buoy in a flattie? Did they go to the Black Craig for wild birds' eggs? Did they whisper in the Kirk on the Sabbath? Did they drape white sheets round them on winter evenings and frighten prim lasses going home from their piano lessons? Did they play football against the Northenders, with an occasional punch-up on the side of Brinkie's Brae?... About all those things Mr Reith might have had to wield his tawse.

There is no one left now alive in Stromness to enlighten us. It is recorded that Provost J. G. Marwick and John Folster were contemporaries of Husky Saunders.

Anyway, after four years the time came for Husky to go back and join his father in 'the Nor'-Wast'. That day in 1889, his friends bade him farewell as the *Ola* left the quay. More than that, they ran along the shore at Ness to wave him a last goodbye.

Husky took the Hudson Bay ship *Eric* of London to Canada. There he became a trapper and hunter. He married and had two sons and six daughters. He made his home at Leaf River and worked for the French company Revillon Frères.

Boy in the Sailor Suit

17 June 1993

Going through that ever-delightful book: *Stromness – Late 19th Century Photographs*, published in 1972 by Stromness Museum, one is struck by how much has changed and how much remains the same.

I picked the book up again to see if the house of Husky Saunders' grandfather could be located. (I wrote about Husky Saunders last week.) And there it was, just across the street from Norland at the South End – a little flag-roofed cottage long since demolished.

There is one intriguing thing about this book, and that is the boy in the sailor suit. This boy appears in photograph after photograph: you get the impression that he followed the photographer wherever he set up his camera more than a century ago, and when the shutter was pressed, there was this boy, well positioned.

Who was this boy in the sailor suit?

Many of the Stromness children are barefoot in the sequence, but the boy in the sailor suit is very well got up, in fine jacket, knickerbockers, long knee-length stockings and good shoes. He obviously came from the upper bracket of Stromness society, and he has a poised assured look, not like some of the children who seem shy of the camera.

Of course it wasn't necessarily a sign of poverty for boys to go on bare feet. Even in the 1930s we ran summer-long without shoes or stockings. The evidence of this book is that the photography was done on a fine summer day. The boy in the sailor suit might actually have felt uncomfortable with his legs enclosed in all that hose and leather... One can imagine a bourgeois mother saying to her son, 'I know it's a fine warm morning, but you will not go over this door until you're decently stockinged and shod... Come, let me brush those hairs and fluff from your sailor collar!'...

And out the boy ran, down the close and into the sun-bright street, and there was a tourist with a tripod and *camera obscura*, taking photographs... Here and there, groups of townsfolk are being asked to pose on the street. They do so, astonished, delighted, and shy. Then the photographer moves on to another street corner or close-end, and yet other townsfolk are bidden to cluster around.

So the photographer, that fine summer day in the heyday of the British Empire, proceeds with his magic box from South End to North End, stopping here and there; but always he is dogged by the boy in the sailor suit, all the way from the Plainstones to what is now the Post Office.

It is too late now to suppose that anybody knows the name of that self-assured publicity-seeking boy.

I think he may well have been the photographer's son: not a Stromness boy at all, but here with his daddy whose new-fangled hobby was photography, and they stayed for a week or two, one far-off warm forgotten summer, in the Masons' Arms, maybe.

The Greenlanders

24 June 1993

The Americans, for some mysterious reason, seem to like enormously long novels, that they call 'blockbusters'. We always assume that Americans like to get jobs over and done with in a hurry. But not, apparently, with the writing and reading of novels.

That quibble over, I must say how much I enjoyed an American blockbuster novel called *The Greenlanders*, by Jane Smiley. Six hundred pages long (almost) it is.

Round about the tenth century, or earlier, families of Icelanders sailed west and founded their own little republic in the immense mountainous glacier-riven island of Greenland.

Folk have said that the name of the place was a great joke, to tempt those colonists away from overcrowded Iceland. But it appears that the south part of Greenland is full of lovely meadows and grasslands, where keeping of livestock – cows and sheep and goats – was no problem at all, though it was impossible to raise cereal crops. And the fjords abounded with fish, seals, walrus. And the bolder hunters went after bears and reindeer. In the good centuries, there was no danger of starvation.

There was a Thing, or law assembly, on the Icelandic model.

The archbishop of Nidaros in Norway sent a bishop to Greenland. There was a Cathedral there, and many priests.

There was a constant threat from the 'skraelings' (Eskimos) further north, but all the time of the occupation, until almost the end, the skraelings could be contained.

There were family alliances and feuds, such as we know all about from the Iceland sagas, but the law-assembly was respected for the most part, though now and again the sessions ended in a pitched battle.

They spoke a variant of the Norse tongue. A Greenlander would have been understood in Orkney or Norway.

The winters were severe, but their cupboards were well stocked from long summers of hunting, fishing, stock-rearing. Like their Icelandic cousins, they loved listening to the long family sagas. But it is difficult to imagine a civilisation getting by without ale or bread.

Then a terrible thing happened to the Greenlanders, not suddenly, but slowly and cruelly over a few generations.

The climate deteriorated. A minor Ice Age closed about them.

It takes a long time to recognise that the winters are getting worse, and the summers briefer and colder. The seal hunting and the reindeer hunting got more difficult; the ever-colder conditions affected the fauna too. The Greenlanders had long periods without a bishop, and the priests were fewer. Not so many trading ships arrived from the west; the Greenlanders had less and less goods to bargain with.

The family disputes grew bitter and rancorous and bloody, and the Things were not so often resorted to. The outlying farms were abandoned. Old people here and there were found dead of starvation. There were ever more accusations of witchcraft – an evil that most Greenlanders had hitherto laughed about.

As Yeats said about a declining civilisation – 'Things fall apart'... There is one last marriage certificate, dated 14 September, 1408, between Thorsteinn Olafsson and Sigrid Björnsdottir ...

Thereafter, silence. It was the end of an old song. The land belonged once more to the northern Inuit, the polar bear, walrus, reindeer.

Until the ice lessened its grip once more, and a few lost or land-seeking sailors made landfall.

Such has been my reading for the past fortnight: a long haul, but enjoyable.

The Longest Day

1 July 1993

Yesterday was the summer solstice – the longest day – and it began well.

We actually saw the sun at breakfast-time, after (it seems) weeks of gloom and rain.

The solstice sun seemed so precious and golden, it tempted me to get along the street – or 'go north', as the Stromness Southenders say.

So I went north, hobbling a bit on sore feet – age begins to put such shackles on one. But, rheumatics or not, it was a joy to be out in the sunshine.

Now the tourists are beginning to outnumber the Stromnessians. Many accents were to be heard along the street.

At last (after a few failures) I think I have perfected the technique of extracting money out of the cashpoint, or 'hole-in-the-wall'.

How good, to buy a wholemeal loaf before the tourists bear them away to make sandwiches of them.

I bought some stamps – I go through a lot of them – with the head of the Emperor Claudius on them, and Queen Elizabeth's head, tiny and silver, on the top right-hand corner, a curious juxtaposition, I thought.

I spoke to a few friends, old and new, in Graham Place – the makers of the *Sails in St Magnus* that look so impressive in the cathedral.

Still the sun was shining, but there was a kind of grey haze now – we Orcadians have seen that portent often enough.

Being a little tired after 'going north', I went for a lie-down in the afternoon. I fell into one of those delicious afternoon drowses that last only half an hour or so and are always an oasis in this troublous life.

What met my waking ear, a kind of plucking, faint plangent notes on the window pane? There was no doubt about it, the June rain had returned.

Rain or no rain, Donald and Dorrie Morrison drove me to Ronald Ferguson's play in the Arts Theatre[1], *Every Blessed Thing*, in which Tom Fleming enacts George MacLeod of Fuinary, great restorer of Iona Abbey and pacifist and social reformer and ecumenist. A magnificent performance it was too, of a script that distilled, with great skill and craft, the work and personality of a good, great, and fearless man.

I don't think I have known a Festival performance to get a standing ovation before last night.

When we drove home, at 10.30, the rain was coming in tumults – 'demptions of rain', the old folk used to speak about. I thought Finstown might be washed into the sea.

Some solstice!

The fire was out but I rekindled it with a few sticks, and seeing that it was getting on for midnight on the summer solstice, I poured myself a dram of 'Grouse' before going to bed.

1 in Kirkwall

Whalers Return!

15 July 1993

It was a great time when the whalers returned from Davis Straits and other points nor'-wast in the nineteenth century.

I have just been dipping into Sir Walter Scott's journal of his trip round the northern and western isles in 1814, in the lighthouse yacht.

The yacht was anchored off Lerwick when the whaling ships were home after their perilous whale-hunt that summer. The whale-men had plenty of money. They hadn't seen drink or girls or green hills for long perilous months among the ice floes and the threshing whales. So they went wild in Lerwick, and the Sheriff of Zetland (one of Sir Walter's shipmates on the trip) had a few of the whalers to deal with – so interrupting what was, after all, a kind of holiday for the sheriffs who were also *ipso facto* lighthouse commissioners.

Roughly the same boisterous on-goings happened when the whaling ships arrived in Stromness. I have read somewhere that respectable citizens were issued with truncheons to defend themselves and their property from the wild men from the whaling grounds.

All those pubs and alehouses in Stromness – think how the proprietors must have unlocked their doors in trepidation on the morning when the whalemen were rowed ashore – in trepidation mingled with keen anticipation, because the harpoonists and flensers had plenty of silver to splash around, and the barrels of ale from Stromness brewery were in fine late-summer ripeness.

The names of most of those vanished ale-houses are lost. But many of them must have had signs over the door. I remember the fisherman John Folster, a contemporary of my father, telling me that he had seen some of those painted signs, some with scenes on them. I expect they were put on to the ash-cart or broken up for firewood. Imagine, if the signs all existed, what a display they would have made in the Pier Arts Centre!

In a story, I called one of those pubs 'The Arctic Whaler', but that was a pure invention.

In a strange mood – a mingling of dread and greed – the proprietor of The Arctic Whaler unlocked his door on the morning that the whaling fleet was sighted sailing through Hoy Sound. And a stir of excitement went through the young men and girls of Hamnavoe. And the merchants put their truncheons in a niche under the counter, where they could easily be reached. (There were no policemen in those days – every householder was his own 'keeper of the peace'.)

The fleet had anchored. There was a barbarous shouting from the ships!

But it wasn't always so. There is the terrible story of the whaling ship *Dee* of Aberdeen, locked up the whole winter in the Arctic ice.

When finally she broke through, next spring, most of her crew were dead or dying.

Among them was a young Harrayman from the croft of Handest, Adam Flett. Amid the suffering and death among the ice that winter, Adam Flett had the mother-wit to keep himself fit by running in that white world every day. He was one of the few survivors to be brought to the improvised hospital in Alfred Place; spectral mariners like those in 'The Ancient Mariner' ... Adam Flett went home to Harray and lived to be an old man.

Such tragic whale-hunts were rare – such terrible landfalls in Stromness.

It was mostly broken staves in ale-barrels – respectable ladies keeping their doors locked for a day or two – a flirtation or two – Bessie Millie waiting for the skippers to come up Brinkie's Brae with their sixpences.

Summer Hesitates into Being

22 July 1993

The poor tourists of June and early July! How many of them will be calling Orkney 'the isles of perpetual rain'?

Not the oldest Orcadian, I think, remembers such a rain-sodden early summer. Certainly not I. Somebody did say, the other evening, that 1979 was as bad. (I'll have to consult my diary!) There they trekked through the streets, the young back-packers.

How could it have been in a tent, with puddles all around? But there again, some Norwegian friends used to stay in a tent at Ness, in former summers, and they fried their bacon and eggs with showers sizzling into the pan – and they actually enjoyed it!

I have never seen so many coloured umbrellas passing under my window... Cars went past, water slurping from the wheels.

I suppose the rain, day after day, drove tourists into bookshops, craft shops, the Pier Arts Centre and other galleries, the Museum, the cafés and the pubs. There was always some place to go to.

Some friends stayed a week in an Orphir cottage. They were wrapped in a rain-cloud for two days. Then the cloud lifted, and for the first time they realised that Stromness, Graemsay, and Hoy had been there all the time. That glimpse, however brief, cheered their hearts a little.

There are other ways of considering this surging seeping soaking summer. Think how people in Sudan, who haven't seen rain for years, would have looked on our month of rain as a blessing from heaven.

Think of the citizens of Sarajevo, the long queues with plastic jerry-cans waiting at the pumps for meagre polluted dribblings of water.

And this rain is rounding out the potatoes for the first magnificent boiling (with butter) in late July. It's the rain that keeps the beer-taps flowing.

Like the tree in the well-known lyric, we Orcadians have 'intimately lived with rain' for centuries.

Yet, I must admit, to wake up for morning after morning to the throbbing of rain on the window-panes drags the spirits down a little, in the end.

The painful thing was, some rainy days recently we knew that the sun was there, somewhere. A silver radiance was struggling through the greyness and the downpours.

Two days ago, the sun came in all its glory, and we woke to it like half-stupefied bees. (The bees, incidentally, have seemingly all been drowned by the long deluge – likewise the butterflies.) Yesterday was bright too. Today the sun is playing hide-and-seek.

It is now, ironically, that you get a nose beginning to drip and a slight huskiness in the throat – as summer hesitates into being.

Pyre at the Braes

29 July 1993

There they lie, somewhere near the top of the pyre at the Braes Hotel, to go up in flames before the end of Shopping Week, the two old armchairs that adorned my bedrooms.

Nobody ever sat in the armchairs, as far as I remember, or only for as long as a butterfly might light on a flower. Somehow, those armchairs didn't invite long sessions.

But they were handy for throwing a coat or a dressing-gown over, or for keeping a plastic bag of letters for a while, or a few books or magazines.

'There might be a few fivers down the side of one,' I said to the men bearing the chairs downstairs to their truck (and it took a bit of awkward manoeuvring at stair-head and stairfoot). But of course there was not a chance of a fiver hidden there, or even a twopence piece, for nobody had ever sat there long enough.

The armchairs were of indeterminate colour – 'dun-coloured' I might have described them, if I had been forced to give them a colour, they were so invested with a fuzz of age – they might have been a muted yellow originally.

How long ago? I can't even tell that. The armchairs were given to my mother by my cousin when she moved to London more than thirty years ago; so I expect they're getting on for half a century in age.

They have been in the bedrooms of Mayburn Court for almost twenty-five years.

The end came for those rather loveless chairs when a friend said, some time last year, 'The chairs are full of woodworms'... She had shifted one, looking for something or other, and a fine dust had fallen from a piece of the woodwork.

There was no doubt about it, the chairs were infested: there was neither hope nor help for them.

Then somebody said they were collecting combustibles for the big Shopping Week fire at the Braes.

So they are to end, after all, not undistinguishedly on the chopping block, but making glorious flames for the revellers of Stromness at the high reach of summer... It might be their richest hour.

Meantime, there are blanks in my two bedrooms.

But plans are afoot to have new chairs there, some time before the Lammas Fair.

Distant Relatives

5 August 1993

It's amazing what relatives we have – all of us – that we know nothing about, except (in my case) after a very long time.

My granny was called Georgina Mackay and she lived on a croft in Sutherland, near a bleak headland on the north coast. Many of that clan had been shifted from the more fertile inland straths to make way for Cheviot herds. They were advised to cultivate the bog and try fishing in the Pentland Firth.

Many of the men had perhaps never seen the sea before, or had scant knowledge of boat-handling or fishing.

It may have been rather hoped that those peasants might get out, as the Irish were doing in their hundreds of thousands, and stake a claim in America.

But to forget their own enchanting language – it must have been like wounding their tongues. Many of the Strathnaver Highlanders elected to stay on, rather than to trust themselves to the perilous Atlantic and the hazards of the American shore.

Georgina stayed, between the barren moor and the dangerous sea. She married and had nine children, in the district of Braal.

But Georgina's sister married a Caithness man called Malcolm and the Malcolms emigrated to New York. And there my grand-aunt lived till she was well into her nineties.

Apart from the fact of the emigration, it seems there was small communication between the two sisters. It was just that people wrote fewer letters in those days.

❀

A fortnight ago there arrived at my door Hal Barker and his wife Bonita from California, on a tour of Britain, which took in Orkney and Shetland.

Hal, my second cousin, is eighty-two. In his youth he acted in Hollywood films, mainly westerns. Nearly always, in those films, Hal was the bad guy, a gunslinger, probably a cattle-rustler or a bank robber. 'How come,' somebody had asked him, 'you're always cast as the bad guy, when you're a pretty nice chap?'

Hal *was* a pleasant man, too, and his wife Bonita didn't look at all like a grandmother. Now they both have second careers, in insurance valuation and insurance legal advice.

Of course, in a stay of about an hour, they took pictures, instant coloured pictures. And we talked a great deal. And my nephew John offered to drive them to Outertown, where perhaps they could see the Strathy lighthouse flashing from the ancestral shore; but it was one of those foggy cold nights that are going to make summer 1993 famous in the weather history of the North.

Next day, my long-lost cousin would be winging on to Shetland.

By now, they will be back in the sunshine of California – glad, maybe, that his grandmother (Georgina's sister) left wet Scotland and the rich archaic language. But, who can tell?

I am too old and lazy to travel myself. I do regret the laziness of my youth that kept me from learning Gaelic and Norse. I wander about in a no man's land between two cultures.

The Tender Tables

12 August 1993

Last Tuesday summer came, the first real summer day of 1993 – August the third – with the sun bright and warm all day. So at last I could shed some of my winter clothes...

Was there ever such a summer as this! Now the tourists were out in their light summer wear, instead of drifting past Mayburn into the Museum, buckets of rain splashing on to their coloured brollies.

Outside, I spoke to a young mother on her way to the 'Tender Tables' with her two bairns.

The Tender Tables – what happy memories the name brings back, of summer afternoons at the West Shore in the twenties and thirties. But very few children, I think, visit the West Shore and the Tender Tables nowadays... Cars can quickly transport kids to Warbeth, Skaill, and Birsay.

It is a curious name: Tender Tables. The 'tables' part is easily explained – it consists of two great slabs of sloping flat natural stone, set one above the other, with easy access up a broken natural stair. (I will have to visit the place soon, to refresh my memory.) One of those parallel rocks was called 'the Pulpit' – probably because from that vantage one could seem to dominate those on the sand below.

But where the adjective 'tender' comes in will have to be left to Norn scholars to decide (it is not in Hugh Marwick's dictionary).

The area round the Tender Tables was a wonderful summer playground for children.

Several narrow strips of sand sloped down from the cliff face into Hoy Sound, and every strip of sand was divided by barriers of natural sloping rock. When the tide was out, the interstices of the rock were dotted with little triangular rockpools in which tiny almost transparent crabs could be found lurking among the tassels of seaweed... We were well warned by our elders not to paddle or swim too far out in those cold waters, or the fast-flowing ebb of Hoy Sound might carry us off.

It was children's territory, the West Shore.

From above, we could hear from the golf course the occasional thwack of a 'brassie' on a golf ball (a 'Warwick' or a 'Spalding') and sometimes a golfer would slice his drive at the 13th hole and plop would go his ball (costing one shilling and sixpence) into the sea.

We warmed our feet in the rockpools before plunging into the Sound, which was so cold it drove the air out of our lungs with audible gasps.

There was a natural break in the cliffs in which a witch, it was said, had lived who had murdered children, long ago. It took some courage to take a few steps into that cave.

Memory plays tricks. It seems to me mainly boys who built the sandcastles and got stung by jellyfish ... The few adults looked after us when we were very young on the rocks above and set out the sandwiches, the 'rich tea' biscuits and the 'Abernethy' biscuits, and poured the bottles of Gowans' lemonade.

Girls – sisters and neighbours – sat on the greensward above and made daisy-chains.

Of course when we were a few years older we wanted nothing to do with adults or girls, round the Tender Tables... By that time, too, we preferred to stretch our legs as far as Warbeth beach.

The West Shore was a place of early childhood.

And oh, the flood tide came in and lapped our feet, and fairly hurled trawlers between here and Graemsay, beyond 'the Beacon' and Ness into the hidden harbour. Conversely, in a strong ebb tide those trawlers could be caught, engines pounding, like flies in honey.

And the sun shone every day and the sky was blue with a few white clouds, and the sea was deliciously shriekingly cold, all those long summer afternoons that went on and on.

Dounby Shows

19 August 1993

The first Dounby Show I remember – aged six or seven – a relative who was going there with an ice cream and fruit stall wondered if I'd like to go.

I turned down the offer at once. I much preferred the piers and closes of Stromness. 'The Child is father of the Man,' said Wordsworth. I've had lots of invitations in the past two decades to go to Canada, France, Australia, Norway, as a kind of literary showman. Nothing doing. My country is between Ness Road and the Pier Head.

But, over the years, I've grown very fond of the Dounby Show. It has become one of the great days of summer, a crown and a consummation. I wouldn't have missed it for anything.

And who knows, I *might* set out for Dounby tomorrow in search of lost enchantment, in that village where the three parishes meet, approximately... It depends a great deal on the weather, in this savage summer that has trampled on everything good and gracious in our countryside.

But even if I do go, I don't expect any of the joys of Dounby Shows in the sixties and seventies.

Two years ago, Brian Murray and I were eager to taste the pleasures of the beer-tent, which in a fresh breeze resembles a galleon in full sail. And what a merry crew were inside, always: farmers who hadn't met each other since the last Dounby Show, the young men (and, latterly, lasses) of Kirkwall and Stromness and the seven parishes, together with astonished tourists from Edinburgh, London, New York, Sydney... Even if there was no Atlantic wind billowing out the sails, there was enough merriment and chanted narrative to drive the beer-tent on its voyage of enchantment – that ended, alas, at 4pm, prompt. And then you had to wade through empty beer cans and broken plastic mugs; and maybe have a glance at the horses, cows and tinted sheep before catching the bus – full of laden laughing ladies, bairns sucking iced lollies, and men who looked as though they might still round off the festive day with a pint at the Ferry, or the Braes.

Two Dounby Shows ago, it was a golden day, just right, most promising...

When we got to the Show Park, the enchanted tent was no longer there; instead, it had been supplanted by a huge ugly permanent structure... I didn't have the heart to go in. Instead, Brian and I drank our cans of lager against a wall, outside.

That day, I caught a bad cold. It can't have been the weather – for, as I say, it was a beautiful summer day. I think the ailment was what they call nowadays, 'psychosomatic', caused by a victory of prose over poetry.

Make no mistake: Prose versus Poetry, that constitutes the great war of our times.

Be sure that you enrol in the armies of light.

The Flitting

26 August 1993

It's almost a quarter of a century since the tenants began to move into Mayburn Court.

What a Saturday morning that was in Well Park (now Guardhouse Park) where I was staying then! Everything had been stacked in readiness for the big move, mostly in tea-chests lent by our neighbour, the wholesale merchant, Mr James Wilson – an extraordinarily kind obliging man.

Hundreds and hundreds of books had been stacked in those tea-chests. In others, ornaments, kettle, tea-pot, light-bulbs, calendars and pictures – such household utensils.

Stowed into boxes, with the utmost care was strong home-brew for the flitting. The labourers were liable to wilt midway through their stint.

Along, in due course, came two vehicles – Bailie W. E. Knight's coal lorry and Dr Johnstone's Land Rover.

A company of hard-working efficient workers turned up. In no time at all, all the furniture, tea-chests, boxes, beds, pokers and pans were stacked on board, and away went the cargo and my friends: Ian MacInnes, Archie Bevan, Jimmy Isbister, Fraser Dixon... I stood at last, alone, in the empty echoing cavern of Number 6 Well Park.

Soon it was time to go to the ex-distillery, now the new-risen Mayburn Court, to see how the flitting was going.

It was going with marvellous fluency and despatch. Within a couple of hours, everything was roughly in the places they still occupy twenty-five years later – the table, the rocking-chair, the straw-back chair, the two beds, bookcases. The boxes of home-brew were set with great reverence on the table, and half a dozen tumblers seethed away sweetly under a fleece of foam. Then the workers quenched their thirst. There was a lot of dust and cobwebs flying around.

And presently, their work done, their thirst quenched, the workers went home, all except myself and another.

We had another glass or two or three of ale, to celebrate the successful house-moving. It was surely an occasion for celebration.

Outside, there was a great noise of clanging, like mighty irregular bells. The blacksmiths were welding the last of the railings on to the balcony. So we brought out some ale mugs to those men of great strength and resonance.

Finally, my friend and I subsided into chairs and snoozed the afternoon away.

Late in the afternoon, one of the 'flitters' called by to see how things were going.

The flitting had come to a halt. The sleepers drowsed on. A dozen empty ale-bottles stood on the table. The celebration was complete, as far as they were concerned.

Next day, there were only a few odds and ends to clean up, and the ale bottles to wash out.

The railings outside were all in place, and secure. Now, twenty-five years on, the ironwork is spotted with red, and has begun to flake, and could do with some chipping and painting. And – since two-thirds of the Mayburn houses are now privately owned – an interesting situation as to the maintenance of the elegant ironwork has arisen.

Posts and Postmen of the Past

9 September 1993

I heard on the radio recently, the price of postage stamps is going up soon by a penny, which makes it 25p to post a first-class letter.

Translate this into 'old money' and 25p means five shillings. Five shillings – a crown – was a small fortune before the war.

(By the way, you never hear nowadays about boys collecting 'foreign stamps'... Many boys when I went to school had stamp albums, over which they pored for many hours every week ... I suppose stamp collecting is too tame in comparison with video games and such futuristic fantasies.)

I'm sure there weren't so many letters written in the twenties and thirties. I think no more than two or three arrived in our household in a week. I can't remember my father ever writing a letter (though he was a postman). My mother wrote regularly to her parents in Strathy, Sutherland, 'by Thurso'.

It cost three-halfpence then to post a letter. A postcard cost one penny. An open letter (unsealed – generally a bill or a summons to a funeral) cost a ha'penny... The funeral invitations arrived in black-edged envelopes. The recipient read, on thick black-edged paper, that he was invited to 'the place of interment' on such-and-such a date... When I was a small boy, I caused a good deal of mocking amusement by reading out aloud that my father was bidden to come to 'the place of entertainment' for so-and-so's funeral.

No airmail in those days either.

The postmen – including my father – were in attendance when the *Ola* glided in like a black swan to the Warehouse Pier about four o'clock in the afternoon. The few bags of mail were heaved on to a barrow and taken to the Post Office for sorting. That evening the letters were delivered. Next morning parcels were delivered, from a barrow with a big wickerwork basket on top. A household was highly unlikely to receive a parcel except round about Christmas... But there was an increasing trade in mail orders from big drapers and clothiers in the South – which can hardly have made the local drapers happy.

The postmen wore hard hats with a peak aft as well as fore; I presumed, to run the rainwater off. They had uniforms with red piping. On winter nights they had lanterns pinned to the lapels of their coats, to read the addresses.

The Post Office has not always been where it is now. I have photographs showing the postal staff at the door of what is now Mrs Black's house, just south of Hellihole. The Postmistress my father first remembered was a Miss Ross.

A letter arrived for some townsman who had died. Miss Ross said to the telegram boy, 'Write "Deceased" in red ink on the envelope'... The telegram boy duly wrote 'Deceased in red ink'.

That was the day's fun in Stromness Post Office, that particular day.

Introduction to Poetry

16 September 1993

A vast amount of verse has been written – more now, maybe, than ever before. Everyone knows how to read and write, and nothing is easier than to set down a few fleeting thoughts and emotions on a piece of paper. Fifty years ago it was more difficult, because verse was expected to scan and rhyme. Those obstacles have been removed, and now it is possible to sprinkle words out on to a page like pepper from a pot and say: 'I've written a poem!'

Alas, poetry is a craft of great difficulty and subtlety. It requires years of continuous application. Even when the poet is at the height of his powers, he realises how much there is still to learn.

We schoolboys had no time for poetry. Football was the art we were out to master, and catching sillocks at Gray's Pier (I was never very good at the latter).

'I have a little shadow / That goes in and out with me.' What boy in his senses wanted anything to do with schoolroom tosh like that, from *A Child's Garden of Verses*?

But we had to take our poetry and swallow it, like medicine – a verse every week to be learned by heart. You had to stand up in the class and recite it.

By and by, in spite of everything, certain verses took root in the mind. One of the first to strike root was Burns' 'To a Mouse'. The language was a thing of mockery to us young Orcadians. What could we make of a line like 'a daimen icker in a thrave'[1]? Yet there was a kind of magic in the sound alone.

'The Burial of Sir John Moore' – now that was something that football-playing boys could respond to!

> We buried him darkly at dead of night,
> The sods with our bayonets turning,
> By the struggling moonbeam's misty light,
> And the lantern dimly burning.

There were other battle poems in the same vein – Thomas Campbell's 'The Battle of the Baltic', and 'Our bugles sang truce'...

Into those little martial symphonies intruded a stark pastoral, Wordsworth's 'Fidelity': it concerned a shepherd who had died in the Pennine snow, and his dog stood guard over him for days, maybe weeks. One can imagine what a sentimental blur might have been made of it, but we were impressed by the austere beauty of the verse narrative.

Aged twelve we were told that we were about to read Shakespeare's *The Merchant of Venice*. We groaned, inwardly. The classics – all noble imperious literature – were anathema to boys who read *The Wizard* and *The Hotspur*.

The play begins, 'In sooth I know not why I am so sad' ... a simple sequence of monosyllables; and from then on the eye of Shakespeare held some of us and would not let us go.

The Scottish ballads enthralled us. I think the first one we read was 'Sir Patrick Spens'.

> The King sits in Dunfermline toon
> Drinking the blood-red wine,
> 'O where will I get a skeely[2] skipper
> To sail this new ship o' mine?'

1 an odd ear of corn in some cut sheaves
2 skilled

We went on playing football and smoking Woodbines and reading *The Wizard*, but there seemed to be something in this poetry after all, we had to admit.

About the age of fifteen, some of us began to take deep draughts of Shelley and Keats – and after that there was no hope for us, the delicious compulsive drug was in our systems and demanding more. Again, as with Burns, it was more the sound than the sense that quickened blood and being with delight.

It takes a whole life-time to squeeze out the ultimate drops of *meaning*.

So, thank you, Stromness Academy, for that introduction to poetry. (I forgive and forget the maths, the geography, the physics and chemistry, music and 'drill', and Latin grammar.)

Mindful of Age

23 September 1993

Early autumn and the falling leaves is the time to be mindful of age – as if there weren't sufficient signs already.

One of the most noticeable is the forgetting of names. This may not sound serious but it can be embarrassing if you have to introduce two strangers to each other, and you forget (temporarily) the name of one or the other, or – too dreadful for words! – of both... Then all you can do is to make a couple of mutters, indistinct blurs of sound, and pray that neither party will wish to pursue the matter further.

For, to some folk, the forgetting of his or her name is a kind of insult... But here's the rub – an hour later, when you're poking the fire or flicking the pages of a book, the name slots in from (seemingly) nowhere, when there's no particular need for it.

So it is, to begin to grow old, and when the year itself is ageing... Ageing or not, we have had three glorious autumnal days, better than any the miserly summer dowered us with.

All I could think about, toiling up Khyber Pass under that intense blue sky yesterday afternoon, with clouds like marble sculptings, and a lovely ruffle from north-east on the sea – all I could think about, ungratefully, was how much slower I could climb the steps and the steep brae than ten or twelve years ago. Lungs and lower limbs have lost much of their elasticity.

Whereas, of course, on such a day we ought to have been overjoyed as Keats ('Season of mists and mellow fruitfulness'...) or

Hopkins ('Summer ends now; now, barbarous in beauty, the stooks rise / Around...').

Not only poets – yesterday was a kind of day for all creation to revel in. It was that kind of day – a marvellous outpouring of the treasures of light. A day for walking to Breckness or Brinkie's Brae. Even the bench at the Pier Head, sheltered from the north-east, would have been a good thing to do.

But what do some old men encased in their daily routine insist on? – They must go to bed and have their forty winks. Over roof and chimney-tops the sky is a rush of richness, and the sea music is all around.

❋

I got some stamps yesterday from the Post Office depicting autumn. I will stick them on the envelopes with a little melancholy: and hope I won't forget the names of the people the letters are addressed to!

This 'Common' Beverage

30 September 1993

Three cups of tea in the morning, the last cup after the fire has been lit by my good neighbour Brian Murray – and the day is off to a good start.

Tea is so universal nowadays that we take it for granted.

But it wasn't always so. I was reading a chapter or two of *The Pirate* the other evening, and the social drink then for ladies was 'cinnamon water'. Cinnamon water was being sipped in respectable Stromness houses in the nineteenth century... The men, no doubt, were drinking brandy and other 'strong waters' in another room of the house.

So, this 'common' beverage, tea, took a long while to get to Orkney and Shetland.

To begin with – imported from China – it was very expensive too. Eighteenth-century fashionable people called it 'tay' (a pronunciation still common in Ireland – see the dialogue in Sean O'Casey's great Dublin tragedy *Juno and the Paycock* ... it is mentioned too, in that same style, in Pope's 'Rape of the Lock').

Possibly smugglers brought the stuff to Orkney, along with tobacco and rum. One can imagine the laird's factor rubbing a handful of the dark grains and saying, 'We won't be having any more of that stuff, that's certain!'... But the laird's lady, inhaling the delicious fragrance, pronounced it better than cinnamon water, by far.

And so it percolated down to 'the lower orders'. And it was getting cheaper all the time, as the great tea clippers brought their cargoes from the mysterious East, where all the great essences and aromas have originated – 'All the perfumes of Arabia will not sweeten this little hand,' laments Lady Macbeth.

I remember a good Birsay farm wife telling me, fifty years ago, that in her girlhood tea was only drunk on Sundays, as a special treat.

In my own childhood, all the women of Stromness were 'tea-aholics'... They seemed to be drinking tea at their cheerful fires from morning to night... At Well Park, all the women in the block foregathered at 11am for morning tea, each of the four homes taking it in turn. How they vied with each other, to set on the plate superlative home-baked cakes and shortbread. Afterwards, my mother read the tea-leaves – coming from the Highlands, she was supposed to be specially gifted in that way. She was always seeing 'tall dark strangers' or 'long-expected letters' in the tea leaves.

'Mazawattee', 'Typhoo', 'Good-as-Gold' were some of the brand names. And it was always drunk with milk and sugar.

Nowadays, of course, there are sophistications. The better sort prefer slivers of lemon to milk. And some declare, sugar spoils the real tea taste. And others will drink nothing but the tea itself – preferably the expensive brands.

There was no sound so homely as the teaspoon rattling in the tin 'tea caddy' on the mantelpiece, and the rush of the grains into the pre-heated pot, and the burble of the boiling water going in... I wonder what the Stromness women of my childhood would have thought of tea bags, lying there in their cardboard boxes like dead grey moths? – I expect they'd have shaken their old wise heads...

Meantime, the husbands and uncles were taking their manly thirsts to the Pomona in Finstown or the Smithfield in Dounby, by bus. (For the mighty legion of women had seen to it that every pub in Hamnavoe was locked and shuttered – for evermore, they hoped; but it only lasted for twenty-five years or so.)

Remembering Ten-Year-Olds' Fun

7 October 1993

When the darkness came down in early October, the ten-year-olds would gather in a cluster at some street corner. And

'Leave-O!' some boy would shout, and off he would rush into the night, alone.

The rest of us would have to wait and count up to a hundred, and then we were up and after him, hot-foot!

It was almost like the hunt, only with boys instead of horses and dogs and a fox.

It might be long enough before the quarry was tracked down, Stromness being such a labyrinth of piers and closes.

But at last he was cornered, and the game was over.

But it started up all over again, immediately. Another boy was given the wild freedom of the night. The hunters counted to a hundred and were off, this way and that, under the hissing gas lamps.

I forget how many hunts and chases and captures there might be before we were all quite exhausted, and trooped off home, each to his own house.

The desolating thought came that there was homework – spelling, arithmetic, history – to be done before bedtime.

How cosy it was, inside the little house! What a soft radiance the lamp shed from the sideboard.

There might be tatties left over from dinner. They were sliced and fried. Thick slices of bread were held up on forks against the glowing ribs of the range, to toast. That was some feast to go to bed on, on an autumn evening, washed down with a mug of cocoa.

And sleep came over us like a great blue-black wave full of stars, nine hours long.

There were nights too wet and windy to play 'Leave-O'.

Then we stayed at home and played games. 'Snakes-and-Ladders' was only for kids. 'Ludo' was a great favourite with ten-year-olds. We might play draughts (or checkers) too, but that was a bit too intellectual, not to be really enjoyed for another year or two.

One year, someone brought a gramophone into the house, and a few records. There were Harry Lauder records, but I preferred Will Fyffe as a singing comedian ('I Belong tae Glesca' and 'Sailing up the Clyde' and 'Dr MacGregor and his Wee Black Bag'...). But there were also cowboy songs: 'Red River Valley' and 'The Wheel of the Wagon is Broken'.

We wound up the machine at the end of every record, but didn't generally change the needle till the voice came out all distorted. And sometimes a record would fall from our hasty hands and shatter on the flagstone floor.

Sometimes we just sat beside the fire and read *The Hotspur* – stories like 'Red Circle School' and 'Buffalo Bill's Schooldays'. Those schools and schooldays were, we were convinced, much more exciting than ours.

Black Diamonds & the Blue Brazil

14 October 1993

When Rev Ronald Ferguson of St Magnus told me the other week that his book on Cowdenbeath Football Club was soon to be published, I said, 'Well, you can't expect that to be a bestseller'... He indicated that it was a labour of love, that mining town in Fife being his birthplace, and Central Park, Cowdenbeath, being the place where his father carried him to watch his first football matches.

Whereas, if the book had been about Celtic, Rangers, or Aberdeen, the fans would have been queuing up to buy it.

But Cowdenbeath – who in Scotland would want to read about that lowly team, about to be relegated to the Second Division after a wretched season?

As it happens, this book is a very fascinating document indeed.

The 'spine' of the book is the football club indeed, but a whole community is involved. The Fife town grew up around the coal mines, coal being the driving power behind the Industrial Revolution, and important right up to modern times.

Work in the pits was hard and dirty and dangerous, but for these reasons it bonded the whole community, so that joy and sorrow – and there was plenty of the latter – were experienced communally (in much the same way that the great Shetland fishing disasters welded an entire Shetland district into a single cry of grief... This community experience goes through the whole of human history... the Greek plays had their chorus expressing the reaction of the common people to the tragic happenings in Thebes or Colonus).

The folk of Cowdenbeath had their theatre too – namely, the football park where they played against the other professional teams of Scotland – but where the chief rivals were neighbouring Fife teams like Dunfermline, Raith Rovers, East Fife.

There, at Central Park, every Saturday afternoon (once Saturday afternoon was declared an afternoon-off, by no means an easy concession to wring from the coal owners) the miners of Cowdenbeath transferred their personal hardships and hopes to the eleven heroes in the blue shirts.

114

The drama, concerning the history of the club, has been a mingled yarn. It is, above all, a tale of the sinister power of money. This area of Fife had more than its share of football talent. Generation by generation it threw up famous names. But as soon as the talent showed itself, in this player or that, he was signed on by the famous wealthy Scottish or English clubs, and Cowdenbeath, hanging in there by a shoe-string, had to nurture yet another new crop of players.

(Nowadays, in the wider field, the situation verges on the insane, with clever-footed young men being bought and sold for millions of pounds!)

A community like Cowdenbeath, rich in football talent, seems doomed to dawdle along forever in the lower echelons of Scottish football.

Not everybody listens with breathless interest to the TV results on a Saturday afternoon. So I hasten to assure admirers of Ron Ferguson's literary gifts that this is a serious study – spiked with humour and occasional anger – of a town he grew up in and loves deeply, at a certain stage of its development.

Educationally, Cowdenbeath threw up as many talented intellectuals as footballers, nearly all of them of mining stock. Politics too, has been the richer for Cowdenbeath (there is even a prominent Tory!).

Through this coal-grimed industrial labyrinth, Ron Ferguson follows the clue that led him through local reporting to journalism in Edinburgh, to university and the theological college, to Iona and St Magnus in Kirkwall.

It is a heart-felt and luminous progress.

Also it is the work of a true craftsman in literature.

I recommend it to many readers who have never seen a football kicked in their lives – and to those who, sitting by winter fires, have never wondered where all that good light and warmth come from.

Not a bestseller? It certainly deserves to be.

Stromness Football in 1930

21 October 1993

To those who have been brought up on the great poems of English endeavour and heroism – for example, the choruses of *Henry the Fifth* – the spectacle on TV last night, of hundreds of English football supporters being forcibly deported from Holland, must have been a shameful sight.

I think the trouble is that a game of football is no longer for enjoyment (both for players and spectators), as it used to be, but it is a huge gladiatorial combat, with enormous prestige and finance involved. When Scotland was involved in past years in the World Cup, the performance of the Scottish team seemed to alter the whole mood and tone of the nation – far more so, than the words and actions of any Scottish politician.

It would be an exaggeration to say that the fate of a nation depends on the deflection of the ball from a goalpost: a centimetre makes all the difference as to whether it goes in or bounces back out. But sport seems to be looming ever larger in the lives of people and nations...

I suppose it may be a substitute for warfare. From that point of view, a few punch-ups and broken windows and baton-charges in Amsterdam are better than Julius Caesar's campaigns, or the Thirty Years' War, or 1914–18.

But what has happened to the delight of football as we ancients knew it in Orkney in the 1930s? Of course we were boys then. But if ever notice of a football match appeared in Peter Esson's tailor-shop window, away we ran on a summer evening to the Market Green.

Stromness Athletic was full of famous players in those days – Hugo Munro, 'Yokko' Johnston, Bill Groundwater, George Clouston, Attie Campbell.

There were only three teams that Stromness could play against: Hotspurs, Rovers, and Thorfinn from Kirkwall (and the most formidable of these was Hotspurs, with fine players like Collier and Corsie in the forward line, and Thomson the goalie).

Stromness was a pretty ordinary team till about 1930. Then they suddenly became great, almost unbeatable. One season they topped the Orkney league, having won every game except for a draw.

What heroes they were to us small boys, that eleven in the white shirts!

I think I was there that Saturday afternoon when Stromness suddenly began to be the best team in Orkney. They were playing Hotspurs at the Market Green. At half-time it was Stromness 0 Hotspurs 2.

We nine-year-olds stood there with heavy hearts. Then the miracle happened. The Stromness players got inspiration in their boots. Goal after goal flashed into the net.

It was one of the happiest Saturdays of my life.

I remember Mr John Shearer, science master at the school, arriving late on in the game and asking me what the score was.

And I said, with stars in my eyes, '4–2 for Stromness'...

That is the way football should be experienced; in such innocent pastoral style.

Was there no nastiness then? Well, we might go so far as to taunt Kirkwall supporters with 'Kirkwall stiggies' (starlings), and they in turn would call us 'Stromness bloody puddings'.

But no punch-ups, no window-smashings, no Sergeant Mainland leading away louts in handcuffs to the cells...

Will there ever be such days again?

'Trowie Body' Is Seventy-two

28 October 1993

I duly reached the venerable age of seventy-two last Sunday, feeling rather crabbit and at odds with the world because I had a cold. But why anyone in a peaceful place like Orkney should feel disgruntled, even with a cold, when we see every night the sufferings in Bosnia, Somalia, Angola, passes rational judgement.

Besides, I had good friends who made the day pleasant for me.

Half a century ago, in October 1943, I never for a moment thought I'd ever get to seventy-two. Even thirty-two seemed doubtful. Because, in that long-past youth, I was a kind of 'trowie[1] body', having been found with TB in 1941, and spending six summer months in the sanatorium at Eastbank.

That was in the days before streptomycin and PAS[2]. The chances were that you wouldn't get better of it. It's strange, looking back, how tranquilly one accepts such a situation. Aged nineteen then, I used to sit in the balcony at Eastbank and decide, somewhat arbitrarily, that I wouldn't get beyond twenty-three. But the prospect didn't fill me with dread at all. The only treatment was rest and good food. It was ration-time in a world at war, but fortunately in Orkney there were plenty of eggs, butter, meat. Nobody told us seriously not to smoke. So I puffed ten Gold Flake or Players every day. Nothing wrong with that, I

1 sickly
2 para-aminosalicylic acid

reasoned. Hadn't I been inhaling Wild Woodbines since the age of twelve, with any funding I could beg, borrow, or steal? (Now, looking back, that early initiation into smoking was almost certainly why I was up here at Eastbank, half a wreck, and waiting to be flung full and finally against the crags in three or four years' time.)

Meantime, they allowed me to walk about, and even to go down to Kirkwall, where the main attraction was Leonard's bookshop... Old kind Mr Leonard always had time for a chat about Tennyson or some other poet.

Soldiers in Orkney – there were 60,000 of them – when they were struck down with TB, were sent to Eastbank too. I remember a few of them: one especially, a Congregational minister who was brought in almost secretly one morning. He was on a troopship bound for Iceland when he had a lung haemorrhage. He was put ashore at Kirkwall, for Eastbank.

Rev Collins-Williams was a nice man.

I used to drop in on his small ward to see how things were with him twice or thrice a day.

One morning I heard on my hospital headphones that Germany had invaded Russia. That was at midsummer, 1941. Mr Collins-Williams, flat on his back in bed, had heard the news too.

'Whom the gods wish to destroy,' said he, 'they first make mad'... I think it was a quotation from a Greek poet.

If you think you're not going to live beyond twenty-three, nothing is of great importance that can happen. Still, it was thrilling, the news.

Now, at seventy-two, the world seems to be quite as mad as it was in 1941.

A few years later, they discovered the miracle drug streptomycin, for TB.

That's why I'm still around, at seventy-two.

Clouston's Pier

4 November 1993

I am glad to have in my house now a painting of Clouston's Pier, Stromness, which used to hang on the wall of John Broom's house in Franklin Road.

It came to me by way of our mutual friend Paddy Hughes.

Clouston's Pier is where I was born seventy-two years ago, in the door next the street, just below Mrs Boyes's shoe-shop; but then I think it was a saddler shop operated by Mr Tom Craigie, who later became green-keeper at the golf course.

My first memories are all of Clouston's Pier.

I was sitting on the doorstep there one day in 1924 or so and looked up to see a tinker woman – possibly Nellie Newlands – standing before me... I dreamed of travelling in a tinkers' cart for miles and miles, across hills and dales, soon after that.

There is an even earlier memory. I am sitting in a pram indoors and my father is outlined against the window, reading a paper or document of some kind...

Legends accumulate about every pier and close. When my next eldest brother was in his pram outside the front door – I must have been very tiny, or even unborn, when this happened – the brake was left off and the pram began to career towards the edge of the pier. Somebody was there to catch it in time... That incident was related over and over, in our family.

Old women cleaned their fish at the slipway. My oldest brother – a child too – sat watching the swilling of the haddocks in the sea. 'Be careful, buddo,' said the fishwife, 'or thu'll faal in'... and with that my brother Hughie toppled over the edge, with a splash.

In summer the boys fished sillocks, or crabs, or they bathed.

And we rowed in flatties across to the Holms.

Fishermen baited their lines outside a black-tarred shed.

One day there was a very high tide – I haven't seen a higher in Stromness. The sea came halfway up the close – it was beautiful, and amazing and frightening.

One day, some years later – I might have been about ten – I was standing on the edge of the pier with my school chum Billy. We were both looking at the old fishermen, when I heard a splash, and there was Billy in the sea. He came out, silver-splashing, and ran oozing sea all the way home.

The gulls would make a sudden terrible outcry. 'Ah,' said my mother, 'the cullyas[1] are crying for rain'... But I can't remember whether such days ended in rain or not.

I was six when we left the pier for Melvin Place.

My old friend Ian MacInnes painted the pier. I hope to hang it over the mantelpiece, any day now.

1 common gulls

Poem for Auction

11 November 1993

There's no feeling so good as to be writing something, there at the kitchen table, with the fan heater purring like a mechanical cat and the little Anglepoise lamp throwing a circle of light.

It's hard to write something new *every* day – so we writers positively long for somebody to order or request us to write something.

It doesn't matter if you know the person or not. So long as you approve of the theme, you can make a start.

And never believe for one moment, about 'inspiration'. A craftsman is given a job to do. He makes a start as soon as he can, eagerly.

Yesterday, a letter came from a lady in a village called Keyworth, in Nottinghamshire. The church organ badly needs repair, but the restoration will cost £16,000. Among the fundraising ideas is an auction. Mrs Jennifer Davie wondered if I would contribute something – a photo, maybe – and sign it.

I don't have that many photos, so I thought after breakfast this morning that a few words on paper would be better – very much better in fact.

You may not think it is a poem – it doesn't rhyme, for one thing. But at least it yearns to be a poem, with images circling like planets about a central theme.

A Poem For The Restoration Of The Organ In St Mary Magdalene Church, Keyworth, Nottingham

Think of the ancestors in sound of the Keyworth organ.
Centuries ago
There might have been fiddle and pipe at Evensong,
As in Thomas Hardy.
Further back, rough true utterances
Of country folk,
Sweet pure mouths of children.
So, obedient to the psalmist
Voices dance across centuries.
'From harmony, from heavenly harmony
This universal frame began,' said John Dryden.
St Cecilia,
Seated at your many-voiced frame
Think still of the Keyworth organ
Seeking now, in age,
To utter its pristine praisings.
Think of the first song thrown upon chaos.

I don't expect I'll ever be in Keyworth, or hear the restored organ in the church of St Mary Magdalene there; but once I copy the poem on a sheet of good handmade paper, and sign it and send it, maybe somebody at the auction will bid a fiver or so for it.

It'll certainly look better on somebody's wall in Nottingham than my signed photograph.

It would be nice if the verse, framed, could be hung between a fiddle and a flute.

It may be because the world is starved of music, that there is so much trouble in Bosnia, Somalia, Ulster, Angola, Haiti – and a hundred other places.

Stone Book of the Dead

18 November 1993

November is, traditionally, the month of dead souls.

One Wednesday afternoon early in the month, I paid a duty call to the kirkyard at Warbeth.

There is a first grave in the new kirkyard, now.

That is sufficient indication of one's own age, because I remember the first tombstone in graveyard number three – It was in memory of John Mackay, owner of Stromness Hotel, who died in 1928, a big block of granite with *Manu Forti*[1] inscribed on it.

It was the very oldest kirkyard that was fascinating to us as boys on summer days – the heavy slabs, some horizontal, with the beautiful deep-cut lettering on them commemorating vanished skippers, merchants, lawyers, ministers. One was for a young girl called Ellen Dunne, with a memorial rhyme that herdie-boys used to learn by heart, seated on the kirkyard wall. Here too was the double tombstone, half in Latin and half in English, commemorating the late eighteenth-century minister, Rev William Clouston, who wrote the fascinating account of contemporary Stromness in the *First Statistical Account*, and was an agreeable tolerant learned man. 'Yes, to be sure the people drink ale, but hard work and the climate make it needful' – so he said, in effect (though I'm too lazy at the moment to turn the pages for his actual wording). He interspersed his account with frequent quotations from Virgil. I think he would have been a pleasant man to spend an evening with.

1 the motto of the Mackays

A few years ago Stromness kirkyard had the same problem as North Fara; there was danger of erosion, so the cliff face was shored up and fortified.

Imagine, if we had seen the foreshore some morning suddenly strewn with skulls!

The great hero hereabout is Alexander Graham, the Stromness merchant who ruined himself by winning Stromness's freedom to trade, unhampered by Kirkwall taxes. But there is no tombstone to our great man in the kirkyard. Was he so very poor in the end that there was not enough money to buy a tombstone? We know that his widow was 'in reduced circumstances'... It was surely a shame on his fellow-merchants that he lies in an unmarked grave.

No need to look for Bessie Millie's name anywhere here. That seller of winds wouldn't have had enough sixpences (her usual fee) put by to pay for a gravestone.

Nor is there any indication of where Gow's fiancée Miss Gordon is buried.

We must remember that the great majority of Stromnessians in the past were interred anonymously.

That Wednesday afternoon, we thought of looking for the memorial stone of John Folster, fisherman, that George S. Robertson (Provost and Postmaster) had put up for his neighbour and friend at the pier at Alfred Street, and had inscribed with his own hand.

But the shadows were gathering fast in mid-afternoon, and we got lost a bit in the labyrinth of stones... We promised ourselves to return some other day, to look for John Folster's tombstone.

The Pier Head Parliament

25 November 1993

Where did the old men of Stromness foregather, in the old days?

There being no pubs, they stood in groups about the Pier Head. Indeed, our teachers handed out to us dire warnings that if we didn't apply ourselves to our studies we would end our days 'holding up the wall at the Pier Head'.

Ancient or feeble or stiff, the old men of Stromness – even after a life-time of work – held up the wall at the Pier Head. Suddenly somebody had a brain-wave. Why not seats at the Pier Head? So the ancients of Stromness, after the Town Council had approved the idea, could take the weight off their feet. The crowded benches quickly became known as the Pier Head Parliament. I began to write a brief column every week for *The Orkney Herald*, called 'What the Pier Head is Saying' – the forerunner of 'Letter from Hamnavoe' and 'Under Brinkie's Brae'.

Former generations gave great veneration to grandparents and great-grandparents, as being the repositories of traditional skills and pieties. In some ways, that attitude nowadays is being neglected. Life is for the young, the jet-setters, the holiday-makers in Ibiza, the fabulous money-makers.

But not entirely. Some caring folk in Stromness, years ago, opened the Eventide Club-room at the Pier Head. Here the citizens can come in from the cold. They can plug in the fire and make themselves a cup of tea or coffee. They can play darts or draughts. They can read the *National Geographic* and other magazines.

Some good Stromness ladies, out of the kindness of their hearts, keep the little cosy room clean and well provided.

We have come a long way from that image of the old men on a winter afternoon standing in a huddle against what used to be called the Custom House wall, smoking their pipes and wondering if they'll go home before the next shower of sleet. And if the wind was in the east!...

We have been talking so far about men. It should be realized that the Eventide Club is open to everyone of a ripe age, including women. And not only the town women, but their sisters in from Hoy and the parishes. It can be tiring to the feet, after a morning of shopping.

The Eventide Club is not an exclusive male club.

So, ladies of Stromness and round about, the door is always open to you. Bring your knitting if you like.

Menus before the War

2 December 1993

Reading the glossy magazines nowadays, you might think that people lived for food almost exclusively, in ever greater refinements.

Think too of the huge popularity of cookery books. You would have to live to be a thousand to taste a new recipe every day.

It might be that we are indeed a more refined people nowadays, with more exquisitely balanced tastes and manners. (But I doubt it.)

Maybe pre-war, the normal Orkney kitchen repertoire was a bit limited, especially for boys who were mainly interested in sweeties and lemonade.

There were variations on about five or six items.

First and foremost was Scotch broth, a thick mixture boiled about a bone, or a chunk of meat. (I only began to enjoy that when I got to my teens.) And there were no exotica like tomato soup. There it was, the plate of Scotch broth steaming on the table at one o'clock – take it or leave it...

After the soup came boiled beef and tatties – clapshot in winter ... I didn't much care for that either. The clapshot was OK.

Another day, there was stew, with onions and carrots. We gobbled it without relish, quickly, to be outside once more playing football... No herbs – just pepper and salt.

(My mother was a good enough cook: it was just that boys' stomachs are not attuned to such savoury diets.)

Another day, there would be mince and tatties. This was an ordeal, too.

There were plenty of fish days – fine fresh haddocks and cod caught that very morning and sold along the street, out of hand barrows, by the fishermen, who weighed the fish on brass hand-scales at sixpence per pound... Even such fish was of no interest to boys. You gave a few patient sighs, and slipped some of the buttered fish to the cat when nobody was looking.

Porridge was a frightful ordeal! And if there were lumps in it...

The elders maybe thought they were wooing us with puddings – Creamola, rice, Farola, sago, with a dollop of jam on top. No way – the puddings were even more repellent than the savouries. The exceptions were apple and rhubarb tarts.

What on earth, then, did we eat? Our digestions seemed to be finely attuned to the products of the frying pan. If there was ham and eggs for tea, we could smell it from half a mile away. And sausages were almost as alluring. Best of all were kippers. Kippers cost a penny each, but were always sold for some reason in pairs, as if one magnificent juicy kipper wasn't quite enough for the normal stomach... A kipper for tea caused one whole day to tremble with excitement: the digestive juices danced with delight.

The day ended with cocoa, another dull drink. Sometimes, if the cocoa tin was empty, you just got hot milk at bedtime, a very repulsive nightcap, especially when the milk cooled and a skin came on top that clung to your mouth.

Roast beef was too dear for working-class households, except on New Year's Day.

There might be a chicken (or hen, as it was more honestly called) once a month or so, and that was good, especially with oatmeal stuffing.

❋

Suddenly, in adolescence, the taste changes. One begins to appreciate Scotch broth, mince and tatties, stew, fish... But I never got round to liking milk puddings.

Since the war, there has gradually grown this huge repertoire of cuisine. It takes a long time to read a menu in a restaurant nowadays.

'The Endless Ballet of the Weather'

9 December 1993

Stromness is wide open to south-easterly gales, and so we suffered last Sunday, but even more so on Monday when the storm rose to a crescendo.

It being full moon, the tide was high, almost as high on the noust below Mayburn as it was possible to reach. The rampant waves marched in, in awesome procession, and tore themselves to pieces on the pier below, with great flung shawls of spray, again and again. Anyone standing at the Pilot's Lookout would have been drenched between one wave and the next.

Watching from the seaward window, it was more than impressive. The harbour was covered with a smoor of spray, all the way to the Holms.

The wind howled about the street corners, hustling people about.

There was no sign of Winston the grey kitten, who seems to like the Mayburn area. Nobody would blame Winston, on such a day, for sitting on a rug beside his own fire, and purring.

Only the bravest cats and people were out and about that day. People going past, under Mayburn, were wet with sea-spray, not rain.

The fire was hungry for coal.

In early afternoon, I decided to imitate Winston and keep warm.

The wind howled, louder than ever. But the ebb had set in, and the combers bursting from the pier below did not rain themselves down so spectacularly.

I wondered, has the sea got into a few Stromness cellars; for these are the conditions, a full moon and a south-east gale.

We might have known, from a few preliminary flickers and waverings, that the TV would falter and fail. Suddenly, in mid-evening, the picture gave way to a perpetual blizzard – a pity, because there was a serial about a she-demon that I was wanting to see. I had to turn to Thomas Merton's autobiography instead, which I'm sure was much better for me. At bedtime, it was still blizzarding heavily across the TV screen.

Next day the wind had shifted to the south-west, and moderated.

Orkney under the new sky looked like a different place altogether. Any new-come tourist must have been astonished at the contrast.

At evening, our tourist would have been utterly enchanted. The harbour lay like beaten silver under the full moon – very tranquil, after the fury of yesterday.

And the TV was restored to us. But it was Budget, Budget, Budget, all night (it seemed). We old folk are not to be allowed to freeze, after all. As few of us old folk have cars, dearer petrol doesn't bother us. And the price of beer (same as yesterday) doesn't worry me as it would have done, powerfully, three decades ago.

Today – one day later – is the first of December. Rain is lashing the window-panes. It looks as if we might be in for a winter of much variety.

A good smell of clapshot is coming out of the pot next door.

The fire wants three or four big lumps of coal on, to make the house winter-merry.

A Christmas Story

23 December 1993

There was an old man who lived alone in a peedie cottage on the far side of Brinkie's Brae.

His wife had died thirty years before. His son had emigrated to Canada and he never heard from him. His daughter had gone to Glasgow to marry. She wrote him a letter sometimes, but less and less frequently as the years passed.

The old man was quite alone. He might say, 'A fine day' or 'A blowstery day' to anyone he met on the road. But that was all. Nobody crossed his threshold. Nobody was encouraged to visit.

He went down to Hamnavoe for his pension on a Monday, and got his few errands. He had a glass of stout, to give him strength for the steep walk home.

On the street he saw a small boy and gave him a fivepence piece. The coin was small as the scale on a haddock...

He had cut peats in May and brought them home in August. He wondered if he would have strength to work the peats next summer.

A blast of north wind woke him after midnight. His room was all a dazzle of light next morning when he got up. The snow was up to the eaves of his long disused byre.

'Well,' said he to his cat, 'we'll just sit beside the fire and keep warm.'

The cat sang on the rag mat.

There was a small boy in Hamnavoe, and he was delighted at the sudden snowfall.

His father came in from the west and put a basket of haddocks on the pier. The sun flashed off the silver!

The peedie boy said nothing to anyone.

He hooked a haddock on his forefinger and he set off up the close, and on up the Kirk Road, and up past Grieveship and over the shoulder of Brinkie's Brae.

Sometimes he was knee-deep in snow.

Here and there a dog barked at him, but it was a cheerful barking, as if the dogs liked the snow too.

Soon the boy saw a cottage with smoke coming from the chimney.

He knocked at the door. The old man opened. The boy gave him the fish. At sight of the fish, the cat sang several ecstatic songs.

The old man invited the boy in to sit for a while at his fire.

A New Year Story

30 December 1993

'Well,' said the old man who lived on the far side of Brinkie's Brae, 'there'll be no visitors this New Year for sure. Who wants to visit a crabbit old man? Besides, all the men and lasses I used to go first-footing with are in the kirkyard. Well, there are one or two left, but they live a good distance away, in Yesnaby and Hamnavoe, and they won't be walking all this distance in weather like this'...

All the same, when he was in the town for his pension on Monday, he bought a bottle of whisky and a round of Westray shortbread and an iced cake at Argo's.

It would never do, to have an empty cupboard at New Year!

He bought some liver from the butcher and some fish from the fish-shop for the cat.

After his mince and clapshot on Hogmanay evening, he sat in his straw-back chair beside a good fire: a bundle of red and orange and yellow flames.

Soon he had nodded off to sleep... This was happening more and more often, this drowsing after his dinner

Sometimes he woke up feeling awkward and at odds with the world, especially if the fire had sunk to grey cinders with only a single glowing ruby at the heart of it – then it was sometimes hard enough to get the fire going again... Then he would be melancholy on winter nights, thinking of all his 'yamils' in the kirkyard.

This Hogmanay, the old man slept longer than he intended. He was wakened by a far-off noise of hooters and sirens from the hidden harbour of Hamnavoe – all the ships in the harbour sounding off. It was midnight.

'Another year,' said the old man. 'Well, I'll just fill the stone hot-water bottle and go to bed.'

Then there was a rush of cold air from the opening door and the dying embers flamed up, and the cat jumped on to the table, and who should come in but Jimmo the farmer of Readypenny that he had gone to school with, carrying a bottle of whisky in one hand and a lump of blue-black coal in the other. Jimmo of Readypenny was followed by two other old men, Richan who kept the ironmonger's shop in Hamnavoe and Knarston the fisherman. All four had sat in the same classroom sixty years before.

They chorused 'Happy New Year!' and threw their lumps of coal on the fire, and asked where were the glasses.

There were no glasses, but our old man blew the dust out of four cups and set them on the table. And he took his bottle of whisky out of the cupboard and there were four little barleycorn soughs as the drams were poured into the cups.

'Happy New Year,' he said. 'But what's the use of you men only coming to see me once a year? You're all too busy making money, I expect. Good health to you, all the same'...

The four cups touched rims, making tiny delicate music.

The flames leapt up in the hearth.

'A Happy New Year to you all,' sang the cat from the rag mat at the fire.

R. T. Johnston, Writer & Cartoonist

13 January 1994

A rare talent there was in Orkney twenty-five years ago and earlier, when the Stenwick stories appeared weekly in *The Orkney Herald*.

The astonishing thing is that the author, R. T. Johnston, was not himself an Orcadian; and yet he had mastered the Orkney dialect so well.

It might have seemed to the first readers that these comic stories were ephemeral, like the newsprint they were written on, although deeply enjoyable.

But The Orkney Press a year or two ago put out a selection of Bob Johnston's stories, in hard covers, and they (I'm sure) were read as avidly as the originals were, every Tuesday all over Orkney.

True enough, they were not meant to be penetrating studies of Orkney characters: they were caricature, and claimed to be nothing more.

But they were true creations, all the same, and Chon Clouston and Godfrey Ritch have something of the eternal in them. Godfrey Ritch especially is as steeped in the joy of life as Falstaff even. He is a creative force.

The whole parish of Stenwick throbs with comical intensity.

We know that these tales are set in the thirties and forties, and Orkney has changed almost out of recognition in the half-century since then.

The question now is, will Stenwick and its folk be treasured by young Orcadians in the twenty-first century?

I think they will be. Orcadians love their islands more than they ever express it, and this comical mirror will make a few more generations laugh, no doubt. Though externals change, essentials remain.

Bobby Johnston in fact belonged to Buckie; though he was married to a Kirkwall girl.

At the same time as he was writing Stenwick – very quickly, week after week – he was contributing a similar series of stories to (I think) the *Press and Journal*, set in the Buchan district of north-east Scotland, with its very different ethos and dialect.

To run two such series in parallel was, in itself, an extraordinary achievement.

The author himself was a quiet laconic man who never wasted words. I spent many a Monday morning with him reading proofs in the little *Orkney Herald* office, and we got on well.

His consuming passion in life was cricket – test matches were great dramas for him, though he rarely showed his exultation in victory or desolation when things were going badly.

He was a great fan of Agatha Christie.

Besides being a literary man, he was a talented cartoonist, under the name of 'Spike', and these impromptu sketches were as popular as the Stenwick stories.

R. T. Johnston will always have an honoured place in Orcadian literary comedy.

Daily Papers

27 January 1994

For a few Saturdays past, I have taken a certain famous newspaper, in order to get the TV and radio programmes.

Such a vast amount of newsprint is delivered – so much, that the mere sight of all those sections (news, finance, sport, business) gives me mental indigestion.

(I think of going hungry into a Chinese restaurant in Edinburgh in my student days, and how the mere look of that hill of cooked rice on the plate banished appetite.)

It's the same with modern newspapers. I often think that the bigger they become, the emptier they get, by some kind of ruthless mathematical progression.

Anyhow, if I have a half-hour to spare, I go recklessly through this famous London newspaper, thinking that at least the many pages will help kindle the fire (which is more than can be said for 'glossies' like the *Radio Times* – no happy little conflagration there, to start the morning, only a surly smouldering that the cut sticks and small coals hold in deepest contempt).

But I do save the television and radio section of *The Times*, so much more terse, readable and succinct than the glossy exclusively devoted to such things.

Ah well, I suppose the vast expanse of newsprint nowadays is a happy hunting-ground for journalists – though often enough they have to gnaw the bones pretty close, and true nourishment is hard to find.

Not many readers remember the wartime dailies. They shrank and shrank until by 1944 or so, there were just four pages. Yet there was always a queue outside Rae's in the early afternoon. People were really hungry for news in those days; with wartime censorship several normal avenues were blocked.

In those far-off days, my mother took a paper called the *News Chronicle*, long defunct now. It was, I think, a Liberal paper on the whole, and it had good book reviews and a frequent highly readable essay by a Wick journalist called Ian Mackay.

Before that, in my father's time, we changed from the *Daily Express* to the *Daily Herald* – my father was to the left of centre, a faithful adherent of the working class, and the *Express* was too Establishment orientated, and jingoistic.

Myself, I regretted the change, not being old enough for politics and cherishing a great affection for Rupert the Bear – the only thing I read in the *Express*, apart from football reports... Whenever a goal was scored, 'the leather was booted into the rigging', a phrase to rouse the heart of a young schoolboy, especially if it was Jimmy McGrory that 'unleashed the daisy-cutter'...

I wonder if my old chum Rupert the Bear is still going strong?

Stormy Burns-Time

3 February 1994

Just when, in mid-month, we were beginning to think, January's a mild enough month this year, compared to the tanker-wrecking storms of last January, the weather must have seen what we were thinking, and noted our complacency, because it turned awkward as only January can.

The wind went in wild skirls over the islands on Burns day, just as it did the day the great bard was born – 'a blast o' Janwar' win'...'

I spent that evening reading Burns poems and songs out of the sumptuous Oxford edition in three volumes. I tried to avoid the universally-known poems like 'Tam o' Shanter', 'The Cottar's Saturday Night', 'To a Mouse' and 'Holy Willie's Prayer'.

I read a few poems I hadn't read before, 'Epistle to J. Lapraik' (a fellow rhymer unknown then to Burns, full of good-fellowship and encouragement); and 'A Winter Night' (you can almost feel the snowflakes on your eyelashes as you read it); and a song or two.

Modern readers tend to sniff superiorly at some erstwhile popular Burns poems, like 'To a Mountain Daisy', as being sentimental and almost mawkish. I had a passing glance at this poem while the tempest howled in my lum, and it seemed to me to be a creation of the utmost tenderness and delicacy – not to speak of the magnificent technical artistry of the piece... One shouldn't pay too much attention to sophisticated modern know-alls. I ought to have capped this Burns reading with a glass of the barley-bree, but somehow I drifted off to bed at midnight with only a cup of tea inside me. (I forgot to say, too, that Scottish TV that night, late, presented one of the best Burns programmes of recent years, for which they deserve all praise. Especially good was the voice of Gerda Stevenson, accompanied on the clarsach by her sister Savourna...)

I confidently hoped the storm, having celebrated Burns with such wild strathspeys and bagpipes, would give us a day or two of mild end-of-winter weather, with hints of spring even.

Nothing doing. The next day was a real ranter, howler and snarler.

I have two friends in on Wednesday evening to see the BBC TV serial *Middlemarch*, one of the really good adaptations from a fine Victorian novel. But Renée phoned in the early evening to say it was too stormy to drive down, and some time later Surinder appeared, to say he thought he wouldn't venture out at 9.30 on such a wild night. As it was, on Ness Road a swap[1] of wind had lifted the sailor cap off his head and whirled it out to sea.

So I watched *Middlemarch* alone, and that isn't quite so enjoyable.

The wind raged, wilder than ever. I had a glass of Old Mull whisky to celebrate Burns, a day late, and the blood flowed merrily for half an hour along the veins.

On the 24th, at Langskaill, I'd had supper of haggis and clapshot. So Burns got honoured, as he deserves to be forever.

The storm *must* blow itself out overnight. At 6am there were blatterings of sleet at the bedroom window, and the wind, every five minutes or so, smote the house mightily.

End of winter, indeed! Never entertain such a hope till the equinox heaves into view over the March horizon.

1 swirl

The Old Black Cat

10 February 1994

Gypsy, the old black cat, is asleep on the couch, with one eye open.

She has just had her breakfast, chicken out of a tin. There was so much heaped on her plate, she had to leave off twice or thrice and return after ten minutes or so.

She loves food, Gypsy. If I stir to go into the kitchen, she assumes at once that that is a summons to her to another meal. She is quite hurt when the kitchen door is shut against her.

Eating and sleeping are Gypsy's great delights. She will sleep anywhere. You'd think she'd prefer the fireside, in such a cold January. But I come on her sometimes sleeping on top of the bed in the cold spare bedroom.

Her favourite place of repose is my rocking-chair. That is difficult for me, because in that rocker I do all my reading. The Anglepoise lamp is there, and all the books. So often I have to lift her and set her down on the couch, a comfortable billet too. But some days, for some reason, the couch is not to her taste. She will stroll away and tuck her paws in under, on the hard floor, and seem quite content there.

It is not easy, sometimes, to enter into a cat's mind.

Gypsy is a very good-natured cat, and purrs away like a little engine most of the time, especially if you stroke her or scratch her under the chin. A well-behaved companionable cat.

But, very occasionally, the strongest throb of energy goes through her. She gets up suddenly and makes a dash round the room as if some fierce dog were after her. Then once more she curls up on the couch, or wherever, and goes to sleep... I think cats know, before human beings, when a storm is coming.

It was the storm, not a hound, that was after her! There have been plenty of storms since she came here.

Gypsy is seventeen years old, and I have known her since she was a tiny black kitten. The only sign of age in her is that now she has three white whiskers, and she is averse to going out on cold grey mornings. This mornlng, however, the sun was shining on to the balcony at Mayburn, and Gypsy actually ventured out on to the balcony for a brief stroll, while my neighbour Brian was bringing in the coals.

In a day or two she will be going home to the East Mainland, after a three-week holiday in Stromness.

There will be nobody to greet me in the morning, with cat-songs, as soon as I open the bedroom door. Nobody to eat bits of cheese or fish from my fingers (for she likes to eat in company, rather than just off her plate on the kitchen floor). Nobody to boss me around, silently.

I'll just have to write her a letter every week, as usual.

Cycles of War and Peace

3 March 1994

It's hardly a cheerful experience, listening to the radio or the TV news nowadays – and trying to guess at the sufferings of Sarajevo, Somalia, Angola, and Haiti.

Indeed, some people go so far as to say that constant exposure to such horrors hardens viewers and listeners... There was no mistaking the relief on the faces of the Sarajevo people these past few nights, when the guns in the encircling hills suddenly fell silent.

What we experience at second hand on TV should make us glad that we live in a quiet place like Orkney.

But maybe we ought to be asking, however foolishly and fruitlessly, why some cities and nations are called on to endure such horrors, while other societies keep the 'noiseless tenor of their way' for generations and centuries.

The answer may well be, that peace and disturbances of the peace move in great historical cycles.

Orkney's time of trouble began maybe in the eighth or ninth centuries, when pastoral communities of Celts were assaulted and systematically exploited by the blond sailors from east-over-sea, and they were men, those conquerors, who didn't believe much in peace, even when they had seized Orkney, Shetland, Caithness, and the Hebrides. There was something wrong, according to their way of looking at life, in peaceful coexistence with neighbours and dying 'a straw death'.

I imagine that the Pictish farmers and fishermen and their women must have endured something like Sarajevo or Angola, when those longships anchored off their shores and nousts.

The peaceful violated pre-Viking Orkneymen! We ought not to forget that those pastoral tribes had themselves come suddenly out of the south and dispossessed an even older people. That invasion and uprooting can't have been a courteous gentle intermingling.

There must have been blood on the rocks and fire in the thatch, all over 'the islands of the whale'.

And before those scattered innocent tribes, there must have been yet earlier communities, all the way back to the final retreat of the ice.

So, then, Orkney has had its savage times too. It is as if the gods of war had said, 'Those Atlantic islanders have supped full with horrors. We'll leave them in peace now, for a few centuries. After that, we'll see what's what...'

There have been minor disturbances, last shakings of the vials of wrath: the Battle of Summerdale, the storming of Kirkwall Castle, the 1940 bombs over the Flow and the Brig-o-Waithe...

The war gods have had more important chessmen to play with – Genghis Khan, Henry the Fifth, the conquistadores in Mexico, Napoleon, Hitler.

The Chinese had a curse to put upon folk they didn't like – 'May you live in interesting times.'

May we be left long in our humdrum times, observing seedtime and harvest, the equinoxes and the solstices, and the everlasting stars in their courses. Who shall ever read their mysterious ciphers? May worldwide peace be written there, somehow, at last.

As for the fierce Vikings – what nations could be more peaceable, this long while back, than Norway, Sweden, Denmark?

Testing Days

10 March 1994

March has come again, and brought spring-time, though the first day was like a really bad winter day, with the wind howling out of the east – the worst airt for Stromness.

The west wind is our friend, for Brinkie's Brae shelters the town.

But still, though wet grey snow was lying in the corners and there were occasional flake flurries, March had come, and the winter was over and gone (seasonally speaking).

I remembered, quite suddenly, some March days in the late 1930s, when we were still at school. For a great obstacle loomed before us, the Higher Leaving Certificate exam, and if we got safely past that obstacle the road to the future was assured, in a way.

But failure meant relegation to second-class status in society: though there was always a chance to have a second assault on the obstacle the following March.

The first subject we had to tackle in the week-long exam at Stromness Academy was 'English'. We had to write an essay in an hour, first of all, and we were given a choice of topics. I remember that I chose to write about what might have happened if Bonnie Prince Charlie had won the Battle of Culloden.

In the afternoon – I think we got a paper on English Literature and Grammar and Interpretation. The Interpretation concerned a very dull passage of eighteenth or nineteenth-century prose. I don't think I did so well at that.

And that was only the first day. Wrung dry, we went home and prepared for next day's ordeal, French or Latin or Maths (I forget which).

Those were solemn sessions, sitting in a high schoolroom, while Mr Christie the Free Kirk minister (the invigilator) opened the packet of exam papers and came by, setting one on every desk ... One swift glance, usually, was sufficient for a student to know whether he would pass easily, or might with luck scrape through, or be sunk in failure without trace.

When the dreaded Maths exam day came, it didn't take me more than five seconds to know that I was in for an ignominious defeat. But I scratched away with my pen, constructing frightful tangles of numbers. Trigonometry – whoever (I thought that day, aged seventeen) dreamed up such a rack for the torturing of young people! Yet some of my contemporaries took it all in their stride, with ease and relish.

All this was conducted in an air of high solemnity. It was like being at some complex austere ritual in a temple of learning. You dared not even whisper.

Twice a day Rev James Christie came tripping on hushed feet down the aisles, dropping a sweetie in wrapping paper – a caramel – on each student's desk, to give him strength.

But that dreadful week in March of the Higher Leaving Certificate was by no means the end of the matter. In May or early June a succession of awesome figures descended on the Academy, out of the clouds. They were His Majesty's Inspectors of Schools, led by one who seemed to have been there from the beginning, Mr Barron, who grilled us in English and Latin. Then, for French, there was lady inspector Miss Ramsay-Ewan; and for physics, Dr Boyle; and for maths Mr Gunn (who, Mr Shearer our maths teacher told us) was a brother of Neil Gunn the Caithness novelist. This interested me, because I had just been reading with pleasure *Morning Tide*.

Mr Learmonth, the headmaster, came most solemnly into our Fifth Year classroom and read out the results, some time in May, I think. We had all failed, except four. (My maths answers must have been a farrago of near nonsense.)

It meant that we also-rans would have to return to the fray the following year, or else follow non-academic furrows.

I can't remember that this disastrous news poisoned the summer for me.

Those summers before the war were oases of joy and peace and boundless freedom.

Pros and Cons of the Phone

17 March 1994

Many houses – probably most houses in Orkney – have a telephone now.

To those who have it, life in pre-telephone days is inconceivable.

Yet for most of my life I didn't have a phone, and I managed somehow without it. The many generations of our ancestors had to manage without it, of course.

I must have been in my mid-twenties before I used a telephone for the very first time. I think someone had to stand in the kiosk with me and show me how to dial the number. In those now-distant days you had to go by way of an operator in Kirkwall telephone exchange, and you had to have your big ancient pennies ready to drop into the box.

It was a long while before I felt at home with it.

Even now I am slightly apprehensive whenever the double ring comes, maybe when I'm having my fish and clapshot, or reading a book... In these streamlined times, it could well be somebody who wants an immediate urgent answer to some question – and I am one of those people who like to sit and ponder things for an hour, and argue with myself this way and that, with all the 'pros' and 'cons', before making up my mind. That's why I'd much rather people sent me a letter, instead of catching me suddenly off balance. Of course, friends phoning from here and there is quite a different thing, and entirely delightful.

And if we old men are stuck in the house by reason of this storm that has blown all through the winter from November to March, how good to be able to lift the phone and get in touch with butcher, baker, doctor, or chimney-sweep.

Let's try to imagine an old couple in Hamnavoe a century ago. The young birds have all flown the nest, to Australia, Edinburgh, Alberta.

How they must have sat beside their fires on a winter night wondering how things were in those distant parts of the world. 'Poor bairns!' says the old woman, as the hailstones mingled with flung seaspray beat on the window. 'Far fae home, and in weather like this too!'

And they put a few more blue-black lumps of coal on the fire.

'Bairns!' says the old man after a time. 'Jock in Queensland is forty-four years aald, and it's high summer there noo, and it'll be that hot where Jock is you could fry eggs on the flagstones. He writes once in the year – what more do we want?'

Just then the door opens, and the postman comes in, his lantern pinned to his official coat, and he sets a letter on the table, and wishes them both a good night, and goes out with his sack of mail, into the storm.

The letter is opened with trembling fingers. Spectacles are adjusted. It is not from Jock in Australia, it is from their daughter Jessie Anne in northern Canada. All's well, she has written, the family is flourishing, they have a new log house – but oh, the blizzards! They're having to dig their way from door to road twice a day. And it's so cold, your breath freezes on your lip. And she hopes they're both well...

'We ought to be thankful,' says the old man, 'that we're here in Hamnavoe, and not out there in that wild icy waste'...

'This letter's taken three months to come,' says the old woman. 'Would it no be fine if we could just hear Jessie Anne's voice again, this instant and the five bairns!'

'Don't be a fool,' says the old man. 'Put on the kettle for a pot o' tea.'

Little did they know, our good old ones, that two generations later their descendants would be in instant touch, by phone, from the farthest corners of the earth.

Outertown Dramas

24 March 1994

Winter has come back, with redoubled fury it seems, as I write this. A blizzard of wet flakes is hurtling against the window – it will last for half an hour or so and a cold sun will look at the white fields and hills, briefly, then another storm will gather its snows in the northwest and come howling over Orkney.

Winter, that fierce king, is fighting a strong rearguard action against the flower-dropping armies of spring.

This is being written not at Mayburn but at the cottage of Don in Outertown (or Ootertoon, as the people of Stromness have called it for generations and centuries). I am staying at Don for a few days, looking out over dramatic landscapes and seascapes.

After the recent storms, the sea along the coast is a smother of white. Hoy, after snow, looks 'like two Polar bears', as a friend described it well the other day.

The Black Craig looms sinister and grey through the tail end of the blizzard.

It is a beautiful dramatic district, Outertown.

It was to this very cottage – a croft at the time – that a strange fisherman came one day a century and a half ago. He had an extraordinary story to tell the folk of Don. His fishing boat had been thrown against the Black Craig. The ship had broken up and the crew had perished. Only this young man had managed to get a foothole in the cliff face and had dragged himself into a cave above the reach of the waves. He had had to stay there for days until the storm subsided, subsisting on a few herring and drops of fresh water seeping from the roof of the cave.

At last the young fisherman – I think his name was Charlie Johnston, from the north-east of Scotland – managed to scale the difficult cliff face and knocked at the door at Don.

The cave he sheltered in was called 'Charlie's Hole' thereafter.

I heard recently that Charlie was, many years later, lost at sea. The old fatalists of the time would have shaken their heads and said, 'Ah well, that was the way he had to go, a sea death was marked out for him'...

It was on the coast below that, out of a calm sea, milky-white, a great wave fell over the houses and fields. It almost washed the horse from under the laird at Breckness who was spurring on up to the higher land. An old woman reputed to be a witch, who lived in one of the crofts above (I think Liffea) stood looking on. The laird's factor, thinking she was responsible for this weird occurrence, struck at her with his whip or stick.

This tidal wave was subsequently blamed on the great Lisbon earthquake of that same year, more than two centuries ago.

Is it possible that an earthquake, however big, could have caused such a disturbance in our northern waters?

The blizzard that was blowing when I began to write this article shows no sign of yielding to blue sky and sun. Instead, it has thickened till there must be a hundred hen-wives out there plucking feathers.

We are three or four miles from the town.

It may be – if this goes on – that we'll be locked in by a white wall of snow, and a helicopter will have to drop milk, beef, bread and coal down on us!

But, even as I was writing the last paragraph, the thick flake-flurry thinned out. The sky is a lighter grey. Maybe we will see a patch of blue soon.

Meantime, I haven't seen Peedie-Don, the black cat, since I came. You'd think it would be fireside weather for cats. But no: Peedie-Don likes the outdoors.

And now it is snowing heavier than ever...

Waiting for Green Benches

21 April 1994

No weather to get outside yet, as I write this, in mid-April.

Any day now, though, I expect the benches, new-painted, to be set here and there along the street, and at the street-facing wall of Mayburn Court. What a relief, when you are a bit tired shopping, to plump down on a seat with your bag of messages and watch the cars going past (while, alas, at the same time getting lungfuls of exhaust fumes).

I hope they don't forget to put a seat at the Museum Pier, and another at Flaws's Pier. Many a contented half-hour have Stromnessians sat there, on summer afternoons, when the places weren't taken up with tourists and knapsacks. Not that we object in the least: in fact, the tourists ought to have priority, for we can sit there any time we want.

How happy the tourists seem, too. Just to watch the comings and goings of the *Ola* and the *Sunniva* and the fishing boats is enough. Not quite enough, for out come the cameras, sooner or later, and the moment is fixed for all time. The young tourists often have sandwiches and Coke, and eating in the open air they must truly feel like travelling folk.

A little rain cloud might drift by, sprinkling a thousand rain drops. The hardy tourists sit the shower out; some, a little resentful of the thoughtlessness of Nature, disappear into the Museum.

So, the placing of the green benches is a sign that summer is on the way.

The daffodils are late this year. No wonder, there have been such relentless downpours of rain, such batterings of cold wind but now, a bit belated, they are coming.

One morning last week I had a visit of a pleasant young man, a student photographer from Napier University, Edinburgh. He is preparing a portfolio of modern Scottish poets. That was where I came into the picture, literally.

When he phoned me the previous week, I was in the depths of misery with my cold, so I stipulated, 'No outside photographs!'

Everything seemed to go quite well inside, with a complication of fittings and wires and cameras, and frequent flashes.

The young man, Fionn, had his mother with him, and she brought a gift of something completely covered in a wrapper. I laid the little parcel in the hearth, near the warmth of the fire.

After all the photography, Mrs Carroll said, 'I think those flowers ought maybe to go into a vase.' So I found a pint beer mug, and in went the dozen or so daffodils, all hooded in their buds.

Next morning they were all out – except one or two lazy ones – there was a circle of little suns all round the beer mug. In the evenings they waft abroad their rich smells. They are the bright tapers of Primavera.

'Ah well,' you say to the daffodils, 'We have survived another winter'... And when the new-painted green benches are in place, we'll know that we've broken through into another summer.

Good Templars and Salvationists

28 April 1994

Brian Murray and I were walking up Hellihole Road last Sunday afternoon and we passed the Temperance Hall.

It seems to stand there, very forlorn and neglected, now.

It's a wonder no local group makes use of it. (Maybe it is used – sorry if anyone is offended.)

As the name suggests, it was built for the local Temperance movement, maybe ninety years ago or thereby. This suggests that the Good Templars were strong in those days. The fruit of all their labour and propaganda happened in the early 1920s when Stromness voted itself dry.

The Good Templars were a Lodge and so, I suppose, most of their meetings were private.

But the Good Templars rented their hall to the Salvation Army, and it is in connection with the local corps of the Salvationists that I always think of the place.

In my boyhood, the Salvation Army always had two officers in charge of the local corps, either two men or two women, and the public meetings were held on a Sunday. There was also a week-night meeting for young people, where we sang rousing hymns and played games: but it never attracted many boys and girls.

The great Salvationist event of the year in Stromness was the week-long visit of the Wick corps, when there were cheerful meetings every night. One of the Wick officers was the great hit of the celebration, for he mingled the gospel message with much fun and good humour. He was called affectionately, 'Happy Harry'.

The Wick Salvationists had a very good brass band, and all that week Hamnavoe resounded and re-echoed with the cornets, trumpets and drums. They played here and there about the street, followed by troops of children.

When they sailed away on the *Ola*, the Wick band played 'God be with you till we meet again'...

But the local Salvationists had their own small band of trumpets, tambourines, and drums too.

When I was very small, I went with my mother shopping on a Saturday night. (The shops were open till late then.) The street was always busy.

One of the delights, while coming home with the basketful of messages, was to stand for a while and listen to the local corps playing their music at the foot of the Church Road. The gas lamps flared along the street. My father came back from his letter delivery. The trumpet and the melodeon mingled their notes between Peter Esson's tailor shop and the Commercial Hotel, as the stars came out silently, one after the other.

A Disappearing Art

5 May 1994

Every weekend I groan, looking at the pile of letters that have to be answered. The replies take one morning at least – more often two.

It struck me one morning last week, I could be phoning my correspondents instead of writing. That would be much less tiring, and cheaper too, considering the postage nowadays.

It may be that the trend is indeed in that direction: the phone instead of the letter.

But the art of letter-writing has an illustrious history, going back to the early Egyptians and Chinese. Letters are mainly written impromptu, without any consideration of art, yet some of the letters written in the past are deeply satisfying and moving, as if they come straight from the heart, without the artistic censor constantly interrupting with, 'What a clumsy way to say it!' or 'The grammar in that last sentence is very doubtful.'

You get the impression, reading the letters of Keats and D. H. Lawrence, that they didn't even stop to re-read what they had written. The letters of Keats are full of mis-spellings and omissions, and yet they are beautiful to read. And Lawrence's letters spill over like molten lava.

This raises the question of whether we are entitled to read these private communications at all, since they were written for one particular person on one particular day and not for the whole wide world to gawp over.

Yet, writer and recipient being long dead, where is the harm?

There's another matter that strikes me. More and more of the letters I get are composed on word-processors.

In a couple of generations or so, there will be no handwriting at all. In the infant classes at school they will have, instead of our slates and slate pencils of the 1920s, little glimmering word processors on their desks. But surely everyone will have to write their signature. Not necessarily. They say that maybe in the future a fingerprint will do.

So, if we are nearing the end of the millenia-old art of the hand-written letter, we ought to be glad that we were privileged to write letters in these latter days.

It may be a nuisance, but it can be a delightful nuisance, if you are writing to friends.

There are at least two good times of the day, when you hear the postman drop letters through the letterbox, softly, like leaves falling. The heart gives a glad leap. Of course the letters may be from the Inland Revenue or a garish leaflet promising you a holiday cruise in the Caribbean, or a fine new motorcar.

Long may the feet of the postmen rise and fall along our streets.

Targets of the Temperance Poet

12 May 1994

Further to our few remarks on the Temperance Hall, now sadly neglected, in Hellihole Road, it appears that the Temperance movement in Stromness threw up a poet, maybe more than one.

(Looking into John Robertson's *An Orkney Anthology*, since the above paragraph was written, the name of the poet is given as Bews, a native of Kirkwall, who worked at Stanger's Boatyard at Ness...)

The hostelries, brewery, and distillery that Mr Bews attacked were The White Horse Inn, the Commercial, Sandy Flett's, Ernest Robertson's, the Masons' Arms, the brewery at the top of Leslie's Close, the distillery of MacPherson Brothers, and Billy Clouston's.

How few the number of pubs in the early twentieth century compared to the full flowering of 1840, when Rev Peter Learmonth counted almost forty when he compiled the Stromness section of the *Old Statistical Account*.

But many of the drinking places of 1840 might have been small private rooms where you could drop by for a mug of home-brew for a penny or so. No doubt these places varied considerably in quality and service, ranging from hospitable women who kept their drinking-room clean and tidy, to awful dens with spiders in the window and mice at the skirting boards.

A time of year dreaded by many Stromness folk and rejoiced in by others was the day in late summer when the whaling fleet returned from Davis Straits off Greenland. Those men had seen no drink or girls since late Spring, and their money-pouches were crammed with sovereigns (if it had been a good whale year). The more respectable town-folk were issued with batons to keep some sort of order along the street. One can imagine broken bottles and blood.

No wonder, in a way, the seeds of temperance were sown later in the century. The Star of Pomona No. 789 Lodge was set up in the end, and they built their hall in 1904.

What concerns me chiefly is that the Old Orkney malt distillery belonging to MacPherson Brothers stands where Mayburn Court is now. I remember well the two great copper stills standing in the yard.

Where Billy Clouston's was is now the peedie shop where I get many of my messages.

My father used to patronise Billy Clouston's when he was a young man. The lads of the South End would sally out with a shilling in their pockets. For that shilling (now five pence) you could buy two glasses of whisky and two mugs (or schooners) of strong ale. A schooner was a measure somewhat between a pint and a half-pint. Merry Saturday nights were passed in Billy Clouston's.

Then the First World War came and Stromness was flooded with Irish navvies and English mariners. Many a wild night on the street below my window was witnessed by the folk of the South End...

Stromness voted 'dry' soon after the war, in 1920.

Here are a few examples of verse by Bews, the Temperance poet:

> All Christian people in the town
> Approvingly will hear
> The name of Clouston's will no more
> On Licensed lists appear ...
> For ever in the way of right
> Good Templars onward press
> Till not a public house remains
> 'Twixt Hamnavoe and Ness ...
> From Alcohol, the nation's curse
> For ever, set it free,
> No more let Stromness Street resound
> With drunken revelry.

The First Houses in Hamnavoe

19 May 1994

The first houses in Hamnavoe were built a very very long time ago, and they weren't stone houses either, they were wooden huts with fishing gear outside. And they were built by stubborn people.

The first longships of families from Norway, who intended to settle on the Pictish fields and pastures at Stromness parish – though it was called by an altogether different, ancient Celtic name then – came ashore about Breckness, on that headland facing the Atlantic.

The chief – the skipper – after the first stormy winter, decided that they ought to have a stone-built farm.

Their temporary timber dwelling had been battered and salt-eaten and roof timbers brought down by the ocean gales.

So the sailors became gatherers of stone from the shore, and afterwards they yoked the Pictish oxen and made their first furrows.

There was much hunger. A few Norwegians put the Pictish curraghs on the sea and set out to fish, as far as Yesnaby.

They were unacquainted with these waters. One or two curraghs were upset and the men drowned. But at last they came home with skate, cod, haddocks.

And the chief nodded in a kind of curt way, but he was not interested in the fishermen. What took all his attention was the plough land and the pasture land. Already the first green shoots were coming up.

Secondly, the chief was interested in the building of his house, barn, byres and stable. Slowly it grew all that summer. The women humped stones from a quarry at Innertoon.

At night a guard had to be kept on the long-house, the curraghs, and the fields. The Picts came out of the darkness sometimes and put flaming torches in at the eaves. (Those Pictish remnants lived in the hinterland, in the wet places, the Loons.)

The fishermen were learning to read the coast and the tides. Twice or thrice a week they brought their catches to the beach of Breckness.

The chief only said, 'I am beginning to grow tired of fish.'

The oldest fisherman said, 'I'm beginning to grow tired of that self-important upstart whose face is green with looking at the barley field.'

There came to be differences and quarrels between the fishermen and the farm workers.

It came to a climax on the night of the great midwinter feast when all the community gathered in the new stone-built hall to celebrate the first harvest and the new steading.

The ale-cup went round. The brewers were pleased with their first ale. There was a good deal of boasting that night by the ploughmen, the shepherds, the harvesters.

The ale-cup was passed to a fisherman called Bui. (Nobody had praised the enormous halibut he had caught that week.) Bui took a mouthful of the ale and spat it out. 'Disgusting filth!' he said.

The fighting went on inside Breckness till beyond midnight.

In the morning the fishermen set off with their curraghs and baskets and lines to the shore with the granite hill behind and the two little islands guarding the harbour from the east.

'This will be our place,' said the old fisherman. 'We will have nothing more to do with the farmers.' They called the place Hamnavoe, 'the haven inside the bay'.

Winston the Cat

26 May 1994

There must be a score of cats at least in the South End, round about Mayburn Court.

There are so many cats that you don't pay much attention to them, except to stop for a word or two when one or other comes rubbing against your ankle.

Stromness has always been a cat town, I suppose because there have from the beginning been fish about the piers, and they guarded the house well against rats (though no one will praise their propensity for wanting to tear music out of the air; that is, go after birds).

But recently one small grey cat has come to the South End, who has quickly established himself by sheer force of personality. I think it was my friend Surinder who first carried Winston into my house. He is small and grey, intelligent and alert and good-looking, and he has a tartan collar. He was at home, at once. Of course, like all cats, he was inquisitive that first day, and had the place 'sussed' in five minutes.

For some mysterious inherent quality, Winston stands out. There seems to be a great wisdom and mystery in his deep diamond eyes, and a boundless trust and faith in human beings (in spite of all the bad things that people have done to cats over the centuries: kicked them, thrown buckets of water over them, set dogs on them, ended them in a shriek of car wheels).

After that first visit of ten minutes or so, I thought I'd never be visited by Winston again. But once or twice he has come knocking on my window – that sounds an easy thing to do, but my living-room window is twenty feet above the street. And such a courteous cat as Winston has to be let in.

Sun or rain, it's all the same to him. One night when it was bucketing rain, there was Winston, absolutely soaking, waiting to have a word with another of his friends who was in the telephone box at the Museum.

One afternoon I returned from lunch to my closed house. There on the rocker, I thought (being short-sighted) I saw a grey movement. It was of course Winston having an afternoon nap.

Windows are no problem to him, if they are merely open to let in some air. Winston can pass through the smallest opening. I think he must have been a cat-burglar in his last incarnation.

What a happy cat he is. His throat is vibrant with songs always.

Yesterday there was girlish laughter in the street below. A troop of non-Orcadian lasses were being shown the Museum. They must have been early teenagers. There, in a group of four adoring girls, was Winston. One girl was holding him in her arms, her friends seemed so fascinated that they were still cooing and chirping over him ten minutes later.

I imagine, for Winston, it must have been a marvellous morning. But then all days and all hours of the day and night are delightful to Winston.

I hope he stays with us Southenders a long while.

Advances in Music Technology

2 June 1994

I have been sent four 'compact discs' now, with the cellophane still on them. I suppose I'll have to get, soon, a machine for playing them on.

There has been such an advance in recorded sound and music over the past sixty years! They tell me that more improvements are pending.

I have seen and heard one or two of the cylinders that astonished late Victorians listened to. 'A marvel!' they thought. 'There is no end to human progress. Nothing can stop it now. Soon there will be no more disease or illness. Soon there will be no economic problems. We have steam-ships now instead of sailing ships. We can eat pineapples and bananas from the furthest ends of the earth. And the British Empire is still expanding, on which the sun never sets...'

This kind of optimism and euphoria was common even among the working classes who earned 'thirty bob a week'.

Only a few philosophers and tramps could see the worm in the apple.

But to return to the phonograph, as it was called, but later, in my time, the gramophone.

I must have been six or seven when the first gramophone came to our house, and for a few days, in Melvin Place, we played the records over and over – frequently forgetting to change the steel needle, so that the quality of reproduction gradually deteriorated ... I can't remember the world-wide favourite Harry Lauder till later, but Will Fyffe enthralled us, with 'Sailing up the Clyde' and 'Doctor MacGregor and his Wee Black Bag'... There were cowboy songs from America, 'Shepherd of the Hills' and 'Red River Valley'. 'Romona' seemed to me to be high lyrical stuff. There was also a very sentimental ditty called, 'You'll Never Miss Your Mother till She's Gone'. I shed a few tears over that one, though my mother at the time was an active cheerful woman.

Those 78rpm records were heavy and easily broken.

Towards the end of the war came the lightweight 45rpm record. Gramophones were more compact than the one the dog listens to on His Master's Voice discs. The reproduction was much better. We tested our toes on Mendelssohn, Mozart, Elgar. The voice of Harry Lauder was not heard in the land again.

'What next?' I thought. A man who knew all about music technology told me: 'Tapes.' That was some time in the late 1940s.

I couldn't fathom how music could be put on a tape.

But it came in due course, the great tape revolution. I have a tape-recorder and a growing mass of tapes, more than I will ever be able to play. How can you read, and watch TV, and talk to visitors, and play tapes, all in one evening?

A year ago, the first compact disc dropped through the letterbox. Tapes were on the way out, ousted by CDs.

Time gets more and more crowded, life more and more hectic, the older you get.

It has reached such a pitch now, that the sweetest thing is to sit on Flaws's Pier listening to the waves and the gulls, and silence.

Every Day had its Flavour

9 June 1994

Every day in the week, when we were young, had its own particular flavour, sometimes pleasant, sometimes unpleasant, sometimes neither here nor there.

I'm writing this on Thursday morning, with the early June sun lying bright on the gardens outside.

Thursday was always one of those in-between days. Every shop and office, pre-war, put up shutters at one o'clock. It was half-day, as they used to say, never 'early-closing day'... At school, on a Thursday, we trudged through Maths and Latin and Geography. Those boys who had twopence to spare bought *The Rover*. Shopkeepers and tradesmen dug their gardens in the afternoon, or stretched their legs as far as Warbeth or the Loons. But Thursday evening was magical – 'the pictures' in the old Town Hall (now the Youth Hostel). It cost fourpence to get in. We couldn't afford it, some weeks.

Friday was always a day of delight, because we looked forward so much to the weekend to come. Between the ages of nine and twelve, we went to the Life Boy meetings at the Old Kirk Hall (now the Community Centre), and I played the triangle very badly in our percussion band.

Saturday was the day of boundless freedom, when we fished from Gray's Pier (now Gray's Noust housing complex) and roamed the countryside, and got free rides on Oag's lorry from Dounby, and ate Mars bars, and rifled blackbirds' nests, and in summer had bathing picnics at the Tender Tables (where, alas, nobody goes nowadays). Good girls and boys did their homework to be in time for Monday. But not us – nothing doing – school and everything to do with it was taboo.

On Sunday, we put on our best clothes and went to the kirk in the afternoon, the whole family, and sat high in the gallery in the UP kirk (now St Peter's).

Bluebottles buzzed in the window. My mother passed round a poke of sweeties during the interminable sermon. But Sunday tea was special, cakes of all kinds, especially my mother's home-baked sponges with either cream or strawberry jam at the centre ... and then – oh misery – a last-minute rush to get the homework done.

Of course there was no football or any other sport on the Sabbath in Stromness. You could walk, or bathe at Warbeth, but no football or golf or catching sillocks.

The misery of Monday morning – the forlorn dragging of the feet to the old Stromness Academy (now artists' studios, and fashion stylists', and a branch of Heriot-Watt University). I won't say any more about Monday, except that the misery was compounded by the fact that Monday at home was always washing day: and in those days the housewife didn't just chuck clothes in the washing machine and transfer them to the tumble-dryer. By no means – it was a day of steam and Fels-Naphtha soap and the range a sullen red with heat.

I will say no more about Monday except that there was always ham-and-egg for dinner and kippers for tea – a consolation.

Tuesday was a day neither here nor there. It seemed to have no character of its own, except that *The Wizard* came out on Tuesdays.

Wednesday was 'the mart day'. Stromness was full of farmers and farmers' wives. The farmers passed the afternoon at the Pier Head smoking pipes and saying a sagacious word or two, or rallied with laughter a farmer from another parish... The country wives with their baskets seemed always to have cheeks like apples.

There was no striking of bargains over drams in the White Horse or Billy Clouston's, for there were no pubs.

A Week in June

23 June 1994

Now the windows and doors are all painted, and not before time, says the painter... The windows were down to the bare wood, here and there.

Whenever will they come and fix our Mayburn railings? If they don't come soon, there'll be hardly any railings left. We joke, 'They're held together by rust'...

A lady journalist spent all this afternoon photographing Peter Maxwell Davies and myself, at Hopedale, after a delicious lunch. The photography had to be done indoors – outside the rain came down in buckets. Ros the photographer very much wanted the pictures taken outside. The indoor photography took a long long time. It was no sooner finished than the sun came out, clear and sparkling. But we refused to endure any more photography. It's more tiring than you think, even sitting still.

Tuesday, June 7: My fire-tender, Brian, has had to go away early for an OIC[1] meeting. Fancy me having a councillor to light my fire!

Up at Quildon Cottage, I had good well-salted soup for a first course – then delicious stew and green salad – then fruit and jelly...

No letters today, for which I'm very thankful – most weeks there's more mail than I can handle. Yet it's lovely to hear the little waterfall of letters through the letterbox, morning and afternoon.

The sun is out, but there's a mighty south-west wind on Quildon Brae, which lessens as I walk home beside the musical May Burn and the grass teeming with daisies. Daisies and buttercups and dandelions along the wall are a constant delight.

Wednesday, June 8: Remember, a few weeks ago, writing about Winston the lovely grey cat, that everyone thought was a boy.

I met Winston's owner on the street today. She told me Winston is a girl and is about to have her first kittens.

I hope they don't change her name. After all, 'Evelyn' and 'Hilary' and 'Billie' are unisex names.

What brought me into town was to get some money. Those amazing cash-dispensers! The world is full of wonder. 'Fax' is another...

A delightful supper at Scorrabrae Inn with that indefatigable worker for the Scottish heritage, Margaret Street, and her son Neil. Another glorious thirst having the fish, soon quenched in two pints of cold lager.

We visited the Hall of Clestrain – sadly dilapidated now – on the way back to Stromness in the bright summer evening. How can restored splendour arise from such a broken chrysalis? ... I wouldn't put it past Ian Heddle and his helpers to achieve the next to impossible.

Thursday, June 9: The lovely light now, coming on for midsummer. It seems to me there's an almost perpetual black cloud over Orkney in the TV forecasts. Sometimes they're right. But often enough, it seems to me, the rain-announced day arrives brimming over with light.

In mid-evening, the westering sun is striking my north window. Another few days and the Johnsmas sun will actually enter the living-room from a few points further north.

A wonderful annunciation of summer. This is an enchanting time of year.

Friday, June 10: A great mountain-range of books on the living-room table, that has slowly heaved up since last autumn.

1 Orkney Islands Council

Came home from seeing PMD off on the plane to Edinburgh, to find Brian Murray clearing the books up and slotting them into place on the bookshelves.

Saturday, June 11: An enormous parcel I found in the lobby, when I got home from a delicious lunch of herring and chips and Beamish stout in the hotel, with the Prendergast family and their guests. Inside the parcel was a thick thesis by a German student on some of the stories I've written. It has earned Berthold Schoene a PhD from Glasgow University. Since I don't like reading reviews, even the favourable ones, of my books, I've passed the mighty tome to Brian Murray. I will have to dip into it sometimes, of course, out of courtesy, and in gratitude to BS.

A Special Day

30 June 1994

June 21st is the longest day but for some reason Midsummer Day is June 24th.

And Johnsmas Eve was 23rd.

The reason, I suppose, is that though the winter solstice is on 21st December, the great feast of Christmas falls on 25th.

It was as if those first dwellers in the northern hemisphere waited till they were quite sure that the light was on the turn before their feasting began.

The Light that was the creator of light and darkness lay in His crib three nights after the deep darkness.

June 21st is always a special day, though.

In 1994, in Orkney, after a dubious start, the sun came out in all its splendour, and with it, a fresh westerly wind.

It was still the St Magnus Festival.

I couldn't get to many events this year, for a special reason, but I was eager to get to the second session of the Johnsmas Foy in the Academy Hall. It was delightful, dealing with the supernatural in past Orkney midsummers, selkies[1] and trows mingling familiarly with men and women, and all framed with music and song.

The fourteen-year-olds didn't flinch from the darker themes either, like the trial for witchcraft of Marian Isbister. And Sir Walter

1 seals, 'seal-people'

Scott's visit to the aged seller of winds Bessie Millie, in her hovel on Brinkie's Brae, was exquisitely done. From Bessie, the Wizard of the North (as they took to calling Sir Walter in those times) got the story of John Gow the Stromness bad boy, which he wove into his novel of 1821, *The Pirate*. Not, alas, a tale to keep late-twentieth-century children from their play, or enthral us old men in our ingle neuks....

That morning the kettle that had boiled my tea-water so faithfully for years went on the blink – I had to boil water in the egg-pot! However, my friend Ian MacLeod drove me home from the Foy and put a 13-amp fuse in, and all was well again. (A poor existence without tea.)

The afternoon was so warm and bright we could drink the after-lunch coffee in a newly-built garden patio...

It is always best not to trust Orkney weather utterly.

A cloud swam in front of that golden King the sun, now just beginning to walk down from his highest throne in the zenith, and the west wind blew colder, and we had to finish our coffee inside.

I had my 'old man's drowse' in the afternoon.

The evening was magnificent, too lovely to watch the World Cup for long, though we saw snatches of Germany v Spain between genteel sips of midsummer whisky...

I had been warning my holiday friends from London to keep well away from Brodgar at midnight, lest the trows got them and they were seen in the land of the living no more – at least by this generation.

Myself, I took a late stroll along Ness Road and spoke to a small shrill-voiced black and white cat on the wall at 'Ruah', and walked round the Double Houses and came home to have a poached egg on toast. The last of the sun was just leaving the Mayburn balcony. In the north, in such a clear sky, the glow would go on all evening, and people and animals would move like tranced creatures, and the birds that had sung all the midsummer day long would be furled in their nests, now at the year's lucent turning.

Approaching Johnsmas

7 July 1994

Grey, and a big west wind one day, bright and mild the next. Whatever we can say about the weather, it never bores us.

June 20: A newspaper photographer wants to take a picture. It's not weather to stand outside, in all this wilderness and wet. So the famous

Irish poet and myself sit in a window seat of the bar of Stromness Hotel, with cups of cold coffee on the table before us – the coffee was there purely for design and atmosphere – and the pleasant young photographer Ian takes a clutch of pictures for *The Independent*.

I like very much the light at this time of year. Tomorrow (Tuesday) is the solstice. For a week or two there's no need to draw the curtains at night.

The kettle boils water for cups of tea, late – then goes 'phut'.

Going to bed, there is a three-quarter moon through the uncurtained bedroom window. The clouds have thinned throughout the day.

June 21: John Gray kindly drives me to the Johnsmas Foy in the Academy Theatre. It was a very fine performance by the fourteen-year-old musicians and actors. It was a good balance, putting the harrowing witch-trial of poor Marian Isbister just before Bessie Millie the windseller and her encounter with Sir Walter Scott.

Plenty of talent there for future St Magnus Festivals.

Ian MacLeod drove me home and fixed the fuse in my kettle.

This morning I had to boil my breakfast tea-water in the egg pot!

June 22: A pleasant young London lady visited this morning with fish rolls from Foodoodles (I had prawns and sea sauce in mine) and a can of Theakstons beer that sent up a fountain of foam when I opened it. The English beer was good along with the delicious rolls.

'Pots' – that's the young lady's by-name, maybe because she works in Sotheby's the London art dealers, is going round the West Mainland this afternoon by taxi, especially to Birsay and the Brough.

I ought to have offered to accompany 'Pots', but I'm sure to be travelling that way twenty times before summer's end. I advised her to go past Yesnaby, to see the westerly gale there and what dramatics it can put on.

June 23: Johnsmas Eve, and the sun splashing buckets of light around all morning.

I greet my Norwegian friends Margrethe and Annetin on the street, who have been coming to Orkney for many summers past. We go to the café for lunch, and it is crowded as a beehive with tourists. We ask for salmon but the tourists must be going for the salmon in a big way, for there's none left. In the end we opt for haddock and tatties, very good too. I have a pint of beer. Suddenly the café is empty. The tourists have vanished! We reckon they must be off on tour buses. We finish our lunch outside, on the pier, in the sun, till the wind begins to blow a bit colder. (Our famous Orkney weather, changing from hour to hour.)

A hundred and fifty years ago, our Orkney ancestors would have been bringing the last of their driftwood and tar to all the hilltops, to light at sundown. And then the fiddles and dancing and feasting all night till the sun rose again in the north-east.

A wonderful sight it must have been, fire answering fire from Ward to Ward, from island to island, in the 'simmer dim'.

We have fallen upon bleak times, as far as ceremony goes, no matter how wealthy we are in motorcars, TV, videos and holidays in the sun.

80 Victoria Street

21 July 1994

Seventy-three years ago Stromness was a different town to the Stromness of today; different, but essentially the same.

The outward trappings have changed.

My first memories are of a house – 80 Victoria Street – half on the street and half down Clouston's pier.

Stromness had reached the sophisticated but necessary state of segmenting its one long street into different names – Victoria Street, Dundas Street, Alfred Street, Graham Place, South End, John Street. (I have often wondered, who is the John from whom John Street got its name? Alfred was the then Duke of Edinburgh, a son of Queen Victoria.)

There I sat on the doorstep of 80 Victoria Street in early childhood, watching the town go by: the fishermen with their creels, the housewives coming and going, the postmen and the dustcart and the many milk-carts. The progress of a car through the street was an infrequent event.

Round the corner on the street, was the saddler shop of Tom Craigie, and round the other corner was J. D. Johnston's draper shop. And there was the Commercial Hotel, and Peter Esson's tailor shop and Bill Matheson's saddlery, and (most delightful of all to a small boy) Janetta Sinclair's sweetie shop: a cave of various delights.

We left 80 Victoria Street in 1926 or '27, just after I had started at the infant school, and moved to 3 Melvin Place, in the vicinity of the Public Library in Hellihole Road.

And from that day until yesterday, I had never been inside 80 Victoria Street.

A Glasgow novelist, Moira Burgess, spends many of her summer holidays in Stromness. Talking to each other the other Sunday evening, Moira told me she had rented 80 Victoria Street for two weeks, with her son and daughter.

She agreed to show me the old place.

Everybody is interested in the place of their first beginning, as the salmon seeks its native stream.

I don't know if my mother would have recognised the house where she cooked, baked, washed clothes, patched and polished and brought up five children. Everything has been modernised – a new door, new window-frames, a new carpeted floor in place of the blue flagstones, an electric fire instead of the black range, a kitchen where cooking is made easy as a song, and laundry day no longer the weary darg[1] of seventy years ago.

I saw the big room above the street where my brothers and I must have slept, but all seems light and airy now, instead of the old remembered shadows.

I would not have recognised the interior either, unless I had been told. But there were a few landmarks. The old kitchen/living-room window was in exactly the same place. I think my earliest memory is of my father silhouetted against that very window, reading a letter or a document of some kind; I was sitting up in a pram watching him.

And the door was in the same place, and the stair went up to the bedrooms above with the same sharp turn in it.

I think it was not the same outer doorstep where I used to sit, but the ancient flagstones of the close are the very ones where I took my first steps outside into the great world.

The modern table stands on the very place where the scrubbed board that was our table stood, a very important place where we ate and played Ludo and where my mother ironed the washing on a Tuesday night.

The Brief Tyranny of Men

28 July 1994

A million women at least all over Britain – maybe a hundred million all over the world were glad when the last kick of the last penalty was taken last Sunday evening, and their menfolk tore themselves away at last from the World Cup on TV.

It must have been a hard time for the women. For weeks they were not allowed to raise their voices above a whisper in their own houses – they, who did most of the talking day in, day out – and they could only make cups of tea and cheese-and-biscuits at half-time. The men would have none of it; these few weeks, once every four years, was their season – the World Cup.

Never had the flames of Women's Lib burned so low, to a few embers, merely smouldering.

The women were content, most of them, to bear it all with patience. They knew that their time would come, in mid-July. Then once more they would take over the reins in every household – issue orders, direct the members of the family about their various errands, this way and that – see to the cooking and the cleaning and the laundry – and also (it has happened from time immemorial) become part of the classical chorus of Hamnavoe women who comment on all that passes between Brinkie's Brae and the Holms.

The menfolk, sated at last with football, are content that it should be so. Poor bodies we men would be without the true keepers of the house: the hand that rocks the cradle and the hand that stirs the pot of broth and the hand that soothes the fevered brow.

On Monday morning – the day after the final whistle had been blown at Pasadena, California – the lovely morning brought me to the Pier Head with hundreds of others. Am I mistaken, or did I see looks of immense release and relief on all the congregated women's faces?

It was more than just the joy of Shopping Week opening ceremony on a magnificent summer morning: but the women, young and mature, girlish and elderly, floated here and there like butterflies in a flower garden – it was in part happiness that the brief tyranny of men was over for another four years.

Summer Attractions

11 August 1994

The year hastens on. It seems like a few hours ago, midsummer and the St Magnus Festival, and the barbecue fire flaming on the steep bank at the Braes.

Then we set sights on Shopping Week in July. Meantime the tourists are arriving by the hundred each day, bringing their cars. Even the quiet Back Road has its flow of cars, engines interrupting the pastoral music of sheep cropping the grass, and sending out a gobbet of exhaust fumes every twenty yards or so to purify the lungs of pedestrians.

And Shopping Week came, in a blaze of sun, that went on all that week but for a shower or two to sweeten the air.

We keep talking about the weather to everybody. 'Yes, what a lovely summer!' ... 'Compared to last July – what a wash-out that was' ... 'Yes, aren't we lucky, compared to the people in the south of England, sizzling in ninety degrees!' ... 'The lovely fresh airs off the sea...'

So, Shopping Week ran out colourfully threaded with skirling pipes. I missed lunch one day, through a mistake, and dropped in by the Lifeboat station, where the ladies provided delicious meat and tuna sandwiches and tea. Cheap it was, too.

What's next, after Shopping Week? The shadows begin to cluster like subtle thieves, almost before we are aware of them, stealing the summer from us. But still there's no need to draw the curtains, though the lamp goes on a few minutes earlier each evening. (If we ignore those first shadows, perhaps their great black King, Winter, will forget about us: so the perverse human mind tries to convince itself...)

Next is the Dounby Show and the County Show and the half-dozen other agricultural shows. I'm sure they are in full swing now, even as you are reading this – for I write my column well in advance.

Well, I used to love the Dounby Show, especially the beer tent with its canvas blowing out like a galleon in the summer wind. That great ship of joy and reminiscence is no more – or, rather, has been modernised.

There is the St Magnus Fair too, in the shadow of the Cathedral. I used to enjoy that, before my limbs got too weary to take me from this tent to that booth, threading through crowds.

What then? Well, the encroaching shadows can no longer be ignored. When the wind drops, the summer visitors who have never failed us in thousands of years, the midgies, come in dense dark clouds in the evening, each carrying a little torch with which he burns neck, face, and hands; like tiny Vikings out on a wrecking foray.

The tourists, at August-end, begin to thin out.

What then? Harvest Home. When I was younger, there was Harvest Thanksgiving in the kirk, on a week day, with plenty of country folk and town folk there. Alas, there's little thanksgiving for anything nowadays – only grousing.

Then the Lammas Market, in Stromness on the first Tuesday in September. But that magnificent ceremony ceased in 1946 or 1947. I have written overmuch on that great event in the past: and I may celebrate it again.

'And' – the old folk used to say – 'after the Lammas Market there is nothing to look forward to but winter.'

Problem Insects

18 August 1994

Clegs in July – midgies in August. But the whole month of July passed without a single cleg[1], which you might think a good thing, for nastier more furtive pain-dealing flying insects it would be hard to imagine.

No warning noise with a cleg. He steals up on you silently, a grey ugly shape on the back of your hand – and then he plunges his poisonous dagger in... And the vulnerable come out in red painful blotches.

So, what has happened to those disgusting little assassins?

I think maybe they have been done to death by insecticides.

The midgies are quite another matter. They laugh at insecticides. People smear themselves in creams and lotions on a summer evening. Some people swear the midgies lap them up and then go in for the kill.

And the midgies aren't loners, like clegs. They go about in dense swarms, in dark, drifting clouds, millions of them. You might compare them to battalions and regiments of alcoholic soldiers let loose among the taverns of a sacked city, after a year-long siege when they didn't have a drop to drink.

Finally, on a warm summer evening when the wind drops towards sundown, the 'city' that is an innocent tourist, or a nature-lover gathering wayside weeds, surrenders.

In flocks, through every breach in the wall, swarm the licentious soldiery (the midgies). It is the stored wine-barrels in the taverns they are after, the heaped beer-kegs, the hogsheads of whisky – that is to say, your blood and mine, wanderer through the last enchanting summer weeks.

The midgies might die of a surfeit of blood, or of the frenzied mauling and scratching you give them – but what are a few hundred midgies among thousands of them, millions of them!

1 horsefly

They lurch on, loaded with drink, to die in the gutters and sewers of the taken town.

Then a few freshets of wind blow in from the sea, and the army of despoilers vanishes at once. It is as if their tiny ears heard bugles that we cannot hear with our dense muddy auricles, and they reel back in various stages of inebriety to their camp, wherever that may be. Many of them no doubt will have to face a charge in the morning. Many a comrade lies slain inside the ruined city.

These passing images occurred to me the other day in the beautiful valley of Rackwick, when we were enjoying sandwiches, wine and ale outside the hospitable cottage of Mucklehoose. Fortunately, that beautiful day, we had only to endure a half hour or so of the midgies' rampaging. A sea wind saved us.

Another thought occurred, concerning reincarnation. Supposing those millions and billions of midgies were to come back as elephants, alligators, man-eating tigers, vultures and sharks, what a dangerous planet it would be!

Suppose – even worse – they were to come back as human beings who have invented atom bombs, cocaine, and pop-music-on-transistors-in-public-places?

What then?...

Music of the May Burn

1 September 1994

The May Burn: over many millennia, it has scooped out a little valley on the south flank of Brinkie's Brae – but so slowly that if some aboriginal Norse fisherman of Hamnavoe could revisit it now, after a thousand years, he would notice hardly any difference.

And it is such a shy little stream, you hardly notice it threading down beside the track, but for faint musical chimes under the summer grass.

Two summers ago, the publisher Gordon Wright from Edinburgh was wanting to take photographs of the burn for the book *Rockpools and Daffodils*, but there was no way of getting at it, no interesting angle or viewpoint – it was just a gleam and a few notes of music among the long grasses.

So it has been, all this long dry summer.

But if I was to labour up to the crest of the brae – for I can't walk as blithely as I used to do, twenty years ago – there *would* be a little change, after the day-long rain deluge yesterday. The little whisperer among the grass would be a lively boy with a penny whistle, making music all day long, all the way from the road above till it gets lost in the culvert, to reappear at the noust under Mayburn Court: and there it mingles its sweet notes with the salt music of the harbour.

And never think that that's as much as the shy hidden stream can do! After a prolonged downpour, a day and a night of it, the May Burn breaks out and becomes a menace to the entire neighbourhood.

He rides a wild horse that goes careering down the Distillery Close, so that folk who live there can't get into their houses till the ferocious creature is safely corralled again. It surges down, foaming, and leaps the steps at the bottom, and swerves past the Museum, and makes a mini-waterfall on to the noust.

The folk of the South End are half aghast and half delighted at the gentle stream's night of outlawry. But that only happens once in every decade or thereby.

That may be, briefly, the natural history of the May Burn; but it has a social history as well. Some time in the nineteenth century it occurred to some knowledgeable person that the innocent water could be transformed into 'usquebaugh', water of life, whisky.

And so a distillery was built where the Mayburn houses stand now, and for a generation or two 'Old Orkney' malt whisky, and 'Old Man of Hoy' whisky gained a certain fame among the enchanting waters of Scotland.

I'm told, there are still in existence a bottle or two of Stromness whisky, here and there.

The shy summer child, the player on the penny whistle after a shower, the wild horseman after a thunder burst: there he is, a golden prince exiled and imprisoned in a crystal cell for ever: a bottle of 'Old Orkney'...

Sweyn's Last Voyage

15 September 1994

Eight centuries ago, about this time of year, a man standing on the beach at Breckness would have seen a longship coming over the horizon curve, bearing east and north. And he would have said, 'There's old Sweyn's ship, coming home from the summer cruise to get harvest in, in Gairsay.'

The same thing had happened, every September, for decades. The man on the Stromness shore had been watching Sweyn's home-coming since he was a boy.

At first, when his eyes had been keen, this Stromness man saw plain the golden beard of the skipper; and the young sailors had sung on ship-board; and the ship had been full-freighted with plunder taken from English and French merchant ships. Deep in the water she laboured home to Gairsay with bales of wool, barrels of wine, chests of delicate jars and pots: whose true ownership could never be proven by sealed and signed bills of lading.

Then, the Stromness man had heard, there was a winter of rejoicing in the north isles. But first, Sweyn had ordered the cutting and carting of the sheaves.

Not every year had been like that one. Sometimes at summer's end Sweyn's ship came limping home, lean and gaunt. There was a breach here and there in the proud curve of the hull. There were one or two empty places at the rowing bench.

But mostly, Sweyn Asleifson was a fortunate Viking. (To be perfectly honest, 'pirate' was a truer word for it, just as it should have been for Francis Drake. But Asleifson and Drake were encouraged, to some extent, by the establishment – whereas John Gow was his own man, a freelance adventurer, with nobody to speak up for him when he was down on his luck.)

The Stromness limpet-gatherer remembered one famous end-of-summer when Sweyn's sail was sewn with splendour, so that no Scandinavian or Frankish King was so richly windborne. That year, Sweyn had captured a cargo of fine broadcloth, and had had the booty sewn on his sail, so that even the whales and skuas might wonder at this ocean-cleaver.

The years passed. The Stromness shore-watcher was growing old. He had to screw up his eyes now to see the Gairsay ship sail out of the wide Atlantic. He reckoned Sweyn himself must be an old man. In fact, there was a rumour all over Orkney that Sweyn had promised the Earl and Bishop that this last voyage was to be the last. When he came home, old Sweyn with the silver-grizzled beard would fold his sail for the last time.

It was late, this year. The oat harvest was under way all over Orkney. Still Sweyn Asleifson lingered in the west.

Then, one morning, the Breckness watcher saw the ship. There was a black square sewn on the sail. There were few hands to see to the navigation. The ship limped on north, beyond Yesnaby.

In the next days, the news went like wildfire through the islands. Sweyn had been killed, defiant to the last, in a broken street in Dublin, Ireland.

There was much sorrow about that. There were a few flagons of joy and relief broached in the merchants' counting-houses in southern seaports.

The Paraffin Lamp

29 September 1994

I suppose paraffin lamps still turn up in salerooms, and are sold as antiques.

Because, of course, nowadays we only need to flick a switch and the room is lit. There are even lamps for the writing table, the bedside and the reading chair.

There was something magical about the paraffin lamp that shed light all winter long from the kitchen dresser.

Of course, it took a bit of work to keep it shining pure and bright. My mother would spend a little while on it every day, breathing on the tall glass funnel and wiping it with a soft cloth. Then the wick had to be kept even, so that it didn't flare up at one corner and blacken the glass. This 'evening-up' was done with a hot poker.

And the coloured glass bowl had to be fed with paraffin once in a while, in the daytime, when the bowl was still cold.

I seem to remember that we were a bit reckless with paraffin in those long-ago days. We splashed it on the paper and sticks and small coals to get the fire going in the stove. A lit match, and the flame went roaring up the lum.

But to return to the lamp. All the year round, it obeyed the dictates of the sun. For the three summer months, it was hardly lit, except maybe on a rainy evening near bedtime. There it stood on the dresser, a patient servant, waiting its hour.

Towards the end of July, the family might cast a look or two at it. It was taken down, given a thorough clean. The wick was inspected. The coloured glass bowl was filled. (How paraffin made the fingers stink for ages! No amount of tap water could take the smell away.

Eventually it just evaporated.) Then the gentle benign light was shed into every corner of the room, enriching everything.

Towards the end of August, we would hear the old folk saying in the close, 'Ah, the nights are fairly drawan in noo'... The lamp was becoming queen of an ever-larger part of the evening. We did our homework for the new school session under it, and played Ludo or 'snap', and maybe just sat looking at the wonder of light.

For, as the sun retreated, so the paraffin lamp made up for that deficiency.

I am writing this on the eve of the autumnal equinox, when the sun and the lamp are held in perfect balance: and only the full moon is a greater wonder, and the awakening stars.

Even as late as this, moths used to dash themselves stupid against the mysterious radiance of the lamp – and that was altogether frightening and disagreeable.

What could the silly moths be seeking, in all that heat and dazzlement? Touch the lamp glass, and it burned your fingers.

Presently, as the nights grew colder, the moths took themselves off, maybe to fly to the stars, as in Shelley's marvellous line, 'The desire of the moth for the star'.

By the winter solstice, that lamp ruled the night and most of the day.

The Hero of Stromness

6 October 1994

I think there ought to be an Alexander Graham Day in Stromness, a holiday and a celebration, every year.

There he stands, in our town history, the hero of Stromness. And yet, apart from the 'fountain' at the Pier Head, we have done nothing about him. And the street where he lived is called Graham Place, of course.

He may have been a descendant of Bishop Graham of Breckness.

He was probably quite a prosperous merchant in the growing seaport of Stromness in the early eighteenth century, with maybe a ship or two – held in partnership – trading out in Scandinavia or the Baltic.

There was no avoiding the missives that came regularly to the Stromness merchants from Kirkwall, asking a share in their revenues, so that the Royal Burgh's tax could be lightened somewhat.

On the face of it, it was a reasonable enough request.

But there came a day when Alexander Graham refused to accept the missive.

And maybe that same day he went round the other merchants of Hamnavoe, advising them that they too should make a stand. 'Return them the demand,' he urged.

And some Stromness merchants agreed with Graham; and a few shook their heads – 'The law is the law,' they said. And others went away, grave-faced or smiling, without a yea or a nay.

They understood quite well that Graham's letter of refusal, once the Kirkwall merchants had read it, would result in a lawsuit, and lawyers' fees were high in those days.

There was more than one lawsuit. There was a sequence of them lasting for years. Money drained out of the tills of the Stromness shipowners, and seeped and drained till some of them cried, 'No more! We'll be ruined men. We will have to sack our skippers, sell our ships.'

But Alexander Graham would have none of that kind of talk. He had put his hand to the plough, he would not stop till the work was accomplished, whatever stones or clods might hinder him in the furrows.

Eventually, there was only one ultimate lawcourt to resort to, the House of Lords.

And the House of Lords came down in favour of Stromness.

If there were any bells in the town that day, they must have rung out from Cairston to Ness.

But what of the hero himself? It seems, he had poured the last of his resources into the struggle, and had bankrupted himself. All we are told is that his widow died some years after him, 'in reduced circumstances'.

There is not even a stone in the kirkyard to let us know where his bones lie.

If his fellow merchants allowed that to pass, it was a great shame on them; and to us too, who have only put up a 'fountain' and given his name to a street.

Stromness, after the disgrace of Gow the pirate, stood in need of a hero at that time.

The words 'freedom' and 'tyranny' were in the air, brought from Europe and America in the ships that called. It was only a short while after that that the American War of Independence broke out: and a decade or so later, the French Revolution.

Publicity Operations

13 October 1994

The world, maybe, is composed of two sorts of people: those who like 'the limelight' and those who want to run for cover whenever journalists, broadcasters, or TV folk appear over the horizon.

I belong to the second group, and always will (and maybe I'm not in a bad tradition, because most Orcadians, especially the country folk and the sea folk, have always been that way, and always – I fervently hope – will be...).

About three weeks ago I was, out of the blue, nominated for a literature prize. Immediately, out of the blue, the media people homed in. I'm not saying against them. They proved to be pleasant people, concerned to do their job efficiently. I don't think they were aware of just how much the poor fish – me – was squirming on the hook, each time.

Anyway, it began a fortnight or so ago with a pleasant man from BBC World Service, Roger Fenby, whose father had been the amanuensis in France to the composer Delius. Roger Fenby knew his job, he got the answers from me without too difficult probing. I almost forgot about the tape recorder. Ten years ago it would have stood there, on the stool between us, like an instrument of torture from the Middle Ages.

(Incidentally, those tape recorders are getting smaller and smaller, till now you get them hardly bigger than matchboxes. Those who worship technology have reason to throw their hats in the air. I tend to have reservations and suspicions. It is all happening too fast – the story of man's cleverness from the wheel to the atom bomb – and the precious delicate human element may be under threat...)

Well, I have neither the space nor the time to tell about all the journalists and all the photographers, but I must say that my work ground to a halt a fortnight ago, and all I have managed to write are letters and, of course, 'Under Brinkie's Brae'.

Every one of those publicity operations leaves us shy folk in a state of semi-exhaustion. But when you go to bed in mid-afternoon, as soon as the head hits the pillow, there the phone rings: another journalist accompanied by a photographer is on the way! Wearily you acquiesce – what else is there to do?

What I dread most is the TV cameras. I've known for days that the TV crew is on the way. Not an hour has passed since that I haven't worried about it. How does one answer questions out of the blue, impromptu, with all those instruments levelled? Politicians seem to thrive on it. Not me.

The TV crew were nice when I underwent the ordeal high up at the Braes Hotel an hour ago. But my mouth was as dry as a cork and my tongue seemed to be trying to tie itself in a knot.

I fervently hoped, the TV interview was the last.

But no. Two schoolboys are coming this afternoon for an interview for the school magazine. Having once been a schoolboy myself at Stromness Academy, I could hardly deny them. But I fervently hope that Finn Aberdein and Darren Johnston will ask me simple civil questions...

They did.

Map in the Marrow

20 October 1994

The 'peedie summer' arrived on Monday (10 October) and it is going on still. Long may it last.

We have (or, at least, the old Orcadians used to have) the weather map throughout the year in the marrow of their bones.

There was 'the gab o' May' – a period of churlish weather before spring began in earnest.

There were 'the borrowing days of March', when – it may be – February with its slush and snell[1] winds trespassed into March.

And the old folk would say after New Year, 'as the day lengthens, the cowld strengthens'.

They knew the vagaries and chances of the weather at all seasons. The farmers knew well, but I think the fishermen knew even better, because their livelihoods and their very lives depended on a good reading of the weather. Many things had to be taken into consideration: the phase of the moon, the ebb and flow of the tides,

1 sharp, biting

the prevailing wind – plus a hundred intangibles the layman knew nothing about.

I seem to remember a beautiful summer morning long, long ago. And I said as much to a neighbour who had lived many years in lighthouses the length and breadth of Scotland. 'A fine day,' said I.

There was not a cloud in the sky. The harbour sparkled with a thousand points of light. It was perfect weather.

'Ah,' said the lighthouse keeper's wife, 'I don't like the look o' it at aal. There's a storm brewing. There'll be bad weather, mark me words.'

How could any storm break the crystal and sapphire of such a perfect day? I laughed secretly at such superstitious weather lore.

But she was right. A storm was breeding under the horizon. Before that day was done, we were struggling with the wind, we were drenched with rain.

Ever since that day, I have respected the secret weather knowledge of the old folk.

Are there any of them left?

Nowadays we don't have to depend so absolutely on that primitive weather instinct. Perhaps it has totally withered away.

We can hear the scientific forecasts on radio and TV. But are they as accurate as all that? I think we Orcadians – according to the TV chart last night – were promised gloomy weather today, with fairly strong wind. And behold, as I sit writing this at my kitchen table, the sun is streaming through the window at near noon, and there is no rattle in the window frames. Of course, the west wind might be strong enough on the braes above Stromness... And the sun might muffle itself in clouds by mid-afternoon. There's no telling.

'A green Yule maks the kirkyard full,' was another saying. But, over a century maybe, the broad weather pattern has changed; and there have been no healthy Christmas snowfalls. And, as far as I know, the death-graph has ceased to depend on the absence or abundance of snow.

I think children now don't enjoy the abundant snowfalls of my childhood. (May it not be a result of global warming! – for if it is, Orkney might sink slowly under the water from the melted icecaps.) But the farmers too wanted a good snowfall every winter, for the earth was warmed by that enormous white overcoat. And the buried seeds were all the more robust when they broke from the furrows, seeking the sun.

The weather lady on TV was right last night, after all. For I had no sooner written the above than the cloud-rack covered the sun, and there came 'a slaiver' (thin dispersed rain) on the wind.

Bleak House

27 October 1994

The sorrows and joys of lighting the fire!

Since my friend and neighbour Brian has gone to Ayr for a week, I have had to light the fire myself.

This great household event, now that I do it myself, takes place about noon, after 'the work of words' is done in the kitchen; that small kitchen space quickly gets heated up, at breakfast time, by a fan heater, and there after the teacup and plate, eggshell and marmalade are cleared away, I can get on with writing.

(This past week the letters to answer have piled up in a toppling heap, concerning a recent literature prize and my birthday, the latter of which has taken me away beyond 'the allotted span' – a thing that, at the age of thirty or so, I thought I could never possibly arrive at.)

But let that be – today I am concerned with the problem of lighting the fire.

I used to be able to get the fire going, in the old days, before Brian came to relieve me of the onerous task.

And surely fire-lighting is like swimming or riding a bike: once learned it is never forgotten.

That's what I thought. That's where I made the big mistake.

Crumple newspapers. Set a 'firelighter', one of those small white flammable cubes. Arrange sticks. Set a few small coals, plus the half-charred cinders from last night, and away it goes.

Away it *ought* to go.

Last Monday morning it was a miserable failure. The newsprint flared, the 'firelighter' flamed, the sticks crackled and smoked, and back I went to the kitchen – maybe to have a shave, or to look in the cupboard for something to eat for lunch.

When I opened the kitchen door again, to see how the fire was getting on, there was nothing in the grate but a wisp of smoke, and one minute flame in the coals that wouldn't have warmed a fly.

There is a remedy for that – a life-giving infusion of oxygen. You hold a spread sheet of newspaper over the opening and the wind rushes up the lum, the coals respond and the flames dance and flap and unfurl, with joyous noises. You can see the ghostly congregation of flames through the thin tissue of newsprint.

Alas! There were only a few sighs, blurps, and whispers, and when I took the newssheet away, a few blue strands of smoke meandering up, fruitlessly.

The fire lighting was an utter failure!

Now, five days later, I have mastered the craft, but not with that economy that characterises the true master of the mystery of fire – I insure against failure by using two firelighters, and a big scatter of sticks, and a brimming shovel of small coals: an excess of combustion.

This morning friends phoned to say they were on the way, at 11am... It would never do, entertaining them at a cold black grate, on a bleak October morning.

So I set that fire at once in the extravagant way, with abundant kindling, and I had just applied the match when they knocked at the door.

Obedient welcoming fire! It threw out its light and warmth immediately. And, though there was a filthy strewment of dust and ash and cinders in the fireplace, my abode couldn't be called – as it could have been once or twice this week – Bleak House.

Benefits of Latin

3 November 1994

I'm told there's no Latin taught in most schools nowadays.

If we had been told that, out of the blue, in our third year in the Secondary, what a cheer we would have raised! We were busy then with declensions and subjunctives, and it was no fun for boys and girls of average intelligence.

The trouble began in our first term, learning that *mensa* was 'a table' and *regina* was 'a queen' and *amo, amas, amat* meant 'I love ... thou lovest ... he or she loves'.

What could we make of a weird language like that? – so different from the English, or rather Orkney dialect of English that we spoke in the playground and at home.

How, we wondered, could the citizens of Rome have got their tongues round such complications of language?

Yet we persevered, under Miss MacPherson, Mr Ritchie, and Mr Cook. We were told by our townsfolk, most gravely, that Latin was very important – very important indeed – we couldn't be said to be wholly educated if we didn't understand Latin. 'How,' we were asked, 'could doctors write their prescriptions without the aid of Latin?'

If we wanted to obtain a Leaving Certificate – the crown of school achievement in those days – we had to secure a pass in Lower Latin, at least. If we wanted to study English Literature at a Scottish University, we had to have Higher Latin.

The thought of such august achievements made the mind reel!

We stuck doggedly to the task.

Bit by bit, a little enjoyment began to seep through. Julius Caesar, for example – that mighty Roman – was a historian as well as a soldier and a statesman. He wrote about his campaigns in France and Germany, in a simple vigorous prose: *'Omnia Gallia in tres partes divisa est'*... That resounding opening is lodged in every schoolboy's memory. Very soon, we began to enjoy translating Caesar's *Commentaries*.

Then there was another historian, Livy, who was almost as good. The Roman orator Cicero: how we enjoyed his splendid denunciation of the conspirator Catiline in the Senate: *'Homo perditus,'* he called him – 'You abandoned man.'

Then came the poets, who were more difficult, but even more enjoyable, once we got into the rhythms of Ovid and Virgil: *'Arma virumque cano'* (Arms and the man I sing) begins Virgil's epic, and further on there is a line with all the sadness of mortality in it: translated, it means very roughly, 'there are tears for this and that event and human affairs touch the heart'.

Later, we came to understand that Latin was one of the great pillars on which the English language stands, the other being Anglo-Saxon.

And so anybody who really wants to appreciate the glories of English, must have some knowledge of Latin.

How can they read one of the greatest of our poets, Milton, without some understanding of Latin and the classical myths? The thunders and sweet sounds of Milton must mean little to modern youth.

And Milton is trebly disadvantaged in the late twentieth century; because so much of his imagery is taken from the Old Testament. What average school pupil reads the Old Testament stories nowadays?

But we pupils of the 1930s knew them well, because such magnificent stories as David and Goliath, Joseph and his brothers, Isaac and his sons Jacob and Esau and 'the blessing', and many others were taught us as part of Religious Instruction in the Primary – one period a week – and we have never forgotten them.

They are a part of the great heritage.

All Saints' and All Souls'

10 November 1994

The first of November, as I sit writing this. Outside, a brisk cold wind, and blue sky, but every now and then a cloud drops rain.

All Saints' Day, today. And that doesn't mean only the canonised saints, like Magnus and King Olaf, and Columba of Iona, but a numberless host of unknown men and women who have led good lives and left the world a little better and sweeter for having lived their lives in it.

We all know a few people, at least, whom we would include in the roll call. Some of them are almost forgotten now – their names faded in the registrar's book, or becoming ever less distinct on kirkyard stones as sun and wind and rain erode them. But they had something imperishable in their keeping while they lived, and that can never be lost. Most of them were poor and had no interest in making names for themselves – rather, any kind of publicity they shrank from.

Millions of such good people there must have been, all over the world, since humanity took root, and apart from that certainty we know nothing about them.

They too, an innumerable nameless host, are celebrated today, on All Saints' Day.

❋

Last night, under the street lamps, little groups were going here and there with pokes of flour and jars of treacle, beautifying the shop windows along the street. It was Hallowe'en, the night of witches and cats and candles.

Indoors, I wonder if many children were dooking for apples in a wooden tub, or cracking walnuts and Brazil nuts in brass nutcrackers?

So we prepare for winter, though autumn has still a month to go. And tomorrow – November 2 – is All Souls' Day.

It is, I'm sure, natural to remember the dead as the nights grow ever darker, and especially as oneself gets older. Another October past, another winter looming.

It is indeed a sure mark of the increasing years, that the dead seem to outnumber the living in an old man's mind.

The town, as always, swarms with young folk – a delightful promise and seal of the future. Those young people have been in Stromness, generation after generation, a perpetual spring: it is impossible to imagine that the fountain will ever dry up.

The disconcerting thing is that I know the names of only a few of them.

As one gets older, one lives in a town of strangers, increasingly. You only know your contemporaries, and those slightly younger and slightly older.

I remember my father saying, more than sixty years ago as we walked along the Innertoon road, with the kirkyard down below, fronting the Atlantic: 'There are more Stromness folk lying there than there are living noo in the toon'...

I was touched to awe at the thought.

All Souls' Day – How many Stromnessians are buried at Warbeth? Maybe fifty thousand, maybe more.

Impossible, in early November, not to think of them, especially those we knew. Some we cared for; some we were indifferent to; some we may have feared or disliked.

But of the true worth of each of them we know nothing; and that is something else to wonder at.

Salute the Hen

17 November 1994

An egg and toast and tea for breakfast – that meal has been going on for a long time, not only in Orkney but all over the country; and may it go on for generations to come.

In spite of what a lady politician[1] said a while back, I know of nobody who has had 'salmonella' from eating boiled eggs.

Maybe it was the explanation of one or two mild tummy upsets in the past – but they may have been, more probably, caused by a sour pint or a slice of mouldy cake.

It seems to me that eggs nowadays – most of them – don't have such rich yolks as in former times, nor such a delicious country flavour. But maybe old men have always thought that, about everything you care to mention. Nothing is the same as it used to be, in the good old days.

Never a croft or a farm but had its flock of White Wyandottes or Rhode Island Reds, dipping their heads all over the farmyard and stepping daintily, presided over by the strutting cock with his crested comb, and a fierce tyrannical eye in his head. There was never a sign of 'hen's lib' in the barnyards.

And then the croft wife would come out with a bowl of oats or bread-crumbs and the demure birds couldn't get close enough to her, rising and fluttering and disputing. And the ferocious tyrant, the cock, looked on with a mad eye; knowing well he could scatter his dames with one imperious strut, and have what seemed to him the best of the nourishment.

That homely barnyard ritual is rarely seen nowadays. Indeed, a town-dweller like me, with a fading memory, might well have got the image all wrong.

But one thing I do know, when you had your breakfast egg, you were convinced that you were absorbing pure Orkney country nourishment.

This leads some curious minds to wonder about those domestic birds. They aren't native to the islands at all. I read somewhere that they originated somewhere in the Far East, among the jungles of Burma.

---

1 Edwina Currie

So far away! Then how, by all that's wonderful, were they brought to Britain; and when?

If I had an *Encyclopaedia Britannica*, perhaps the mystery would be explained. (I might drop by the Stromness Library some afternoon, and do a bit of research there.)

It can't have been the Romans who took the first few hens across the Channel – Burma was too far away even for the Romans.

But there were ships, and traders, and merchandise. Over centuries, it is possible to imagine how those birds that couldn't fly but only flutter, and laid plenteous warm glowing eggs shaped like shore stones, gradually spread into Europe and so north to Britain. And further north, to Thule.

What can the first Orkneyman have thought when a merchant uncovered a basket, and offered a bevy of hens, dominated by their fierce neck-stretching clarion-crowing tyrant?

Being Orcadians, for a week or a month they would probably have thought they had made a bad bargain, until the taste of a morning egg – over a week or so – wore down their resistance.

When I was in an Aberdeen hospital four and a half years ago, I had to have no food at all for days round about the operation day.

'How are your days passing?' said the surgeon one morning.

'I'm thinking all the time about sausages and eggs,' I said. 'And apple pie.'

Saint Andrew

8 December 1994

St Andrew's Day today[1], and a brighter more tranquil end to the month of November we could not have.

We must wonder how the apostle Andrew came to be connected with Scotland.

We know that originally he was a fisherman with his brother Peter in Galilee, and afterwards became a disciple of Christ until Good Friday, when, unlike his bold brother, he did not stay for the trial and execution.

Did he hide among the vennels of Jerusalem, or did he make for the shore to be safe, and to be soothed by the wash of waves?

1 the last day of November

His courage came back in full measure and he ate the fish that the risen Christ grilled on the shore, with the other disciples.

The tradition is that he died on a saltire cross at Patras in Greece.

So where does Scotland come into it?

Imagination likes to follow Andrew as he travelled north, beyond the Swiss lakes and the coast of Brittany, where he would have understood well what the fishermen in those places were busy about.

But this was not the particular place for him – though, after his martyrdom, every place on earth was his to bless and benefit.

Alba, Scotland: how was Andrew to get there? On the ocean between Europe and Britain he saw whales that might have been descendants of the great fish that gave Jonah sanctuary for three days, and cormorants skimmed across the sea like dark arrows, and the bonxies[1] lifted and tilted on the wind.

This sea was colder and rougher than Galilee or the Mediterranean.

He stepped ashore and spoke to the fishermen at a little sea village.

(Once death has been shrugged off, all languages are open to the good pilgrim – what were the confused tongues of Babel become a universal music.)

Yes, said the fishermen, the name of their country was Alba and this part in the east of Alba, was called Fife, and as for their little scatter of houses and bothies, it didn't have a name yet.

No – they said – they intended to build a church, but the fishing took up all their time.

Fish and stones: viewed with the eye of eternity, they have an equal beauty and value.

So, this stranger went herring fishing in the little boats of the Fife men, and he helped them and their women to gather stones for the building of a church.

It was a child, of course, who discerned with the pure eye of innocence who their guest was.

And the boy told them, on the very day that the Bishop came to dedicate the finished church. 'He is St Andrew, of course, the one who saw the boy with the two small fish the day the multitude was fed on the hillside.'

But by then the man from Galilee had moved on.

The Bishop hadn't known till that moment whether to call the new church St Fergus or St Mungo or St Ninian.

1 skuas

But now he called it, solemnly, while the bell rang and the incense fumed and the candle-flames fluttered: St Andrew's kirk.

And the sea village was called, from that day on, St Andrews.

False Flu

15 December 1994

I woke up early yesterday morning and felt wretched and shivery at once.

'Here it comes,' I said to myself bleakly, 'the flu.'

I managed to heave out of bed at 8am, the usual time, and thought, 'Well, if a person has flu, he doesn't want to get up, in fact he can't get up.' But still, it felt like flu as I boiled the kettle for breakfast tea and put bread into the toaster. I actually caught myself in the act of putting a lovely big farm egg in the saucepan.

The last thing you want to know about, when you have flu, is egg and toast. So, with inexorable logic, I said to myself, 'You don't have flu' (though the shiver was still on me).

I even enjoyed my egg, toast, and tea – which is not possible when you have flu.

At last it struck me that it was time to switch to the winter quilt.

I have two quilts – a heavy one for winter and lighter one for summer.

Since April or May I've been sleeping under the summer quilt – with, of recent weeks, an extra woollen cover.

And now, in December, it's time for the winter quilt. That's why it was so cold last night.

Old people hate change, in even the slightest thing, as though change reminded them of their mortality, their last and final change. 'Change and decay in all around I see,' we sang blithely as boys in the kirk on Sunday evenings – not understanding one syllable or letter of the hymn we were trilling and trebling on about...

So, at midnight, I heaved the great bulk of the winter 'downie' through to my own bed, and slept much better than the chilly night before that.

To make doubly sure, I switched on the storage heater, which had stood idle in the bedroom since March, and woke in the early hours to see the red eye glaring at me – but in a friendly fashion, to be sure; it's just a way those non-human things have of appearing inimical.

So, I know I don't have the flu after all – not at the moment of writing, anyway. Who knows what tomorrow will bring?

(I think comfortingly of the flu jag I got last month.)

The sun is shining through the kitchen window, and all seems well under the shelter of Brinkie's Brae.

But the weatherman on Radio 4 spoke about storm-force winds this morning early.

That's another thing we old folk can be doing without: storms.

How we enjoyed them as boys! (I must write an article about that some time – on the theme that the world is made for the very young.)

The Universal Winter Song

29 December 1994

Today as I'm writing this is the shortest day of the year – the winter solstice – December 21.

There is the consolation of knowing that from tomorrow or the day after, the light will begin to grow, to mount higher and higher with the sun until it nears the zenith on June 21.

It is a clear pleasant morning as I write. If the weather holds, I expect there might be quite a few folk at Maeshowe wanting to see the last ray of the sun setting over Hoy, strike through the long passage and linger briefly near one of the tombs. (Near, not *on*: because, I've been told, in five thousand years since Maeshowe was built there has been a slight wobble in the earth's axis.)

I've seen the Maeshowe midwinter sunset glow, and it is a marvellous thing to experience. It is as if those ancient people had a deeper sympathy with the movement of star and planet than we 'educated' moderns do; and they were able to tap a richer vein of symbolism, the victory of light over night in the heart of the kingdom of darkness itself.

It was a tomb that the golden key gave entrance to.

Light: all the ceremonies of this dark time of the year are concerned with light.

There is young Saint Lucy, who is celebrated today in Sweden (though in the rest of Europe and Christendom her feast is

December 13). Her eyes were torn out because she refused to marry the suitor proposed for her, and her eyes (those precious stones) were her loveliest feature. But there are other lights than the light of the body, and to that greater light she was true.

In Swedish houses the youngest daughter got up early and dressed in white on St Lucy's Day, and woke the rest of the family with coffee, rolls and a St Lucy song.

Not much is known of our own St Tredwell, who has a loch in Papay named after her, but I seem to remember that Tredwell had a story parallel to Lucy's – a chief or a king desired her, especially her most beautiful eyes, so she sent him her eyes with a thorn through them. We need not accept the story literally – it would be too awful to dwell on – but it is a fleshing-out of some perdurable inner symbol.

St Thomas' Day is also December 21. Thomas is the apostle who doubted the Resurrection until he was shown the physical evidence. After Pentecost, the tradition is that he evangelised eastwards, as far as India, and was martyred there. What, though, does St Thomas have to do with December 21? In the east is the spring and fountain of the light, and from this midwinter darkness the sun, earlier by two minutes or so every morning, proceeds to rise a point or two towards the east at the vernal equinox, at the pivot-point of light and darkness.

The Shetlanders, our neighbours, kept a purer and longer tryst with the midwinter ceremonies than us sceptical Orcadians. We have a full account of what went on in Shetland crofts and fishing bothies a hundred and fifty years ago, when people had a more poetical view of life than us readers of *The Sun* and viewers of *EastEnders*.

On the shortest day, no work was done, so sacred was the time (and sure, they deserved some tranquillity, after a long year of toil). The Shetlanders had this rhyme:

> The very babe unborn
> Cries, 'O dule! dule!
> For the breaking o' Tammasmas Night
> Five nights afore Yule.'

Certainly the Orcadians had the same song; only we got rid of it early and unrecorded, so anxious we were to fatten our geese and hoard our silver, and forget the mysteries.

And here, now, today, I catch myself at work. But only vaguely – to compose this small essay is to take part, after a fashion, in the universal winter song.

Hogmanay, 1950–70

5 January 1995

This is the half-dead time of year between Christmas and Hogmanay, when the shops are just beginning to open their bleary eyes after the holiday.

To start its rejoicing the east wind has begun to blow, loaded with cold rain. But at least there's no flooding in Orkney, as there is in Wales; as there was a few days ago in Paisley. (Occasionally the May Burn overflows and sends a torrent rushing down the Distillery Close: but so far this winter it has behaved itself.)

Thirty or forty years ago, despite the trough between Yule and New Year I thought it a great time. I had saved up enough in Peter Drever's whisky club – half a crown a week – to be sure of a bottle of whisky and a bottle of rum or gin for the great Scottish feast.

Let the storm rage or the snow come in sheets, we were ready for anything in those far-off days.

Always at Hogmanay, there was a magnificent supper at the house Springbank where Gerry and Nora Meyer resided and still reside.

After the *Pole Star* had sent up showers of golden and silver rockets and every boat at the piers had sounded their hullabaloos, it was time to resort to Well Park where I resided then, but now they call it Guardhouse Park.

Then it was time to first-foot the neighbours, and there were plenty of them in the Ness housing schemes. These visits were paid in a deepening golden trance, into which laughter and choruses intruded. But soon it was time to visit a few more distant neighbours, with the swiftly-ebbing bottle stuck awry in the coat pocket.

Those who have read and inwardly digested the poem called 'Tam o' Shanter', by one Robert Burns, will know what can happen sometimes. Ambition takes wing – there is a cottage in the country that ought to be visited. There is snow on the ground and the black wind is howling. Perhaps better leave that visit till morning? 'Oh no,' cries the reckless spirit of Hogmanay, 'There is only one place to visit, and that is the cottage on the parish border. There and nowhere else!'

Scott of the Antarctic never set out so resolutely.

The road is long and dark and deserted.

What strange thing has happened now?

I am lying in a ditch of softest snow – snow the pillow and the quilt – the wild night the bedroom and a star the bedside lamp.

The few senses left suggest that it might be a good idea to struggle out of this nest of snow and forget about the desired cottage and weave a way home again... There is still enough wit left to suggest that I might be present at a breakfast, but I would be the breakfast myself, and the hoodie-craws the feasters.

At the Ness houses, there were still plenty of lights on, plenty of doors opening and shutting, plenty of scattered cries: 'Happy New Year', and here and there a discordant rendition of 'Auld Lang Syne'.

That was a typical Hogmanay and New Year, any time between the late fifties and the mid-seventies.

Alas, the ageing frame will not endure such intensities at festival now. There will just be a few formal calls, a few quiet callers, a longing for peace and books and the fireside, and the first crocuses.

Edwin Muir

12 January 1995

Today's the third of January, and I think there will be no more first-footers: not that there have been many, as in the old days when we used to look intensely on the Barleycorn when it was yellow.

Now the Barleycorn stingeth like a serpent, in age.

The thought of late merrymakers at the door with bottles! – They are, nowadays, more like bandits with drawn swords.

As Wordsworth said, 'The things which I have seen I now can see no more'...

So I won't be going, later this month, to any Burns Suppers, where the 'usquebaugh' goes like a torrent among the trenched haggis, and much sentimental important nonsense is spouted by men in kilts.

Nor yet will I be faring north to Shetland for Up-Helly-Aa, for the final European midwinter fling. I have heard a rumour that once Up-Helly-Aa was held in other places than Shetland, and consisted mainly of blazing tar barrels being dragged through the street ... I think the Up-Helly-Aa revellers could be doing with some better words to their choruses, incidentally.

While we're on the subject of Burns and poetry, it strikes me that thirty-six years ago, on this very day, Orkney lost her greatest poet. Edwin Muir died in England on January 3, 1959.

I think I must just have been between two bouts of New Year celebration when my mother told me that news of Edwin Muir's death had been on the radio. Well, that was calculated to sober the most reckless of celebrators.

Edwin Muir wasn't a drinking man, in the tradition of Burns, Hogg, and MacDiarmid. I think a glass or two of wine was the extent of his drinking.

Instead, he was a meditative poet, in the tradition of Vaughan, Herbert, and Wordsworth; poets who drank at the pure streams of thought. It was more than just thought that overbrimmed their chalices, it was the essence of thought, the almost tasteless pure draught of meditation... The inebriation that such wine induces leaves no regrets and no hangovers.

I only got one reproof from Edwin Muir at Newbattle, and that was when I had been at a well-known Eskbank tavern called the Justinlees, and had looked on the Barleycorn when it was yellow, and suffered that questionable enchantment... I got a mild telling-off from the warden of Newbattle the next morning. Almost at once he was as friendly and kind to me as ever, and continued that way till he and Willa returned from America and went to live in Swaffham Prior near Cambridge, where he died.

Not for Edwin, had he been born in Deerness or Wyre eight centuries ago, the foaming ale-horns when they went round the drinking-board, and the skalds began their vauntings and their long genealogies.

Instead he might have gone over to Eynhallow and begged leave of the doorkeeper to be a guest there till the Yuletide celebrations were over. There, among flickering candles, the milder chants would have mingled with the calls of seabirds and the waves' rhythms.

'An Hour's Difference'

19 January 1995

Today as I write is the 12th of January – not any particular anniversary, but I remember the old Stromness folk saying in my childhood, 'By the twelfth, there's an hour's difference in the light' – calculating, of course, from the winter solstice on 21st December.

And indeed there is that extra piece of light at the end of each day, especially noticeable if there's a clear sky.

People living at Ootertoon, Stromness, will notice sunset moving from the Coolag hills in Hoy to get, at last, a free drop into the Atlantic. It is all very dramatic and beautiful – if the whole splendour isn't ruined by blizzard or storm winds...

For, it is well known that the worst weather comes after the solstice. 'As the day lengthens, the cold strengthens,' was one of the many Orkney weather sayings in my youth. (Nowadays, with central heating and thermal clothes, we don't notice those things so much.)

But, a century ago, what heroes the islanders must have been – and indeed everybody in the northern hemisphere – to thole¹ such winters. They had to go outside to get water and see to the livestock, the fishing boat and the peatstack, in blizzards and north-easterly blasts. Indoors, the crofts were full of peat-reek and hen-flutters in the rafters and pig-squealings from the back of the fire, and a lamp-glim too feeble to read by.

No wonder they delighted in visitors from the village or a nearby farm. Even Skatehorn the tramp would be welcome to a bowl of porridge. If somebody called who could take down the fiddle from the wall, and play, then there was an element of enchantment ... Old Grand-da was cherished for his treasury of stories and characters long dead.

But the cycle of life went on, winter or summer. Old Grand-da died, a child was born under the same roof.

It was in a January tempest that Robert Burns came into the world ... 'a blast o' Janwar' win' / Blew hansel in on Robin'...

The month of January was dreaded, true enough, for its storms and blizzards. And yet the people knew, far more vividly than us

1 bear

pampered folk of the late twentieth century, that in a true sense the worst was over; darkness and death had been dealt a mortal blow, for the daylight was drawing out at each end of the day. That much was clear to everyone, even the animals could sense it, even the seeds under the snow were beginning to make their first faint tremulous pulsings.

In a month or so, after the solstice, the Coolags of Hoy would not be snuffing the lamp of the sun in the middle of the afternoon. The sun would drop sheer into the Atlantic. They had not read Milton, but they would have appreciated more vividly than any scholar the lines from 'Lycidas':

> So sinks the day-star in the ocean bed,
> And yet anon repairs his drooping head,
> And tricks his beams, and with new-spangled ore
> Flames in the forehead of the morning sky.

We are speaking about Orkney folk of two centuries ago or thereby.

Four thousand years ago, the Orcadians of Maeshowe knew even more about those mysteries.

Signs into Sounds

26 January 1995

Every day I write something, for better or worse, with one or other of my ballpoint pens.

I have a hoard of ballpoint pens, chiefly black which I prefer to blue or any other colour (but there are a few blue ones too).

The ballpoint pen has improved a great deal since the early days in the late 40s, when you might take a quite expensive one out of your pocket to find your fingers all stained black and the inside of your pocket a black indelible splash... Then, when you came to write with the thing, it smudged the paper with excess ink.

A letter, so written, was not a thing of graphic beauty.

Still people went on buying ballpoints, maybe because they were less labour than filling the old 'fountain pen' out of a bottle of ink: maybe just to be in the van of progress.

And the scientists in the ballpoint factories went on working on this new wonder of the world, and gradually they rid the pen of its floodings and smudgings.

The whole world of letter-writers must have been won over, because the pens got progressively cheaper, until finally you could buy one for under a shilling.

And yet complete perfection has never been achieved. There is no uniformity. Some pens go like a song till they suddenly perish in the middle of a word. Some of the same make and name, absolutely identical, are just awkward. They turn coy halfway through a sentence and utter faint faraway syllables; then for a few paragraphs they might decide to be cooperative. Such pens rarely achieve old age. They get cast, in a sudden burst of irritation, into the dustbin.

How far away from the pens that we learned to write with in the primary department of Stromness Secondary School! There, in serried ranks of pupils – there were fifty in our class – we fitted nibs in penholders, and some boy or girl thought worthy of the task was sent with a large bottle of ink and he or she filled the little white porcelain inkwells with a blue-black dollop. The inkwells fitted neatly into a hole in the top right-hand corner of each desk.

Then we had to write in our copybooks, in 'copperplate writing', some proverb or other – 'Too many cooks spoil the broth' or 'A burnt child dreads the fire' or 'A stitch in time saves nine'... Thus, in addition to acquiring a fair hand, we were meant maybe to absorb the street wisdom of the ages.

The really remarkable thing about those copybooks is that each pupil acquired his or her own style of writing, as unmistakeable as a fingerprint – despite that attempt to impose uniformity on us.

Further back, beyond ink and paper, the discipline of writing began.

This was in Miss Matheson's infant class, in the mid-20s. We sat two to a desk. Slates were slotted into grooves, a slate pencil was put before us.

Miss Matheson wrote the letter 'a' on the blackboard and said, 'This is the school cat and it says "ah".' So we wrote the lower-case 'a' on our slates with our slate pencils, and the classroom was full of tiny squeaks like mice, as we five-year-olds laboured to get a toehold in the written language.

Miss Matheson wrote an 's' with chalk on the blackboard. 'This is a snake and it says, "s-s-s-s".'

So we began to make signs into sounds, a long time ago.

King Snowman

9 February 1995

The snow has decided to be awkward this winter, like a skinflint doling out bits of silver and taking them back.

Yesterday morning I was convinced the snow had gone for good – at least, till next December.

I was having my old person's snooze on the couch after lunch of smoked fish and clapshot, and a glass of Muscatel (very posh), when I was wakened by artillery of hailstones in the lum.

And when I went – painfully, because nowadays I'm beginning to have rheumaticky pains here and there, and am glad of a walking-stick outside – to look through the window, there was the street grey with sleet and hailstones.

That's why the snow is a penny-pinching miser this winter, like some kind of pawnbroker with a thin red snivelly nose and blue broken veins on his cheeks... Not at all like the generous jovial snows of childhood.

'There he goes again,' I can hear some youthful readers saying, 'always on about the old times! I bet it wasn't like that at all!'...

The youthful readers might be right, but one of the blessings of memory is that it transforms everything so that the summers of the early thirties, for example, were one long blaze of sun from June till the day after the Lammas Market. And the winter snow didn't come in dribs and drabs, but in one generous dazzling benison, that lasted a week or so and then vanished like a dream.

For that week the snowman was King (I have never seen a right snowman for years). The snowman had a very formal dress. He ought to have had a battered bowler or top hat, but they were few and far between, so a cloth cap had to do.

The snowman's eyes were bits of coal. He was a very fat jolly person. Grandma's tin box was rifled for buttons; for the snowman's white quilted coat had to have a row of many-tinted buttons of various sizes. The cupboard was searched for a scarf with one or two moth holes in it, to wind round the snowman's neck, for it would never do if the snowman went down with pneumonia.

The snowman, alas, was a smoker. Cigarettes were no use to him, the wetness would have ruined cigarettes in an instant. No, the snowman insisted on a pipe – an old rank pipe cut (it seemed) from a larch forest in Finland. This pipe was stuck, a bit awry, into the snowman's face.

Nobody ever actually saw the snowman lighting up or puffing grey smoke. Possibly, he only smoked at night, alone, in the garden, under the stars.

Between his pipefuls, he probably sang winter songs, till dawn, in his deep cheerful voice, while we children were asleep.

Did we, or the snowman, know what was in store for him – how brief his beautiful dazzling reign would be?

For – as I said – the great snows of childhood suddenly vanished. There came a thaw on the night and all that was left of the lovely snowfall were a few grey tatters at the side of dykes. Orphir was covered with thin frayed wretched lace, that yesterday wore a gleaming gown.

And the snowman? He had died in the night. Nothing was left of him but a sodden cap, a scattering of various buttons, two chips of snow, a scarf fit only now for the ashbin, and a pipe that could never be smoked again.

I had meant to write about snow fights, the sledge-runs from Oglaby to the street below the Library, the red laughing faces of boys and girls, the music of their banter under the brightest stars of the year.

But it turned out that I couldn't get past that snowman.

'Seventh Age' Has Come upon Me

16 February 1995

In my childhood, only a few very old men went with sticks (or staffs, as they were called, echoing the famous 23rd Psalm).

There they were, the old old men, going on their sticks.

There being no notion of time in childhood, those ancient Stromnessians had always had staffs, and they always would have.

We had no notions at all of birth or death.

And of course we could never imagine ourselves, in any circumstances, using a walking-stick.

We lived in a perpetual childhood.

And here, for the past fortnight, I've been going here and there helped by a stick.

Shakespeare's 'seventh age' has come upon me.

But it had been coming, slowly, for a few years now.

You notice, first, that you no longer walk in a straight line. There is a slight bias to left or to right. There is a certain wavering in the footsteps.

Everyone has to turn, suddenly, in the course of daily events. I discovered, over many months, that if I turned suddenly, I staggered, and all but fell sometimes. (I am speaking quite without reference to alcohol; of which I take very little nowadays, in any case.)

These little aberrations occur on surfaces with normal friction. This winter there seems to have been an abnormal number of frosty days, with saltings of new snow over the shiny patches. It behoved even the fittest person to walk with care ... One morning last week, Brian Murray warned me not to set foot on the Mayburn balcony: it was a solid sheet of ice.

That afternoon, my kind hostess at Quildon suggested I should have a stick of hers to walk down the brae, in mid-afternoon.

It was extraordinary, what confidence that flimsy cane gave me. I could pick my way with ease through the icy patches, and down that steep series of Faravel steps, without a care in the world.

Not a stagger – not a single lurch to port or starboard! True as a compass, the stick led me home.

Ever since, I haven't ventured out without it.

The stick does more than steady one, it gives a certain abandon and joy to one's going. It takes about ten years' heaviness off one's step.

You must have seen Charlie Chaplin half dancing over the hill into the sunset, swinging his cane ...

Well, now I understand a little how Charlie faced every threatening situation with a brave heart. His stick gave him courage and humour and panache.

It all goes back, maybe, to our jungle ancestors in the treetops. Look, in the next David Attenborough film, how splendidly and fearlessly and with superb timing they swing from branch to branch.

In old age, we remember again the feel of trusty wood on our hands, the thrust and the recoil, far back at the dawn of time.

A Busy Week

23 February 1995

Wednesday, February 1: Bitter cold day. I bet not many folk have sampled smoked fish and clapshot for lunch, plus a glass of white wine.

The clapshot season is almost over. We must make the most of it.

On TV, *The World at War* – Hitler's suicide in his Berlin bunker. In what region of the *Inferno* would Dante have put such a monster?

The remarkable Attenborough series on plants. Not gentle green fountains at all – every bit as fierce and predatory as tigers and eagles, some of them.

Thursday, February 2: There's to be a book of Orkney photographs by Gunnie Moberg some time next year. My pen is to supply texts.

Yesterday I did two small poems – 'Pebbles in Ice' and 'Flowers on Ice'. These poems will keep me busy for a week or two.

No time for them today, however.

Confine writing to a merry little essay on building a snowman in childhood, for *The Orcadian*. The balcony at Mayburn is a sheet of ice. Decided not to trust myself on it, so stayed at home... I've taken to watching every afternoon a TV game of words and numbers, *Countdown*. It's a very good-natured game, with pleasant people.

A story I wrote twenty years ago was on Radio 4 today – 'Silver' – but I missed it.

Friday, February 3: Suddenly smitten with earache, for the first time since childhood. Like needles jabbing. Fortunately it subsides to a dull ache. It may be the icy grip of winter: a frosty draught has found a way through the walls.

Have lunch at Hopedale. Max Davies has come over from Rackwick, in preparation for 'a publishing tour' in USA, conducting orchestras here and there. Afterwards he's going to award himself a 'sabbatical' – a year of perfect freedom to do what he wants. I reckon he deserves it.

Two young writers visit briefly in the evening, and enjoy pints of the famous dark rich Ness brew – Duncan MacLean and Robert Alan Jamieson from Shetland who's reading tonight in Pier Arts Centre.

Saturday, February 4: The oranges are good this winter, full of juice. Bananas are good too, but I always think they taste better when the skin is beginning to show black splotches: then the full flavour is released.

Watch from the couch two rugby internationals – Scotland beats Ireland, and England beats France (the latter a decisive victory).

It seems to me rugby is a much more physical game than soccer, which seems a bit namby-pamby in comparison. But when a week later I watched a rugby league final – Wigan v St Helens – on a rain-soaked pitch, it was a wonder to me that such vast men could come alive out of such violent tackles, like a war of Titans.

Sunday, February 5: Today there was a birthday party – the ninety-fourth – for our friend Renée Simm of Quildon Cottage.

Surinder had prepared lunch at his peedie cottage, Stenigar: a deliciously spiced soup, baked salmon.

Afterwards Christopher and Matilda and young Joshua came for the cake-cutting, and cups of Earl Grey tea.

A magnificent fragment of the prophet Isaiah at the Mass lesson this evening, concerning the seraph with six wings that touched the prophet's lips with a burning coal of fire.

Monday, February 6: Two more poems in the morning to accompany Gunnie's photographs: the Martello Tower (one of two) at Longhope and Cubbie Roo's Castle at Wyre, taken from the air ... this is the ruin where Edwin Muir used to play as a child.

Cubbie Roo (Kolbein Hruga) was apparently a stern strong chieftain eight hundred years ago. Mothers would warn ill-behaved children, 'Cubbie Roo'll get thee!'

Cubbie Roo had a son called Bjarni, who later became Bishop of Orkney. He was a famous poet in his day. It is intriguing to think that two great poets in such a small island sat at the same hearth of The Bu[1], twenty-four generations apart.

Last Week of Winter

2 March 1995

So, this is a good feeling, to know that we are in the last week of winter. February, I always think, brings winter to a close. But I expect there will be a few wintry days yet, like last year, with a little

---

1 farmhouse near Cubbie Roo's Castle, believed to be the homestead of Kolbein Hruga

blizzard in mid-March (when we were isolated, moreover, in a cottage in Outertown, with a dog, and a cat that was a fleeting shadow merely; but it was a delightful cottage, above Hoy Sound, and in the shadow of the Black Craig – it was a pity, though, that the snow came before we had managed properly to operate the stove).

There are in fact no fixed boundaries for the four seasons in a place like Orkney. Magnificence can descend in the depths of winter; there can be long dreich days in July or August.

It is, with us, more a question, of light than of storms and stillness.

January, and even more February, sees this swift rising of the fountains of light.

The miracle of renewal is happening so quickly before our very eyes.

A cold wind blows, with sleet, from north-west. But, when the cloud goes at last, we see that the late afternoon sun has cleared the Coolags of Hoy and is setting in the open Atlantic...

In the end, everybody decides when winter begins and ends for himself (or herself – I hasten to scribble, lest nowadays I be put down as anti-feminist; you can't be too careful).

I think the three months, December, January, and February are true winter months.

Spring begins, not quite precisely of course, on the first day of March, and ends on the last day of May. And then, with June, comes summer...

But, if that's the way things are, why do we call the 24th of June 'mid-summer', when summer has only taken a few golden steps and, in fact, the light is beginning to shorten?

It is a strange puzzling business, this arrangement of the seasons. The Orcadians of four generations ago lit the Johnsmas midsummer fires on every hilltop on the midnight of the 23rd June, when the sun was just past its high meridian. (We ought to agree at once that winter and summer were much more vivid experiences to earlier generations – winter darker and more cruel, summer the cup overbrimming with promise even if, most years, the achievement fell far short, in the way of harvest and gold put by.)

We have drawn the teeth of winter, with our electric light and our storage heaters, etc. We can fly out to Majorca, to get even more of the sun than we are entitled to; though the sudden shock may not be all that good for us and our pale boreal skins.

So, the seasons are not of so much importance to us in the late twentieth century.

It's somehow still a relief, though, to know that I'm writing this in the last week of winter; and that, by the time you read it, spring will have begun.

Boots Shoes and Bends

16 March 1995

Stromness is slowly changing shape. Two afternoons ago as we drove through the street, there was a great digging going in what used to be a blacksmith's yard in Dundas Street (in my childhood there was a lot of rusted iron there, from a former generation).

Further along, a once well-known footwear shop, at the beginning of Dundas Street was covered with scaffolding and sheathing, and again outside Rae's (stationer) in Victoria St... There are, it seems, to be a few more flats in the town.

The leather shop – John Wright's in Dundas Street – has appeared in many photographs and sketches, chiefly because of the legend it bore in big black letters – BOOTS SHOES AND BENDS.

Being children, who accept everything, we never once paused to wonder what 'bends' could mean.

It was only later when visitors paused to read this most conspicuous sign of all the shop signs in Stromness, and wondered 'What are "bends"?' that we had to admit that we didn't know what 'bends' were, either.

A few visitors would remark facetiously that the only 'bends' they had read about were afflictions that befell deep-sea divers deprived of oxygen.

It never occurred to anybody to go into the shop and ask Mr Wright the shoe-maker for an explanation.

But indeed the sign seemed so ancient and mysterious that even he might not have known.

At last I had to resort to the Oxford Dictionary, and there, among a hundred other meanings for 'bends', I found this – 'a shape or size in which ox or cow-hides are tanned into leather'...

I suppose, with reference to Mr Wright's shop, it meant that you could buy a length of leather and do your shoe repairs at home, which made much more sense for country people who couldn't afford the time to hang about Stromness for half the day while their boots were being soled.

We won't be seeing that famous shop-sign any more, and to us oldsters it seems as if a piece of Stromness is being lost forever.

Well, but flats for people to live in are more important than bits of nostalgia.

I like to think of that shop, though. It had a good atmosphere. As soon as you went in, you were enfolded in the smell of leather. Either Mr John Wright was soling a shoe behind the counter: or, if he wasn't there, he soon would be, appearing from inside, where his living quarters were. And a more friendly genial man there wasn't in Stromness.

It didn't matter if your errand was only for a twopenny pair of shoelaces, or a tin of Kiwi shoe-polish, he was as pleasant as if it was plimsolls you were after in the golden days of July, or Dunlop rubber boots in the deep snows of January; or even, I suppose, as if a farmer with a whole squad of kids to shoe for school came in for a roll of leather, a 'bend'.

And there, in serried ranks on the shelves all around, were the boxes of shoes in every size conceivable. And there behind the counter was the 'last', the strong, curved needles and the resin.

Now we wait with some impatience to see what shape will emerge from the chrysalis of that ancient building that is no more Wright's shoe-shop, at the foot of Dundas Street.

Lenten Reading

30 March 1995

Yesterday – 21 March – ought to have been one of the most thrilling days of the year in the Orkney calendar. It was the spring equinox, when light and darkness hang in perfect balance. But from 21 March on, the light increases and the darkness crumbles. We are on our way to Johnsmas and high summer.

Alas, that wonderful day, the equinox, had a bleak grey west wind blowing through it, and a smirr of rain, so that it seemed like any wretched day plucked from the middle of January. The only heart-enhancing thing about it was that the light lingered till 6pm or so – curtain-drawing time.

And we have the certainty that from now on, our islands will be increasingly invested with that enchanting boreal light: one of the great rewards of living in Orkney.

You might not have thought it was much of a place to live in, listening to the weather forecast at 6.30. Fine bright weather in England and Southern Scotland; the Northern Isles wrapped in dark clouds.

When I got up this morning at 8.30 and drew back the curtains, a mild golden light lay everywhere. My morning visitor, Surinder, informed me that it had rained heavily on the night. So the dark clouds must passed over when we islanders were all asleep.

So splashed with variety and uncertainty and surprise is our climate! It is – take one thing with another – one of the pleasures of living between two great oceans: this bewildering unpredictable dance of the weather.

The sun is still shining as I write, and I hope another black cloud doesn't blow up before 1.30pm, when I'll be taking my walking-stick and hobbling over the brae for a bowl of soup.

These Lenten days, I've been reading some of those magnificent stories out of the Old Testament: how Jacob stole the blessing from his brother Esau; how Joseph in his many-coloured coat told his dreams of power to his envious brothers; and of the renewal of the poor widow's oil jars...

A few days ago it was the story of Naaman, the Syrian general who was a leper. His wife's little maid servant was a Jewish girl, who said that a prophet of Israel, Eliseus, could cure Naaman's leprosy. 'Wash seven times in the Jordan,' said Eliseus. Whereupon Naaman said that the rivers of Syria – the Abana and the Pharphar – were purer in every way than the Jordan. But in the end the great general consented to go seven times into the Jordan, and his flesh was restored 'like the flesh of a little child'...

The moving part of the story is the little Israelite girl, who had been captured in a raid and brought back to Syria. The sweetness and wisdom and goodness of the child tastes like honey in the starkness of the tale.

One feels, reading, that it is out of such innocence that the dreadful wounds of the twentieth century and indeed all history will be cleansed and healed.

I think it is a great pity that those magnificent stories are no longer a part of our way of life. It is an inheritance that we have – alas! – put away from us.

I can't help thinking that that treasury would be much better for people of all ages than *Neighbours* or *Coronation Street*.

'New' Writer of Genius

6 April 1995

One of the joys of living is to discover a new writer of genius. (When I say 'new', I mean new to me; this writer died in 1952, aged ninety-two.)

You somehow assume, at my time of life, that you have read all the writers you care to read, and mean to stay with that good gang.

I had of course heard of the Norwegian, Hamsun, and heard a novel of his called *Hunger* praised. But somehow I never felt the urge to read Hamsun, especially since I knew he had collaborated with the Nazis in their occupation of Norway between 1940 and 1945, and spent the brief remainder of his life in disgrace and financial ruin.

Surinder and I have been looking after a dog and a cat at the beautiful cottage of Don in Outertown. Gunnie (who of course owns the place, with Tam) has left a biography of Hamsun, and a novel of his called *Pan*, on the table.

I have dipped into the biography here and there. The last years of the novelist's life make painful reading: how he rejoiced at the rise of Nazism in Germany; how he hated the English for shady financial dealings harmful to Norway in the last century, and for the relentless unnecessary bombardment of Copenhagen by the British Fleet in 1805... What Hamsun envisaged was a great Pan-Germanic union of all the northern states of Europe, those whose languages and legends spring from a common root. The German Nazis made full use of him during the war. Goebbels was delighted to find one great European writer in full support of Nazism. The old novelist was even taken to meet Hitler; and after Hitler's death, when all was lost, Hamsun wrote a eulogy in high praise of the dead leader...

No great introduction to a writer's works. Either the man was foolish, or incredibly thick-necked and stubborn.

I picked up *Pan*, and was immediately enchanted. It is a wonderful early work by Hamsun, and 'it has the dew on it'. It is a love story, concerning an affair between an army officer on extended leave, who spends his time alone hunting on the mountain and in the forest, and a young girl who is alternately devoted to him and cold and forbidding to him; so that, among all those magnificent lyrical passages (of nature and the ebb and flow of human relationships) the officer Glahn is reduced to near madness.

The novel is like a long tragic beautiful ballad. In its original language, it must be even more lovely.

Gunnie has a little collection of Hamsun novels at Don. Yesterday I took down a long novel called *The Growth of the Soil*, quite different in style and content from *Pan*. It is the story of a farmer who breaks out virgin soil among the east Norwegian mountains to make a farm – a hard heroic encounter, but full of joy and achievement.

It is wrong to make a league table of writers. But this extraordinary man Hamsun seems to me to be the equal of Thomas Hardy, and almost as good as Tolstoy.

I am glad to have stumbled on a new gold mine.

Drama of a Day's Weather

11 May 1995

Suddenly, yesterday, after a long cold delay, came spring.

The TV weather forecaster wasn't quite so sure that it would happen north of a vague line passing through Sutherland and Caithness. The main part of Britain would be sweltering but not the islanders and the dwellers among bogs – they would be troubled with haars[1] and showers, and much cooler.

What they don't celebrate is the wonderful variety of our climate.

Who would want to swelter in the mid-seventies Fahrenheit in the middle of Birmingham or London?

When I got up passing eight on Monday morning, there had been a slight shower, the street was wet but quickly drying out, and the sun was somewhere through the thin diffused haar.

A great wonder, and, a sure sign of spring – the windows that have been wedged tight all winter are opening, some of them anyway, and the sweet airs of early May are beginning to flow everywhere through the house.

1 sea-mists

I have a lot of work to do every morning at the writing table, but on this special morning, having made a dutiful beginning, I went out in the sun with my friend Surinder along Ness Road to his flat at Stenigar – the 'studio flat' they call it, because it was Stanley Cursiter's studio, and has the great window half in the roof and half in the east-facing wall, where Stanley did his painting in the fifties and sixties. Through this window the fishing boats come and go, and the *Ola* entered superbly at 1.45pm. Stand in another part of the view, and there is the whole of Stromness from north to south in full sunlight except where the Double Houses at Ness block out a little of the South End.

Another sign of spring – I walked there and back without my quilted winter jacket... And inside my house, it is so mild that I've had to turn the storage heaters low.

In the fresh beautiful sun of May, a million daisies are rushing out, like stars in a tropic sky. The dandelions are showing themselves, rugged and shaggy. The primroses cluster on the banks. The daffodils have stopped 'fluttering and dancing in the breeze', and stand there, in every garden, radiant presences taking their fill of light before they leave us again for the hall of Dis[1].

Old men rest in the afternoon, and I did too – a bit resentful at having to leave the sun. Then, through a half-slumber, I heard a roll of thunder!... How lucky we are, to have such drama and variety in one day's weather; compared to the sweaty-sticky inhabitants of Birmingham or London!

The Thousand Flags

18 May 1995

What has happened to the thousand flags that used to be in Stromness, shut away in chests in attics?

I suppose they must have been brought home to Stromness over a century and more by sailors, to show what brave seaports they had anchored in, in foreign parts.

In a Stromness living-room, after six months or so at sea, he would open his kist[2] to let the family see what treasures he had brought home from his latest wanderings – and there, among brass rings from Zanzibar and Mexican scarfs and Tasmanian

---

1 Roman god of the underworld, also known as Orcus, Pluto

2 chest

boomerangs, was this huge flag from Norway or Chile or China – a thing for his younger brothers and sisters to wonder at; it being so different from the Union Jack they were so used to – that imperial flag that one day 'would fly from Cairo to the Cape' as the town-crier Sam Stockan announced at the time of the Diamond Jubilee of Queen Victoria in 1897.

This same Sam Stockan, who kept a shop near where Couper's Stables is, at the south end of the Back Road, had quit the scene by the time I was a small boy, but he was the town crier before James Leask (known as 'Puffer') and John Johnston ('Soldier John')... He had, it seems, a stately presence and a clear intonation, making his announcements along the street: so much so that one lady tourist said, entranced, 'What a poetical-looking old man!' This word was brought home to the peedie shop near Couper's Stables, and for the next while Mrs Sam Stockan let it be known that the grand English gentry lady had called her man 'an owld poetry'...

Well, then, very many Stromness houses had flags of all the nations hidden away.

I saw them first, in all their glory, decorating the street at the Silver Jubilee of 1935. It was a delight, walking under that dense foliage of flags strung between the chimney heads all the way from the South End to the North End. Out they came again, for the Coronation of 1937, as thick as ever.

They slumbered in attics all through the war, until VE Day in 1945, and then, after those lengthy austerities, that grey arid desert of time, they were brought out again and they seemed more glorious than ever. I can't be certain at this distance of time, but I'm sure I saw the occasional German Eagle and Japanese Rising Sun among the lavish bunting; which shows how easily Stromness folk forgave their enemies. Anyway, nobody objected: it all added to the riot of colour.

The first Shopping Week in July 1949 brought out the multitudinous flags again. I think Provost G. S. Robertson made a count, and there were over nine hundred flags. There have been forty-five Shopping Weeks since.

Time and rain and wind and moth and rust have taken their toll, and now we have only little triangular coloured pennants to celebrate great events.

A glory has departed.

Sleepless Depression

25 May 1995

They say, as a person gets older, he doesn't need so much sleep.

If that is true, it is a rather unpleasant truth.

I would much rather be asleep than lying in the early hours, in a mild wakeful depression – and that after having taken a sleeping tablet at midnight.

The first thing I do on awakening is switch on the radio. There it is, morning after morning recently – not Radio 4 or Radio Orkney, but the World Service. Yesterday the man was talking about famous pop groups, the appalling noise of which I endured, hoping that the programme would soon end and that we would be treated to a reasonably intelligent talk or an entertaining story. But the hideous excerpts went on and on...

In the end I switched off and waited for 'getting up time' – 8.15am.

What drink on earth is there so good as the first cup of tea at 8.30?

Yesterday morning I could endure that dawn awakening no longer.

> What hours, O what black hours we have spent
> This night! What sights you, heart, saw; ways you went!
> And more must, in yet longer light's delay...

That's what the nineteenth-century poet, Gerard Manley Hopkins, wrote about his sleeplessness – only, he had a much blacker depression sitting on his pillow than I had.

Anyway, in a sleepy rage I opened the bottle of sleeping tablets and swallowed a second one, and almost at once oblivion came down like a wave.

When I woke again, the nine o'clock news man was finishing his bulletin. I could hear, down below, my overnight visitor, setting the fire.

The morning was half done and there was, as always, so much to do!...

A disgrace...

In a half stupor I fumbled into my clothes and felt my way downstairs.

There blazed the fire, all broken gold. (There has been much need of a fire all through this coldest month of May that I ever remember, in spite of the storage heaters installed two years ago.)

I managed to do such daily mechanical things as boil the kettle for tea and make toast. All I could manage in the way of bright morning talk was an occasional monosyllable.

All I could manage in the way of work afterwards was some base copying of rough work already sweated over and rejoiced in.

Washing the face and combing the hair required a certain amount of resolution.

After lunch, in a friend's house, I slept on the couch for two hours! I think I've been too sad, up to now, to report the death of Gypsy the famous cat, at the age of eighteen... In this afternoon nap, I had a dream. There was the smallest kitten in the world, smaller than a mouse, and black like Gypsy, a Lilliputian kitten. There it was, in my Nitrazepam-induced drowse, and as suddenly it had gone again.

I took my stick at 5pm and tottered down beside the singing waters of the May Burn.

'Working till 2pm'

1 June 1995

It's nice to have strangers knocking at the door, especially when they flatter your vanity by wanting you to sign a book. Some even produce a camera and suggest the taking of a picture outside; or, if it's too rainy and windy, the old rocking-chair will do. (I never like being photographed.)

Writing is a trade like any other, and I have preferred times of the day for work – nearly always between breakfast and lunch.

Then I cloister myself in the kitchen and set about what Dylan Thomas called 'the work of words'.

Last year I think there were a few morning callers – a few, but enough for me to print on a square of white paper WORKING ALL MORNING. And I stuck the notice with Scotch tape to the front door.

It seemed to work, too.

For almost a year now the sun has curled the edge of the paper. It has been beaten on by snow and sleet. It has been soaked by rain. East winds have clawed at it.

And still it is hanging there, on the door panel, a sorely battered document, with the lettering much faded though still legible if you pore over it as you might over an ancient Egyptian papyrus.

You would not believe a manuscript could hold out so long against the furies of the Orkney weather.

Yesterday I had to answer the phone at mid-morning. (That's another disrupter of the peace, at working-time, the phone – but it rings so rarely that I'm usually glad enough that somebody wants to speak to me from a distance...) I forget what the phone-call was about, but in the middle of the conversation I heard a knock at the door, and, shouted 'Come in!' – for you can't phone and answer the door at the same time.

A bearded middle-aged stranger put his head round the door, and asked in a mid-European accent if I would be so kind as to sign a book, please?... So I did, and he left in the rain to visit Skara Brae and Brodgar. 'You cannot do such visits in a hurry,' he said.

As he was leaving, I could see that my notice was impossibly curled and stained and torn. To a foreigner, it might have been a notice to the birds not to mess up the balcony, or a prohibition to rag-pickers... 'The notice will have to be renewed,' I said to myself. 'It's time'...

This morning I had another work-time caller. A very pleasant man who is spending weeks in Orkney researching his ancestry among branching names and very intricate kinship, going back a century and more, and he has kirkyards and other records to examine. It was his hobby; he enjoyed the work very much. He would have much fruitful information to carry back to the other side of the world.

Then he saw clearly that I had work to do, too; though I'm sure we could have spoken with profit for the rest of the morning, at least...

I have found that little pad of thick white pages and have printed on it WORKING TILL 2PM... Will it last till May 1996? I will Sellotape it to the door as soon as I finish.

I think I will keep the ruined winter-battered notice and file it among other precious documents.

The Use of Poetry

8 June 1995

Today is the 1st of June, and there is a poem called 'The Glorious First of June' about a naval battle in which Nelson of course was victorious, but I always get that battle mixed up with another Nelson victory, the Battle of Copenhagen, celebrated in Thomas Campbell's poem:

Of Nelson and the North
Sing the glorious day's renown,
When to battle fierce came forth
All the might of Denmark's crown,
And her arms along the deep proudly shone...

I don't know how poetry is taught in school nowadays, but in my time we had to learn poems by rote, and repeat them in the classroom.

It may be argued that this is not the best way of inculcating a love of poetry in young minds. It could even be argued that it is a ruinous method ... But I am not so sure.

After sixty years, my memory is still stored with the great poetry we had to learn then, and I am often thankful for it. Especially five years ago, when I was recovering from an operation in Aberdeen and had many sleepless nights, the time passed tolerably (enjoyably, even) remembering 'The Hound of Heaven', Wordsworth's 'Immortality' ode, the magnificent dialogue on death in *Measure for Measure*, 'Sir Patrick Spens', 'The Scholar Gypsy', 'Death and Doctor Hornbook', 'The Deserted Village', and many others.

So, nobody dare ask me, 'What is the *use* of poetry?'... It can sweeten long dark hours, besides feeding the inner spirit with honey-dew and the milk of paradise.

But, I agree, boys would much rather be playing football and rowing to the sillocks on an early summer evening, than committing stretches of Wordsworth or Shakespeare to memory. And so we kicked balls and plied oars before we opened the poetry book with a groan.

And the poetry period in the classroom was every bit as bad as the geometry or the Latin period. We were tough, insensitive adolescents.

There fell one day when Mr Paterson, our English teacher, decided to read a poem to us. It was called 'Sohrab and Rustum', by a Victorian poet, Matthew Arnold.

The poem is written in blank verse, in the epic style, and tells of a battle between the Persian army and the army of another eastern nation. A challenge is issued and accepted. Let a champion from each host be sent out to do single combat in no man's land... Let those two chosen ones decide the outcome.

The Persians had a famous veteran warrior in their ranks, invincible, Rustum... A young man from the other army volunteered to do battle with him. Sohrab was the name of the rash young warrior.

It so happened that, at every pass-of-arms, Sohrab outdid his famous rival; until near the end Rustum, baffled and desperate, cried 'Rustum!' and then Sohrab knew that he was battling against his own father. He dropped his guard momentarily, and Rustum thrust him through... At last, on the brink of death, father and son saluted each other, beside the banks of the great river Oxus.

'But the majestic river floated on...' and the brief epic draws to an end.

We tough no-nonsense fifteen-year-olds sat transfixed throughout Mr Paterson's recital.

'If only all poetry was like that!' said a classmate to me later.

Communal Ceremonial Beauty

15 June 1995

A hundred and fifty years ago, about this time of year, the young men and women of Orkney would have been engaged in out-of-the-ordinary activities.

They would have been going back and fore between the highest hill in every district and island with caisies[1] on their backs, full of combustible materials – old broken oars and creels, worn-out ploughs and cribs, flotsam and jetsam, as much peat as could be spared. And there, on top of the hill, a pyre was built.

Secretly, the bone of an animal was inserted into the heart of the pyre.

Maybe some whale tallow was added. Maybe some old wife poured over all a jar of rancid butter – anything to get a flame going.

The thing was, to have a good fire burning on the night of 23rd June (Johnsmas) – a magnificent fire to shame the many fires burning in the neighbouring parishes.

The excitement grew as the great day approached.

The women of 'the toonship' were busy for days beforehand getting food and ale ready for transporting to the hill.

The parish fiddler took down his fiddle that may have been hanging on the wall, in the peat-reek, since the last days of Christmas.

1 creels, panniers

The people kept looking anxiously at the sky. If only it didn't rain!... A rainstorm on the night of the 23rd would have washed out everything.

And finally, the great day arrived. Everyone in the parish who could walk, run, or hobble to the hilltop was there in good time. The weather had kept faith. The sun had shone all day, with one or two random showers only, and the sun was still there, a glow buried under the northwest horizon.

In the midsummer 'grimmlings', people moved like shadows here and there on the hilltop.

Somebody must have been the master of ceremonies, and ordered the torch to be lit and thrust into the pyre.

And soon the whole hilltop was ablaze!

What cheers went up then from the parish folk!

As the flames leapt higher, the young men showed off their daring by jumping through the flames, again and again.

The fiddler plied his bow as though he had half a dozen elbows.

Then the hampers of food and the stone jars of best ale were opened.

All round, as far as eye could see, the Johnsmas fires burned on all the hilltops of Orkney.

Before the big fire burned out, a crofter would light a private torch from the glow and carry it to his own house and steading and fields, as if he was performing a kind of cleansing ritual for the growing crops, and the harvest to come; and for the beasts beyond the dyke.

That is a communal ceremonial beauty that has vanished forever.

The Darkling Thrush

22 June 1995

Everybody agrees that it has been the coldest bleakest spring for years.

And yet the hidden blackbird in a nearby tree doesn't think so. Morning to night he pours out an anthology of joyous song – a pure fountain, jet after jet, unending.

They say he's only defining the bounds of his territory. 'Keep well away, you other blackbirds! No trespassing! I'll do you an injury if you come too close'... That's roughly what knowledgeable bird-folk say that the bird is singing. Likewise the lark 'at heaven's gate' which we heard at Don garden, Ootertoon, a few afternoons ago... All those birds, in short, are selfish aggressive territorialists.

I don't believe a word of it. Or, at best, there may be just one syllable of selfishness in those long outbursts of song. The remainder is pure God-given joy in the beauty of the summer world; however grey and cold the June day might be.

The birds seem to have a wisdom, a foresight, a gratitude that is not all that common in human beings; especially in an affluent age.

Even in the hardest times, they sing. I'm sure they sang among the ruins of Hiroshima, Dresden, and London.

I am reminded vividly of a great poem by Thomas Hardy. Written on the afternoon of December 31, 1900: the last day of the nineteenth century.

Hardy was abroad for a walk on that bleak winter afternoon. He was not an optimistic man, at the best of times – except when he was writing his marvellous poetry, and then craftsmanship makes sorrow beautiful.

Out among the Wessex fields that miserable afternoon, Hardy heard a thrush singing. The fading stormy light was glorified by burst after burst of ecstatic song.

The poet could see the bird on the branch. It was an old 'blast-beruffled' bird, with little future in front of him. (Possibly the January frosts would finish him off.) Yet the ecstasy of the song went on and on, as if he was proclaiming 'Some blessed Hope, whereof he knew / And I was unaware...'

If only that old happy thrush, on the very eve of the twentieth century, could have known what was in store for mankind: the First World War, Stalin, Hitler, Auschwitz, the atom bomb, Rwanda, Palestine, Yugoslavia...

What broken branch of a tree could that ancient storm-tossed bird be seeking to defend: 'Keep away, you other thrushes!... This is my neck of the woods!... Dare to light on this wintry tree, and I'll tear every feather from your wing, old as I am!...'

No, says Thomas Hardy (who was an agnostic) he seemed to be rejoicing over and over and over again, in midwinter and in all of nature.

I agree with Hardy and Wordsworth and Chaucer. Birds sing mainly because they are happy.

And so I thank the blackbird with the magnificent voice who has been singing around Mayburn for a fortnight now – and reminding us that this summer, for all its north wind and grey skies, is here, to be accepted, and thankfully.

Halcyon Summers

6 July 1995

I wonder if we are going to have a good summer, after nearly a week of full warmth and brightness.

This morning again is full of promise – a muted early light, but as all elderly Orcadians know, that's all to the good.

(This is being written on a morning in late June, and by the time you read this – a week later – there may be rain lashing the windows and wind growling in the chimneys. Such is the variety we have come to expect...)

But, very occasionally, the summer follows an almost unique pattern. And whether such halcyon summers come in such wide cycles that only the oldest islanders recognise them, or whether there is no real pattern at all, who knows?

One of those golden summers was 1947.

Of course memory plays one false, and it may not have been a blaze of sun for six weeks on end, from mid-July to early September, but, looking back, it seems that way to me.

The mornings that year began usually with sea-haar. There is something mysterious and beautiful about Stromness, when standing on one pier you can't see the piers on either side, or only ghosts of piers. And gulls cry out of the fog. And the Holms are blotted out.

By noon in 1947 the sun had burned the sea-haar away. It lay in dense folded banks beyond Hoy. And all the long afternoon and evening Stromness was lapped in light and heat. Folk swarmed out to the West Shore and Warbeth. There were few cars in those days.

At Warbeth the long line of surf gathered and broke, gathered and broke all afternoon, and the picnics and bathing were parts of a timeless idyll.

We told each other legends – how long the ancient mineshaft was at the far end of the beach, where lead was mined a century and a half before. 'When the miners stopped digging,' we were told, 'they could hear "the tings" (tongs) rattling in the fire-place at Clook farm...'

And we were told that somebody fell over the Black Craig, that loomed in the middle distance westwards, once every seven years ... And we were told that nature had sculpted the profile of Sir Walter Scott on the Kame of Hoy across the Sound – though I never saw any likeness myself...

At late evening the dense fog banks that had been lurking around moved in again. Stromness was a town of ghostly houses, with lost voices calling out of the silence here and there.

So it seemed to go on, day after day, in that *annus mirabilis* of 1947.

The farmers must have been worried at the lack of rain. Mr Cursiter, who kept an eye on the waterworks, must have been worried. But we revelled in the lavish prodigal gold.

A few of us were on the putting green at Ness one afternoon in early September; I rather think it was the day of the Stromness Lammas Market.

A few drops of rain fell on our suntanned hands.

The marvellous six weeks were over. The autumn rains and winds were about to begin.

I'm sure the pattern in 1995 will be quite different. But you never know.

The long summer of '47 was all the more welcome because the preceding winter had been very harsh.

Stromness Votes 'Wet'

13 July 1995

It will soon be time to celebrate – forgive the word, you Temperance folk – the half-centenary of the opening of the first pub in Stromness after the quarter-century drought.

This happened on a Saturday in May, 1948, when there was (I've heard) such an overspilling of beer-men that they were drinking round Alexander Graham's fountain. The bar was at Stromness

Hotel – a long narrow place no longer in use. There was also a 'cocktail bar' where the Flattie Bar is now.

But of course Stromness had not been entirely dry since 1939 when thousands of soldiers set up camps all round the town, and soldiers – as such poets as A. E. Housman remind us – are thirsty men; every camp had its wet canteen, and citizens could drink there, if signed in by a serviceman. There was only beer to drink in the 'Ordinary soldiers' mess', at ninepence a pint.

The young Stromness women weren't seen in such places. They were treated to 'gin-and-its' or various cocktails in the officers' messes – anywhere from Castlegate Camp to Craigmillar Camp, and camps between.

In 1945, the soldiers' camps were 'struck'. The barrels ceased to roll. It was then that the local men realized what thirst was, and they longed for the day of liberation. Simultaneously, the young Stromnessians who had been serving in the Army, Navy, and Air Force began to come home. 'What!' we can almost hear them crying. 'No place to drink, after five years fighting Hitler!'

They weren't long in getting the petitions in order, and signatories for them, proposing that Stromness be no longer a dry town, but have a bar or two like every other village and burgh the length and breadth of Britain.

And so, in November, 1947, Stromness voted itself 'wet' once again – but six months passed before the two bars opened at Stromness Hotel; and Drever and Boyes, licensed grocers, opened their door in Dundas Street.

Things happened fast after that.

The British Legion was set up behind the coal office, where you could play 'housie-housie' (now called, rather flashily, 'bingo') on a Saturday night.

The Royal – that had been Mr Hardy Leask's draper shop – opened in the mid-fifties. It was said to be interiorly designed like a street corner in Hamnavoe, if you allowed your imagination to play with the image freely enough.

There followed the Braes, with its magnificent balcony, a few years later. And later still, the Ferry Inn. And later, the Oakleigh.

(For old chaps like me who liked to drink their pints in a silence broken only by the story or the comment of a drinking friend, all modern bars are spoiled by too much noise in the form of jukeboxes and taped music. But those who are to flourish in the twenty-first century want it that way, and there is nothing left for it but that we old traditionalists seek our silence in other ways. Silence is a wonderful and a blessed condition.)

Of course, many famous hostelries and taverns had been swept away in the 'dry' triumph of the early twenties: all the hotel bars, and far-famed establishments like The White Horse (Maggie Marwick's), Flett's in Dundas Street, Billy Clouston's at the South End, the Masons' Arms, (where, as T. S. Eliot had it concerning Billingsgate, fishmen lounged at noon) ... The smell and taste of such vanished places – their ambience – can never be restored.

Problem of Space and Shelf-room

20 July 1995

When I was young, I thought what a grand thing it would be to have a house full of books.

There were a few books in the house in my childhood – I chiefly remember one called *From Log Cabin to White House*, about the humble beginnings of some American president, possibly Lincoln.

But we were not an illiterate family by any means. My father in his latter days read a book every day from the Library. My brother Norrie had devoured all Dickens' novels by the time he was twelve.

My taste ran more to the productions of the D. C. Thomson house, of Dundee – *The Wizard*, *The Hotspur*, etc. But I borrowed regularly from Peter Esson's Library too, and I was specially fond of stories about English Public Schools. How – aged twelve – I'd have loved to go to a Public School! Now I realise what a lion's den I was spared, judging from the accounts of actual experiences of vulnerable boys in such places. Stromness Primary was not ideal, but a child could always get to the comfort of his own home, and to the freedom of the piers and shores and hills.

In 1935 Penguin books began to be published. I saved sixpence whenever I could to buy a new Penguin. The first Penguin was a biography of Shelley by André Maurois. Penguin number 3 was *Poet's Pub* by Eric Linklater. I still possess both of them – fairly rare items after sixty years, I should think.

So books began to accumulate, all through the forties and fifties and sixties and seventies. Towards the end of the latter decade, the strain was beginning to show. I was rapidly running out of space. Books were coming in, in a steady flow that sometimes increased to a cataract. Bookcases had to be bought at sales, shelves specially built.

And still the books kept flooding in.

People who visited this house in the seventies and eighties remarked on the chaos of books everywhere – as if a literary volcano had erupted and deposited tomes and volumes and pamphlets everywhere, in tottering stacks and strata.

It was proving enormously difficult to find a particular book – up to an hour sometimes.

It was fortunate for me that Brian Murray came to Stromness, and to the rescue. Patiently and expertly he arranged the hundreds of books in order; and still, nowadays, as new deposits of books arrive, he sees to it that everything is under control.

And he has done the same good office for my papers and manuscripts; but that is another story.

The problem of space and shelf-room is not so easily solved.

Occasionally there takes place a pruning of books, a culling. There are many books in my house that I know I'll never want to read again. Eventually they will go.

I suppose, if I was pressed hard enough, I would agree that I could see my time out with forty or fifty much-loved books. Why not read those great utterances over and over? We don't think it wrong to play music tapes twenty or a hundred times.

Besides, there are far too many books being published.

Cricket in the Rain

27 July 1995

Down came the rain, a steady 'outcast', as we drove back from a car-tour of the West Mainland last Saturday afternoon, my two friends from Oxford and myself.

Earlier, there had been sun. We had lunch at Merkister. The bar was full of trout-fishers. Was it too bright maybe for fishing?

There, outside Merkister, was the Orkney flag flying, based obviously on the Scandinavian flags, a cross with the transverse elongated.

It was mild – I half expected thunder – there were clouds building up from the east, battleship-grey clouds. They covered the sun. Rain began to fall steadily.

Setting out soon after 1pm from Stromness, we had observed that a cricket match was in progress at the Academy playing field.

(The delicate summer plant, cricket, had been rooted in Stromness since last summer. Could it flourish in our wet windy climate?)

The cricket match was still going on, in the rain, as we came home.

My Oxford friends, Hugo and Magnus, are both interested in cricket, so we stopped the car beside the cricket pitch, in the pouring rain.

When you watch cricket on TV, as soon as there are a few drops of rain, the merest sprinkle of a passing shower, the players make for the pavilion and the groundsmen are out, unrolling the covers.

The northern cricketers are made of sterner stuff. Down fell the rain, heavier than ever, but the game went on. The bowlers bowled, the batsmen defended their wickets and frequently had the fielders chasing over the wet grass after well-struck balls.

Nor did the waiting batsmen, and the supporters, have any cover. But they stood there stoically, waiting their turn to bat, applauding the boundaries and the single runs. And all of them must have been wet to the skin.

Some of the cricketers were far from home, too. It was an Orkney v Caithness match, a kind of warm-up for the real Test which would be played the following day, Sunday.

Well, I thought, it's time those brave cricketers had a shed or a hut to shelter in, on such rainy afternoons.

'Play up, play up, and play the game', was a poem we learned at school, aged nine or ten, and we knew next to nothing about the game called cricket that was being celebrated: chiefly, the poet Newbolt argued, that it imbued the nascent spirit of boys with grit and character.

The poet Newbolt should have seen the cricketers of Orkney and Caithness at play, in really adverse conditions. For in the softer milder regions of the South, as soon as a passing cloud bursts, like a bag of raindrops, off go the intrepid sportsmen to pavilion or tent.

Nay – as prose-writers used to exclaim, but don't any longer – nay, let but a batsman or a bowler complain of 'bad light' (a thin haar drifting over the sun) and the umpires consult their light-meters and off they all troop till the sky is clear again.

But those Orkney cricketers, one feels, would bowl and bat through hurricanes or earthquakes.

A Bleak Magisterial Voice

3 August 1995

It's said – and truly – we never think about time in childhood: or if we do, it's in a way quite different from time as adults experience it.

Edwin Muir said it wonderfully: 'My brothers and sisters were new creatures like myself, not in time (for time still sat on the wrist of each day with its wings folded) but in a vast boundless calm ... as if there were only one day endlessly rising and setting. Our first childhood is the only time in our lives when we exist within immortality'...

I suppose no one can pinpoint the day when we change from the child's view of time to the adult's.

But I remember an afternoon in July, maybe in 1931 or 1932. We – a few boys and myself – were returning from a happy afternoon at Warbeth. (It was a delight in those days to run or saunter all the way to Warbeth and back.)

A boy said, 'In three weeks, we'll be back at the school.'

Three weeks! Up to that time, three weeks had been almost an eternity. The notion of 'three weeks' had had little meaning for us. We existed in the heart of each day – of each hour, in fact – whether we were happy or miserable. But happiness outweighed our misery, by far.

But that bright afternoon, the words, 'In three weeks we'll be back at the school', fell out of nowhere like a sudden chill. It was a bleak magisterial voice – though a boy had uttered the words carelessly – and I heard it as a prisoner in the dock might hear a sentence passed on him.

In three weeks we would all be back where we did not want to be. (School, I know, is not so much of a prison nowadays.)

But that innocent summer afternoon, I must have passed from child-time into man-time, where everything begins to be different.

I don't at all mean that life began to be hard and difficult from that day on.

Not at all; it was just a passing cloud, one 'shade of the prison-house'...

I'm sure the next three weeks of the summer holiday were filled with the Warbeth rockpools, fishing sillocks and crabs at Gray's Pier, buying pennyworths of sweeties at Hutchison's or Ma Couper's, driving in Tommy Firth's milk-cart from Castle Farm, blowing dandelion clocks, rowing out into the *Ola*'s bow-wave, scrambling among the ruined walls of the Holms, watching the English tourist-ladies as they sat painting watercolours of Melvin Place, kicking a twopenny ball in the narrow field above the Temperance Hall, enjoying ham-and-egg for dinner on Monday (washing day) and kippers for tea.

And all this in the freedom of no shoes or stockings. Sandals, maybe, if it was 'a coorse[1] day': but I don't remember any coorse days (though there must have been as many in those far-off summers as now).

After that ominous mention of 'three weeks till school', the sands began to drop inexorably through the hour-glass. We were conscious as never before of time passing – Two weeks'... 'A week'... 'Four days'... 'The morn'...

There they were waiting for us one morning, the shoes and the stockings for going to school, and the decent breeks and jersey.

There they were, waiting to be put on, the shackles and the chains; and the gate of the prison open to receive us.

Packaged Goods

10 August 1995

I seem to spend a good deal of time wrestling with packaging.

The manufacturers of foodstuffs have wrapped up all their goods so efficiently, it seems as difficult as for a burglar to break into a house.

There I – and I'm sure a thousand others – stand before breakfast-time, trying to break into a pristine box of tea-bags. I nearly break my fingernails. There seems to be no way in. I know there is a little blue tag that ought, gently pulled, to let me in. No, it is as unyielding as the rest of the transparent armour! Finally I jag it with scissors, and then I can break through to the packet. But it is such a crude way of going about it, I am half ashamed and half irritated.

1 foul (of weather)

And, of course, it isn't only tea-bags. Cornflakes, oatcakes, pies ... They might say it's hygienic packaging, but a ten-minute wrestle with the more obdurate of those packets is not good for the soul.

I have a problem with milk cartons, too. (Who hasn't?) More than one splurge of milk has leapt out on to the floor before I effected entry (as they say in lawcourts). All's changed, with milk, from the days when I poured milk from Tommy Firth of Castle Farm's tin pail into the jugs on the doorsteps, covered with a saucer and two pennies. (For twopence was the price of a pint in those days.)

Nowadays, parcels arrive with an immense amount of green sticky tape around them. I have, in the last few years wrestled with such mummified parcels for twenty minutes or so before they yielded. Sometimes, if I'm tired, I give up the struggle till the next morning when I feel fresher.

I long, in the midst of such frustration, for the parcels of my youth, that arrived tied excellently with string. Most people made a good job of tying parcels in those days... The more reckless recipients cut the string with scissors. The cannier folk undid the string knot by knot, and put it by in a tea caddy, for 'You never know when it'll come in handy.'

When I trotted into the grocer's shop, aged five or six, at my mother's heels, it was like going into a cave of sweet smells: apples, tea, biscuits, liquorice, treacle. There was no pre-packaging in those days. The kind shopkeeper with his silver spectacles weighed out everything on his scales, then emptied the purchase into a stout brown-paper poke, and tucked the lugs in securely. Of course every purchase took some time, but that was part of the joy of shopping.

Finally, to seal the bargain, the grocer put his hand into the sweetie-jar and came up with a couple of butter-nuts or cream caramels, and gave them to me for nothing.

That Saturday evening – for my mother did her shopping about 8pm – I would have sworn that there was no more delightful man in the world than Geordie Spence the grocer in his peedie shop in John Street.

Peter Esson

24 August 1995

Someone has asked me to write a note about Peter Esson, to be included in an anthology of poetical epitaphs over the centuries. Why, readers of the anthology would want to know, write a poem about such a man?

Even in Stromness, nowadays, most people don't know who Peter Esson was... But, fifty years ago, every Stromnessian knew.

He had a small tailor shop at the foot of the Kirk Road, its door opening on to the street.

I visited there from the age of four onwards, because my father worked part-time beside Peter and his brother Willie Esson and his daughter Effie Esson.

There I went on urgent feet every Friday to get what those tailors called my 'pension', a halfpenny: immediately translated into sweeties at Janetta Sinclair's sweetie shop on the other side of the street.

In the evening men would drop by and sit on Peter's bench. Most of them were retired seamen. The stories went on for hours. (When those legends were being wrought, I was of course curled up in bed at home.)

Tailoring was a trade in decline in the twenties and thirties. People were buying their suits ready-made.

So Peter had a secondary job. He was the town librarian, issuing books twice a week – I think, Wednesdays and Saturdays – from the library that is still there at the foot of Hellihole Road. Peter and his wife lived in the flat above.

But tailoring and giving out books were, in a sense, secondary mundane activities.

The most important place in Peter Esson's life was the Free Kirk that towered over the adjacent buildings, including the tailor shop.

It might be said that Peter was acquainted with every stone in that building. He revered it, with a deep devotion. He knew all the ministers who had led worship there. (In fact, I have never known anyone who was so thoroughly acquainted with the highly complex history of Presbyterianism in Scotland, with all its schisms and branchings and reunions over four centuries.)

Peter was a Kirk elder. The expression on his face on Sundays seemed to be different from on the other days. There was a kind of earnestness and veneration.

Towards the end of each week the minister, Rev James Christie, entered the tailor shop carrying a bill concerning the Sunday service for Peter to put in his window. That was always a hushed half-minute in the general tone of genial levity that prevailed, until Mr Christie left again.

I have had to indicate something of the above – but far more briefly – in the note to be appended to the sonnet I wrote called 'The Death of Peter Esson, Tailor, Librarian, Free Kirk Elder', written soon after that most worthy Stromnessian died in 1954, I think.

Stromness Water

7 September 1995

Strange, how we take the simplest natural things for granted, like water.

There's no need ever to worry about water, we think. There's always plenty of rain in Orkney and the north. Too much, in fact, when the dark clouds pile up for days on end and discharge their cargoes.

It was only towards the end of August that some of us began to worry, and not only the gardeners and farmers. Weeks of hot bright days in succession, blue skies, the sun wheeling up near the zenith. A delight to children – who never worry about anything, anyway – but a matter of some concern to elderly people who are inclined to worry about too many things.

Thoughts like this come into the mind. 'What if this drought went on for months? What if the bottles of the heavens were stayed, indefinitely (as it says somewhere in Scripture)?... It is not inconceivable, considering the frightful insults we are subjecting the atmosphere to.

There was a fisherman in Stromness who said, two generations ago, that the weather had not been the same since they invented wireless!

There have been severe droughts in Orkney – such as 'the year of the short corn' some time in the nineteenth century.

I think there are enough deep wells in the islands to see us through the driest of times.

But think of the great cities of the south, with their millions of people. Faced with a ruinous shortage of water, what mass panics and stampedes would break out everywhere!

As I write, it seems that the first rainclouds might be moving in from the Atlantic.

❁

One thing about a dry time is that we learn, some of us for the first time, what a beautiful and precious thing water is.

I think I got to know this in Rackwick thirty years ago, when I had to cross two fields with plastic buckets to fill up at the burn. This had to be done at least three times a day ... it was no burden, it was a delightful ritual – much more meaningful than turning on a tap in the council house at Well Park, Stromness.

It is easy, of course, to romanticise. A century ago Stromness was crowded with public wells, with women queuing up to draw water, and all kinds of unspeakable effluvia were leaching into some of those wells, according to the public health officials who were reporting on the situation in those days,

So, up at The Loons the great reservoir was constructed (which we always knew as 'the waterworks') and the good and the bad wells were closed down, one after the other, until only Login's Well at the South End is left, as a tourist attraction.

There is another, on the road near Broonstoon farm, and it was called 'the mineral well' when I was a boy. More than once I was sent to this well with a tin pail, because some of the old folk swore by its curative properties. (I think my mother drank it for her asthma, which troubled her most summers.)

'The mineral well' tumbled into ruins, but now I'm glad to say that a few years ago it was built up again. The well head is there but is there water inside?... I don't suppose, in this scientific age, it would stand much chance against aspirin and bronchodilators.

I thought of the first rainclouds, a week ago, as friends, when they came out of the Atlantic at last.

A Magical Day

14 September 1995

I wonder how many Stromnessians remembered that yesterday (Tuesday, September 5) was Stromness Lammas Market Day?

I myself only remembered just in time.

But anyway, it didn't matter, because not a vestige of it remains, except (fleetingly) in the memories of a few aged townsfolk.

And this is a great pity, because the Lammas Market was a magical day – as wonderful in its way as Christmas – almost as lyrical as the first day of the summer holidays.

It began with the neighbours giving you 'a fairing', some a sixpence that shone like a star. Talk about people winning the National Lottery! We had been saving up for a few weeks, we might have as much as three or four or five shillings in our pockets – we felt as rich as Rockefeller or Croesus!

It was a holiday from the school, of course.

As I drifted north from the quietude of Melvin Place, the crowds on the street thickened, and near the Pier Head I thought all of Orkney must be there! The buses from Birsay and Orphir were bringing in the country folk, and the folk from the South Isles had landed from the *Hoy Head*, or smaller boats... It was hard for a small boy to wend his way through.

And there, suddenly, was the Fair in all its breathtaking delight! First, at the Custom-house wall, the sellers of fruit and sweeties. Pitched, perilously, on the seaward side, were the shooting booths, offering gaudy prizes.

Against the North of Scotland Shipping office, the 'roll-the-penny' stalls – the strength machine where you struck a wedge with a wooden mallet and, if it was struck powerfully enough, a bell rang at the top of a column... Also, there was the Prince of the Congo who licked a red-hot poker and said in a deep rich voice, 'Sugar!'... But dominating this section of the Market was a stout red-faced angry-voiced man who whirled a roulette wheel and was forever barking, 'Last card!... Last card!'

Under the Warehouse wall was the coconut shy... A veiled mysterious lady read fortunes, if you first crossed her hand with silver. Girls came and went, giggling, from her booth.

Poised above the inner harbour were the swingboats, twopence a ride. Most boys delighted in those airy ups-and-downs. But the one and only time I tried, I felt frightened and sick, and was never so glad to step on solid land again!

Further on, at the North Pier, were the spectaculars, which might be a travelling boxing booth, or else the Wall of Death, with Smoky Joe speeding round and round the perpendicular wooden wall on his motorbike. 'A mile a minute!' cried the booth man... How could any mortal hurtle along sideways at a mile a minute? It was a marvel to us boys.

Along the South Pier was a line of Indians selling silks from open suitcases.

Round Graham's fountain a 'cheap-John' dazzled the crowd with cascades of beguiling verbiage.

Through it all walked Guilio Fuggaccia, with his hound and his ice-cream barrow, intoning, 'Cheap today, free tomorrow.'

There was also a little photographer who darted here and there taking instant photographs.

Most mysterious and poignant of all was the blind fiddler, who took another route through the crowds.

All this took place, for small boys, in a storm of sweeties, fruit, ice-cream, lemonade, apples, chocolate.

Going home for dinner (1pm) and tea (5pm) were resented necessities. We wanted back to the place of magic.

And the early autumn darkness came down, and then, yet another enchantment, Naphtha flares were lit here and there at the fairground!

Weary, penniless, surfeited with sensual luxuries, we dragged home to bed. No home lessons done, and the prison-house of school to be faced in the morning.

We did not know – innocents that we were – that we had been participants in one of the great feasts of the year – *Hlaf*(loaf)*mas*, a time of rejoicing that our winter bread had been secured, after harvest.

Earl Rognvald's Commission

28 September 1995

The most intriguing character in the *Orkneyinga Saga*, I think, is Rognvald Kolson, Earl of Orkney. He was a man of many talents, as he tells us (not boastfully) in one of his poems – 'Chessboard, tilt-yard, trout stream, ski slopes, I'm a master at those. I can sail a boat and play the harp. I'm a blacksmith too, not at all afraid of hard work...'

He took pride in all that he undertook, including labour with hammer and anvil, and fishing with his fishermen.

Earl Rognvald's two great undertakings were the building of the Cathedral in honour of his uncle, St Magnus – and the crusade with fifteen ships to Jerusalem in 1151–54.

A marvellous book could be written about this greatest of Orcadians; but it will have to wait for a younger writer than me, and one with knowledge of ships and architecture and the complex politics of the Mediterranean lands in the twelfth century.

Until that historian comes along, I sometimes imagine Rognvald Kolson writing a letter to a master mason in England, inviting him to make the hazardous voyage north to Orkney, him and all his workmen in stone.

Who were those church builders? A great number of magnificent churches were being built all over England and Scotland in the twelfth century. Were there teams of travelling masons who went from bishopric to bishopric building only churches?

Earl Rognvald probably reckoned that not many church builders would want to travel so far; so he would have used golden words in his letter. Such as: 'You build great poems in stone, and your fame has travelled into our northern seas. I am telling you this, for I am a poet myself, only I deal in harp-strokes that die on the air almost as soon as they are uttered... Renowned builder of churches, it is not among savages you will be coming, but among civilised and hospitable men. You and your subordinate poets-in-stone will be well looked after while the work is in progress, and you will be paid regularly golden crown pieces... This kirk in Orkney is no mere whim on my part, or the Bishop's, but I know that in England you have heard of the blessed martyr Magnus of Orkney. The kirk is in honour of Magnus, and "to the greater glory of God". It is time.

You and your masons will have a few more grey hairs by the time the choir is built, but builders in generations to come will follow your master-plan (making due allowance for changing modes and fashions)... Sir, we have here quarries of the best stone, including the fine red sandstone of Eday island, which is the colour of fire and blood, the hue of martyrdom... If you and your workmen were to come in carts to the shore of Leith in Scotland, with ladders, scaffolding, plumblines, squares, compasses, planes, nails, chisels, hammers, a fine ship will be there on Easter Monday – St Magnus day – to carry you across the North Sea to Orkney... As soon as the foundation is laid I intend to sail to Jerusalem, with fifteen ships, for a blessing on this undertaking of ours. For this venture also, charts will have to be made. Word has come to me that you have lately been working on a magnificent minster in Durham. Your fame has gone before you.

'I have entrusted this letter to a reliable skipper. A horseman will meet him at Lindisfarne, and bear this plea and invitation the rest of the way to Durham...'

Reading for Winter

5 October 1995

You notice it now, how chilly it is in the morning when you get out of bed and come downstairs. It will soon be time, after the long warm summer, to switch on the storage heaters.

And you notice, in the evening, the shadows gathering earlier and earlier. Winter is there, just under the horizon. We are – as I write – a week past the equinox, that marvellous fulcrum of the year when light and darkness hang in perfect equipoise all over the world.

It is time to make plans for reading in the long winter nights – though reading gets more and more fractured by watching worthwhile programmes on TV, like *Pride and Prejudice* and *People's Century* and nature programmes by the likes of Attenborough.

Also, I've discovered over the decades that the list of winter books you draw up is rarely adhered to. Other books are brought to your attention, or tentatively bought or borrowed, and generally these are the books that, unexpectedly, make the profoundest impression. (I can think of one immediately, *The Third Policeman* by Flann O'Brien, that seems to me one of the great novels of our time, a vision of hell that is, at the same time, extraordinarily funny... The Irish are particularly good at this interweaving of sorrow and laughter.)

But, to draw up a tentative list.

I suppose one should read a Shakespeare play. How about *Antony and Cleopatra*? Last year it was *Hamlet*.

I have often thought about Boswell and Johnson's different accounts of their journey together through the Highlands in the late eighteenth century. I have never tackled the complete Oxford edition, any more than I've read Boswell's *Life of Johnson*: which is, after all, a book to dip into.

(One recent winter I neglected Orwell's famous *Nineteen Eighty-Four* and *Animal Farm*, the two famous Orwell novels, in favour of one with an unalluring title *Coming Up for Air*, and found it much much better. With books, you are constantly getting surprises.)

There are so many things you feel you ought to read; and, tasting, have found difficult. I don't think I've managed to read one D. H. Lawrence novel right through (except *Chatterley*), but his short stories and his magnificent nature poems, and his letters, are endlessly fascinating.

Should one have another go at 'A Drunk Man Looks at the Thistle'? Better stick with the jewels that stud that long MacDiarmid poem here and there ... Nor would it be advisable to read Edwin Muir's *Collected Poems* from beginning to end. There are the twenty or thirty poems to marvel at – 'The Labyrinth', 'The Transfiguration', 'The Return of the Greeks' ('The veteran Greeks came home...').

And what of the Americans? A decade ago, I was sent a copy of Flannery O'Connor's *Collected Short Stories*, each one a galvanic shock... But maybe there's enough gloom in Europe and Asia to be going on with.

Dickens? Two winters ago I read *Bleak House*. There remain many unread Dickens novels.

Scott? Nothing doing! We were overfed on 'the Wizard of the North' at school in the thirties. Last winter, for the fourth desperate time, I gave *The Pirate* – about Shetland and Orkney – another go. And I don't propose to read it any winter more.

Old Games in Stromness

12 October 1995

Do they play the old games in Stromness, the kids, now October is here and the nights are drawing in?

The equinoctial gales are past, and there's a brief mild spell lasting ten days or two weeks before the Hallowe'en storms begin: what we know as the peedie summer – a mild mellow time when there's still a kindling in the sun and the last leaves on the tree remember, wanly, the lost glories of summer.

We remember those evenings of peedie summer, when we closed our homework books and jotters early and went out into the gathering shadows of October.

We played very ancient games like 'Hide-and-seek' and 'Leave-O', that must have been played, in one form or another, for generations, maybe for centuries.

Perhaps they were ancestral memories of war and the hunt. 'Hide-and-seek' was a simple game. The central figure, the hunter, stood at a wall with his eyes covered while his companions scattered here and there, in some doorway or close-end. The seeker counted to 'ten' or 'twenty', aloud – then he turned and set out on the chase... The idea was to touch as many players as possible, but the players had to elude capture and return unhindered to the wall or the stone where it all began. Then they had won, then they had got their freedom.

It was possible to play many games of 'hide-and-seek' before hunger and weariness took us home for supper. Supper could be toast and cocoa, or there might be tatties left over from dinner-time to fry.

'Leave-O' was a more far-flung game, in which greater distances were covered and the hunt was more complicated... I don't quite remember the sequence of 'moves', and I wonder if it is still played...

Sometimes, the demon of mischief would get into us boys, and then we thought it great fun to knock at people's doors and run away – but not so far away that we lost the pleasure of watching the householder or his wife opening the door and finding nobody there.

There was a very cruel game whereby we fixed a black thread to a knocker; it would only work with houses that had knockers; and then, holding the other end of the thread, we played the trick. Only in this game it was more cruel and maddening, for no sooner had the old person gone back in, baffled, but 'rat-tat-tat!' went the knocker again, and again.

This we thought was the height of amusement.

But I remember the look of anger, mixed with fear, on the face of one old woman in Dundas Street.

Such tricks constituted more than a nuisance, they were a cruel menace. I hope nothing like that is played any more by the kids of Hamnavoe.

But such were a few of our pastimes before the snow came in December and we blew the cobwebs away from our sledges and 'clogs'.

Skills and Schools

19 October 1995

Wednesday, October 4. I made a pot of soup today, the first for almost a year – so many kind friends invite me out for lunch; and much appreciated they are.

I made my Scotch broth the easy way, using two beef stock cubes, and chopping up a huge Langskaill tattie (unpeeled) and a carrot and two onions, and of course half a cup of 'broth mix'... The result was delicious – I'm glad I hadn't lost the touch – and I had it with thick buttered oatcakes... There's enough broth left over for another meal.

Thursday, October 5. Time to switch on the storage heaters, after the warm summer that is just petering out.

Another skill I have obviously lost is setting and lighting the fire. That's because my good neighbour Brian has done it every morning this while past. Afterwards we sit and drink a cup of tea beside the new flames, and talk about such things as football, poetry, etc.

But the fire-attendant has gone south on Council business, so I have had to be seeing to the fire myself.

This morning it was maddening! I tried twice, and twice after abundant flames and smoke, the fire died on me. I know what happened. In my impatience I poured on too much coal and choked it.

In the end, Margaret, who cleans my house so efficiently every Thursday afternoon, got it going, while I was up at Quildon enjoying another good lunch.

Friday, October 6. How age steals up on you, like a sinister thief.

I had a lot of things to see to in the town. Five years ago, it would have been an enjoyable outing.

It was about the start of 'the peedie summer' and I had put my winter cardigan and jacket on, plus a Pakamac in case it came on to rain.

After I had got all my messages in two bulging plastic bags, it was time to turn for home.

It was a warm windy afternoon, and the half-gale kept whipping the loose Pakamac from my shoulders, and the two bags got heavier and heavier.

Getting near Mayburn at last, I was trudging doggedly like Scott groaning towards the South Pole in 1912.

I was glad to lie down for two hours.

The right way is not to complain, but to be glad that there are messages to buy, and that you have enough money to pay for them; and that, being tired, you have a comfortable bed to lie down on.

Saturday, October 7. What lovely schools there are nowadays, compared to 1926 when I first sat in Miss Matheson's classroom.

The new Stenness Primary School is a small marvel of school planning, full of light and variety and colour; a youngster not stimulated in such surroundings would be 'dull of soul' indeed!

Later that afternoon, under the sun, we saw the rampant shining waves throwing themselves from the open brimming Atlantic on the beach at Warbeth...

At night I caught a glimpse of the full moon on the harbour water. It was pure enchantment, seeing it unexpectedly through the uncurtained window.

A London publisher has sent me a new book called *Sleeping with an Elephant* by Ludovic Kennedy.

Parts of it are very interesting, e.g. the story of Bonnie Prince Charlie and the 1745 Rebellion.

The author, aware – as we all must be – of the romantic handsome tragic prince who almost seized the throne for his father, concentrates on 'the downside' – his stubbornness, his incipient alcoholism, his lack of gratitude to the Highlanders who fought so loyally for him... All true; but yet the heroism and splendour remain, especially when he was being hunted like a fugitive through the islands of the west; the prince's constant cheerfulness – and he had been brought up in luxury in Italy and France – in the teeth of hardships that would have broken most men.

On Being Seventy-four

26 October 1995

Yesterday I was seventy-four, and when I was twenty-four I never thought to see such an advanced age.

And when I was fourteen there were a few old old men on the Stromness Street, with white whiskers, seventy-year-olds toiling along on a stick. And you thought nothing of them – they were just there, along with small children and shopkeepers and housewives, unchanging. Only, you could never conceive of yourself being one of the ancients.

On my mother's fortieth birthday, I being then ten, I remember thinking, 'What an old woman she is now!' Anybody over thirty-five was entering the autumn of life.

Once over seventy – 'the allotted span', as folk used to call it – you realise what a clutter of material objects you have surrounded yourself with – books, music tapes, plates, writing material, cushions and curtains and blankets, coats, a drawer overflowing with socks, enough sweaters and gansies[1] to stock a little wool shop. And more, much more... It's all nonsense; how can you wear more than one jersey at a time? It's impossible that all those hundreds of books will ever be read again – a few will, but most of them are building sites for spiders' webs.

So I resolve, once a week on an average, to get rid of a lot of that superfluous junk, mindful of what Shakespeare said: 'Thou bear'st thy heavy riches but a journey, / And death unloads thee...'

But mostly I forget, and sit comfortably among increasing accumulations, until the day before my birthday this mid-October, when I began to be showered with goodies.

There was a new life of D. H. Lawrence, a thick fat book, for which there is really no room at all on my shelves. That was from a good friend in Manchester, Dave Brock, a great admirer of Lawrence. And then came a big wadded bag containing tapes of all of Mahler's symphonies, a new interpretation (though I have most of them already, in other styles and modes...). And cakes, lovely

---

1 guernseys (seamen's jerseys)

wine glasses and whisky glasses, and candles. And a storm of birthday cards and letters that left me dizzy and disorientated.

Best to go to bed and forget about all that goodwill, all those luxuries, for an hour or two. But even in bed there was no let-up. Whenever drowsiness promised, 'falling shade by shade,' the bedside phone would startle me 'like a guilty thing surprised...'

As for the birthday weather, it was a rather ferocious day, with blusters of tempest and torrents of rain, and bright brief sunbursts between.

'Do not tell me about the wisdom of old men,' said T. S. Eliot, oversetting a whole superstructure of lore about age and wisdom that goes back to the Old Testament and beyond. T. S. Eliot is quite right in a way. What one does get more clear-sighted about is the folly, vanity, waste, cruelty, injustice, the evil woven into time and history, that shows no sign of amelioration – matters one knew and accepted fairly cheerfully for the first fifty years: but now matters like Yugoslavia, Rwanda, terrorism, cast more sombre shadows.

It seems we might have to wait a long time for Burns' prophecy to come to pass – 'Man to man, the world o'er / Shall brithers be, for a' that...'

It will be – the men of vision, Isaiah, Shakespeare, Blake, Burns, will be proved right. But not this year, or the next, I think.

Stormy Nights

2 November 1995

On Tuesday, there was a snell wind from the east, that didn't let up all day.

It was still blowing hard when I went to bed at midnight. There had been rain, too – the street at the South End was all dark gleaming mirrors.

The storm must have worsened in the night, because next morning when I was getting my few messages, the women were saying here and there, 'What a night it was!'...'What wind!'...'There were slates blown off the roofs!'...

I had slept through it all. In fact, I slept an hour or two longer than usual, till 7am rather than two hours earlier. I'm glad about that, because I don't like storms any more. Inside the house I get uneasy like a cat or a dog, who can sense storms in their bloodstreams long before human beings (our instincts rendered dull by the trappings of 'civilisation').

All children, on the other hand, love storms. Among the happier memories of childhood is lying in bed listening to the black storm outside raging among the chimney-pots and setting the waves a-surge against the piers below... There was a feeling of utter warmth and security; then the kindliness and gentleness of sleep.

I wasn't in Orkney for the great tempest of January 1952. I was reading a book inside Newbattle Abbey College when a fellow student told me what he had just heard on the radio, that Orkney had been half ruined by a storm. I said something like, 'We get a dozen or so of them every winter.'

But, even at Newbattle, in the mild Lothians, we must have been on the fringes of that tyrant among storms, because the big old beech tree in the garden, that seemed so firm-rooted, was blown down.

As more news of storm damage came on the radio, our warden, Edwin Muir, seemed fascinated, remembering the storms he experienced in childhood in Wyre and Garth and had written about in *The Story and The Fable*. ('What a night! How the wind whips the pane!') Later, there was a radio programme about the storm in Orkney. Willa Muir was very much entranced by the story of the old spinster's love letters that had been blown all over the island. (But that story had a sad touching side to it, as well as being comical – the spilling of heart's treasure...)

Anyway, the tempest of early Wednesday morning was a feather in the wind compared to the henhouse-wrecking blowster of January 1952.

When I got up at 8am, the harbour was all a-glitter with sun – it might even have been a day in 'peedie summer'. But the clouds gathered and the wind freshened all day, and by mid-evening was moaning in the lum again.

I had had the foresight to make a small pot of Scotch broth – the easy way, with a stock cube.

Broth is one of our defences against winter. And porridge too – come November, I'll make porridge for breakfast some mornings, well salted. And now comes in the clapshot season too, when the neeps are ready to mell with the tatties, with a golden wedge of butter to crown and mell with all.

Sudden Small Disablings

9 November 1995

After the first rains of autumn, the windows of the house are glued tight all winter till April.

This means of course that smells of broth, candle smoke, soot, fish linger for days in the house, without the sweet clean airs of heaven moving through.

Occasionally I keep the front door open – when the wind isn't in the north – and then there is a movement of air, a brief cleansing.

At the same time as the windows glue up, the storage heaters have to be turned on (having lain dormant all summer). You come down to a warm living-room in the mornings but of course the heart of the house never really begins to heat until Brian applies a match to the newsprint and driftwood and coal.

I watched the last part of *Pride and Prejudice* last Sunday, in common with ten million other people.

It is a sumptuous production – all those grand houses and Regency costumes helped with the tortuous stylised love story.

I could not help thinking: how strange those people are, in their bubble of time and class and custom, so hugely different to life as it has been lived in Orkney for centuries.

We seemed to be looking at creatures who lived on a different planet.

I had to read all Jane Austen in Edinburgh, and I never got hooked on her.

But it was a sumptuous production and enjoyable.

Age doesn't steal on a person gradually. It is more disconcerting – a series of sudden small disablings and put-downs.

A year ago I could walk to the Pier Head and back without undue effort. Quite suddenly it has become like one of the labours of Hercules.

One should be able to get on to the rocking-chair and enjoy a good rest, after such a footslog. But no – nothing doing. A stiffness has gotten into the lower back. And you can twist and turn as you please – there is relief for only five seconds or so before the clamps are put on you again.

I'm not complaining: a hundred ills have passed me by. Those that do afflict are of the minor sort, that can be cured by a couple of aspirins (though I haven't tried that yet). Blindness, deafness, gout, poor appetite, sleeplessness – Shakespeare's 'age, ache, penury, and imprisonment' – have hardly touched me, or only glanced in passing.

As the old folk used to say, 'We hev a lot to be thankful for...' But I was a boy when that wisdom was uttered; and the words made no sense to me.

For a few nights past there have been bangs and cracks in the darkness outside – the young folk getting into their stride for Hallowe'en.

I had a visitor last night, on actual Hallowe'en, who had been trying to phone from the phonebox below. And behold, he discovered his hands covered with stickiness: treacle and flour.

I didn't hear the swish of broomsticks passing over my house, the witches going on to their coven.

I'm sure Bessie Millie, the seller of winds, was resting in peace at Warbeth.

Poetry in Words and Football

16 November 1995

How baffling it is – what a waste of time – to lose one's reading glasses!

The longer you look in the obvious places, and fail, the more infuriated you get!

I had them on a half-hour before... They must be somewhere close at hand... Without the reading glasses, I'm a fish out of water; I can neither read nor write.

Last Thursday morning I lost such a lot of precious time looking for them.

And there – when bafflement had reached danger level – there the spectacles were, lying innocently on a pile of music tapes...

What a joy!

The solution is, always put your glasses down on one definite place – then there will be none of this trouble.

A simple solution. Only I've given myself the same sage advice a thousand times in the past, in vain.

A sports editor has asked for a Christmas story that should have a football match in it... I got the same request last year, and after a half-hour of puzzlement (how can one yoke together Christmas and football?) I managed to come up with something acceptable.

The bird sings a passable tune from the page, as the winged pen passes.

But how to do it a second time? I thought of the Ba' game in Kirkwall. That, by the way, featured in a recent TV programme on the history of football...

Anyway, I made a start yesterday, and it might just work.

There has been a lot about Keats in 'the media' recently, because it is two hundred years since 'the marvellous boy' was born in London. He died in Rome, aged twenty-five.

Into one year – 1818 – he crammed the greatest of his poetry – 'Hyperion', the five odes, 'Isabella', 'The Eve of St Agnes'. His manuscripts 'Hold, like full garners the full-ripened grain'.

Keats is the poet who fascinated me at the very beginning, in school, where we read 'Ode to a Nightingale' and 'La Belle Dame sans Merci'.

The words were intoxicating, like wine. I went about the house muttering over and over these magical phrases: 'beaded bubbles winking at the brim...'; 'The sedge is withered from the lake, / And no birds sing...'

It is only much later, when the first effervescence has died down, that the wisdom of the poetry communicates itself, gem by gem, nugget by nugget. 'Beauty is truth, truth beauty...'

To end with football, which was my great love before I encountered Keats and the 'pale kings and princes' of poetry.

It was sad to see last week, the great Scottish teams – Rangers and Celtic – so humiliated (and at home too) by Continental teams.

The Continental footballers have achieved a level of pure artistry which either we never had, or have lost in the last decade or two.

It was poetry, in a way, to see how the Italians and the French wove the fabric of the game with skilful open well-directed passes – no movement but had a thought behind it – and so built up to inevitable goals, and victory.

Come soon to poor Scotland, another Jock Stein.

Withered Leaf of Memory

23 November 1995

I've been lucky with my reading lately. In early autumn I enjoyed very much *Native Stranger* by Alastair Scott, which begins in Shetland and Orkney and perambulates all over Scotland, the author going with a bike and a tent and a little cooker. It is a very funny book. Three locations out of a possible hundred were done on TV; so much fine material had to be left out.

A few weeks later, the post brought Ludovic Kennedy's *Sleeping With an Elephant* (the elephant being a simile for England, a constant irritant to the bedmate Scotland). It is another alert intelligent estimate of late-twentieth-century Scotland ('Stands Scotland where she did?'...). History keeps intruding, as it ought to – we are given refreshing profiles of Mary Queen of Scots (the tragic woman), of her direct descendant Bonnie Prince Charlie (another tragic Stuart), of Burns and Scott and Hume, etc.

Last weekend I was given a loan of a truly wonderful travel book, *The City of Djinns*, by William Dalrymple. The city in question is the capital of India, Delhi, which has been conquered and destroyed and rebuilt times without number – in which many glorious and many horrible things have been done – and which still lives in the fascinating characters, Hindu and Moslem and Sikh, that Dalrymple met and mingled with familiarly, only a couple of years ago.

The City of Djinns is as good a travel book as I have read.

I think I must have met the author, when he was still a very young man, a dozen or so years ago in Orkney, when he was here with a group of archaeologists, staying at Binscarth. (But then my memory is such a withered leaf nowadays that it may have been quite a different person that I met...)

Workmen are busy putting a new roof on the Museum, just across the street from me.

In the storms of last winter the roof was getting dangerous, with old slates whirling away on the wind.

Maybe now it will last for another century.

Strange, how one tends to ignore precious buildings next door. I have been making a mental note for weeks, to visit the Museum and see the new extension, which is very fine by all reports. (That was another date I forgot recently, to go to the official opening of the Pilot's House, etc... It is galling, to be reminded about those things a day or two later... The memory again – another withered leaf.)

Many memorable things have happened in that museum in the South End. Originally it was more than just a museum. The amazing exhibits were lodged upstairs. The ground floor was the Town Hall, where public meetings were held – where the magistrates of Stromness sat in judgement on delinquent townsmen – where the historic meetings of the Crofters' Commission sat, and the crofters came with their complaints from the parishes of the west, and the South Isles – where John Johnston gave graphic lectures of his life in the Indian Army, and in Africa under Lord Roberts – where schoolboys were taken every New Year's Day to see the Wild Man of Borneo and the penny-farthing bicycle, under the watchful eye of Mrs Lyon, the curator.

Stern Realist Crabbe

30 November 1995

The first Christmas card – a robin redbreast – has just flown through the letterbox.

How many robins will there be in this house, plus stagecoaches, log fires, Santas, before mid-December?

Christmas seems to get earlier and earlier in the build-up, till by the actual date much of the excitement has been dissipated.

The TV adverts have been at it for weeks.

What can it be, for the two or three children of an unemployed man, to watch all those expensive treasures being offered (as if it was the inherent right of every child to splurge in such luxuries)?

The true treasure of Christmas is elsewhere, and doesn't have very much to do with money and possessions.

Let generosity flow by all means at the darkest time of the year. 'But does it bring the heart?' as the poet Browning said.

It's always a wonderful discovery when you think you've read nearly everything worthwhile, to come on a new author.

I've been very lucky this year. In March, at Don Cottage, I was much impressed by the Norwegian novelist Knut Hamsun – *Pan*, *The Growth of the Soil* – a name to put beside Thomas Mann and Tolstoy.

My neighbour Brian brought me a secondhand copy of *The English Parnassus*, an anthology of longer poems from Chaucer to Fitzgerald... I used to have a copy of it years ago, but it got lost.

I began to read, idly, a poem called 'Peter Grimes' by George Crabbe. (Crabbe was a poet we never read at school – maybe he flourished at an unfortunate time, between Pope and Wordsworth – and so tended towards diminishment between those two mighty pillars.)

I discovered a great storyteller in verse. After the tragic 'Peter Grimes', I turned to a poem descriptive of rural life in late-eighteenth-century England. We are apt to see that way of life – peasants and small tradesfolk and their masters – sentimentalised, even by great poets like Oliver Goldsmith and Burns ('The Cottar's Saturday Night') – all is steeped in a pastoral innocence and natural worth and charm. The stern realist Crabbe shows the opposite side of the coin. It is not a comfortable experience for the reader, especially when he concludes that life in every age and class and society is pretty much the same...

Maybe that's why we weren't given Crabbe to read at school – whatever happened, we were about to enter 'a vale of tears'.

If that were all, Crabbe would be simply depressing. He is redeemed by superlative craftsmanship, and a sense that, however much evil there is in the world, there is an abundance of good to contain it, like the 'chorus' of women in 'Peter Grimes' with their salves of pity and sorrow.

The other evening on TV there seemed to be little but Princess Di (the rich and privileged as well as the poor have their troubles – Crabbe was right), and the peace treaty between the Croats, the Bosnians, and the Serbs.

Maybe it required a strong man, like Tito, to hold such diverse cultures together.

Whatever happens, may the new-wrought peace last for a long time. (Yugoslavia reminds me of what Yeats said about Ireland – 'Much hatred, little room...')

A Stone Hymn to the Sun

21 December 1995

Today is the shortest day of the year – Winter Solstice – and it must have been a time of great worry for the first Orcadians, those who came after the retreat of the ice.

Ever since midsummer – a time they had greeted with dancing and fires – the sun had begun to dwindle. True the grass patches were long and lush, and the new lambs were growing, and there was abundance of fish and birds.

But the sun was making an ever-narrowing circle through the sky. Instead of going down to the northwest of Birsay, its setting-time was drawing closer to Hoy, as the summer passed and the shadows clustered.

In its shortest passage, the sun made a red and gold pyre on the Coolags of Hoy.

True, every winter hitherto the sun, after the time of bright stars and snow, had begun to revive, making wider arcs through the sky: and though the days were very cold and stormy (the very worst weather of the year) there was no doubt that the sun was renewing itself. It would, as every year, keep tryst with the new grass and the lambs and the shoals of fish and the wild flowers. Even the people who were older by a year, felt the new resurgence of life within themselves: old men sipped once more from the cup of spring-time and youth.

And yet the thinking men of the tribe – those with imagination, who looked before and after, and pondered the mystery of things – reasoned that this cycle of the sun might not necessarily last for ever. Nothing lasted for ever. Children became shepherds and fishermen and mothers, then they began to droop slowly deathwards. At last they lay silent and cold, among witherings and scant white hairs, and it was time for the ceremony of death to begin to be enacted.

For the dead islander, there was no new beginning, other than in his children and grandchildren... He himself was, if anything, a thin ghost in the cold and dank of death.

So it might happen with the sun.

There might come a winter in which there would be no miracle of renewing. No, the winter fire of the sun would cool to a glowing cinder and then go out, finally and for ever. And the tribe would perish in that last ice.

So they reasoned.

And to show that they had the welfare of the life-giving sun at heart (as well as, incidentally, their own welfare) they consulted with the quarry-men and the hewers of stones and the mightiest mason among them sketched plans on a sheepskin with a charmed stick.

They built, over a generation, a stone hymn to the sun on the moor between two lochs.

Then they attempted what seemed impossible, the building of a great sun-temple six or seven fields away. It was no easy task. Maybe two generations lavished their skill and strength on it. They made niches in the walls where dead chiefs and young dead princesses were laid.

There, along the corridor of Orkahowe, the sun entered at the solstice, and touched, with a golden finger, a tomb with the dead jewelled bones in it.

We must imagine, perhaps, a great cry of lamentation changing to a chorus of joy. The sun would not die. And even the dead would taste the chalice of immortality (who knows how?).

The New Year in the 1930s

28 December 1995

Hogmanay came in the early 1930s and it was nothing much for small boys.

Nothing happened in our house in Melvin Place except that a few neighbours and friends dropped by on New Year's Day, usually after dinner-time (roast beef, the only roast beef of the year).

Some years there was quite a crowd in the living-room. My father liked to sing Edwardian music-hall ballads, when he had drunk two or three small glasses with that yellow stuff in them. 'I'll Stick to the Ship, Lads', he sang, and 'A Beautiful Picture in a Beautiful Golden Frame', and 'Sweethearts and Wives'.

Jimmy Bruce the postman was forever urging my father to sing 'The Bible at Home', a very sentimental piece of religiosity. And, Jimmy Bruce would say, sipping the mysterious yellow liquid in his glass, 'I think that's the bonniest song that was ever written...'

Once, when my father was on his feet singing maybe 'Brighton, Brighton, I'll never go there any more', I decided to enquire deeper into the mystery of this yellow drink that impelled men to sing and tell extravagant stories, and behave in uncharacteristic ways, such as kissing ladies, laughing uproariously at nothing, or wiping a tear from their eyes...

So, I took a tiny sip out of my father's glass. Hellfire and brimstone! Poison and burning acid!... Ah, surely my tongue was burned in my mouth beyond mending. Surely my throat was so corroded I would never be able to speak again.

There and then I took a vow that never, should I live to be a hundred, would that dreadful drink called whisky pass my lips! Never.

I was glad to wash my palate out with my mother's home-made Crestona ginger wine.

Since then, I have to confess that I must have, over four or five decades, drunk a hogshead of whisky at least, and much trouble and distress it has caused me and my friends. But also it has given me hours of great joy, in which the world and all its tedium and grief were caught up in a wild Scottish reel. Life was worth living, after all. But I always went to bed with a bottle of Alka-Seltzer and a glass of water on the table.

Always, on New Year's Day, my father, in his Sunday suit with the ivory cross on his watch chain, took my brother Norrie and me to the Museum.

I think a lot of families did that on the 1st of January,

There, on her chair, sat Miss Lyon the curator.

Solemnly we paced past a row of Buddhas. We regarded the first clock ever in Stromness. We didn't think too highly of Hugh Miller's fossils, though my father looked at them with reverence, having a high regard for Hugh Miller.

The moth-eaten birds sat stuffed in cages. The mad eye of a hawk glared at us.

Ah, here was the exhibit we had come to see – the Wild Man of Borneo! He was carved out of wood, and most hideous to behold... It was worth a visit, just to see that primitive sculpture.

Going home, we met a boy in 'the grimmlings', who gave me a wallop on the head and ran away, chanting, 'A happy New Year, a bottle of beer, and a box on the ear.'

Homewards we trooped, to slices of Scotch bun and glasses of Crestona wine.

Warmth without Electricity

4 January 1996

How pleasant it was, last Sunday night, just to sit and do nothing.

Outside, the famous blizzard raged. There was no electricity, therefore no light (except for three candles), no radio, no TV. It's next to impossible to read by candlelight...

So I just sat on the couch all evening and did nothing, except to rake about the embers of memory, that flamed out here and there, now and again: much more delightful images than what might have been on the TV.

A kind neighbour, knowing that I have no gas, came at mid-evening with a flask of tea... Later, Archie and Anne Bevan came with my Christmas present, and we had a dram before the fire... What, incidentally, about the misguided folk who had opted to go all-electric? – What a fix they must be in; once the power lines get blown down by the blizzard...

Pour on more coal! – There are more delightful shows in the leaping lights and shadows in the grate than Christmas Eve on TV.

When Archie and Anne left, the blizzard had stopped but the ice on the balcony of Mayburn Court was like polished armour.

It seemed, said Archie, that there might be more snow.

Back I went to the contented dream-world on the couch, and the candle flickering like a small angel on top of the TV.

It was only next day that I heard of the roads blocked, the abandoned cars, the travellers lost in deep snow. That afternoon, at 4pm, I had been lucky to get the last taxi from Quildon to Mayburn Court, through the heart of the sheeting blinding shouting blizzard...

And then – a small domestic drama repeated all over Stromness, though not in the outlying parts of it – the Anglepoise light came on, and at the same time, the radio. That was about 11pm. I was able to hear the Midnight Nativity Mass from Bridlington, which was better than hearing no Mass at all...

'Go to thy cold bed and warm thee,' as poor mad Tom says in *King Lear*... Cold bed or no, I had one of the longest sleeps for a long time.

On Christmas Day we usually go to Langskaill in Kirbister, four miles away, for dinner. But there was no way of getting to Langskaill. The roads to the hinterland were all blocked.

Even Judge Stephen Tumim, who had come with Mrs Tumim to visit their daughter Matilda and her family at Outertown, couldn't get through. They had to abandon their car, too. 'Ah well,' said Judge Tumim over a dram of MacAllan malt (while I sat beside my half-built unlit fire), 'I'll be able to get on with the book I'm writing on prisons'...

My fire is responding quite well to my feeble efforts, considering that the regular fire-tender, Brian is away in Ayr for two and a half weeks... Thank goodness, all the same, that I got those storage heaters in two years ago – there are tides of warmth flowing everywhere through the house, while the snow piles even deeper outside.

One strange experience. I lay on the couch one afternoon watching a long programme about stage and TV comedians, the very cream of their humour... I thought to myself, 'Many more hearty laughs I've had in the Stromness bar and round the Pier Head with Attie Campbell, Billy Evans, John Broom and Arthur Swanson ... and with others in the old days.' Spontaneity is everything, the rich laughter that comes from the very sources of life, unbidden.

Even in the heart of winter.

Afternoon TV

18 January 1996

Being housebound for a few days, with little energy, not even to read, I watch too much television.

On TV, there is a group of Australian families caught up in some perpetual string of dramas. It is called *Neighbours* and is very popular with young people. I'm glad that, in our little neighbourhood in Stromness, there are few of these heart-wrenchings and deceptions, rages and reconciliations.

Maybe there is a human need for such goings-on: and, if so, it is better to watch it on the box than to have one's life touched by it... *Neighbours* has got me all mixed up, for I haven't got the complex relationships sorted out. Anyway, I don't intend to watch it more... The dialogue is not exactly spellbinding, nor is the Australian accent the most beautiful on this earth. Compare it for example, with the lovely Caribbean or Irish cadences, to which you could put poetry very well.

I suppose Australian is a bit better than South African, which is English at its ugliest, or nearly so.

Another quaint group of programmes, from America, are the 'confessionals', in which youngish men and woman sit before a studio audience and tell the most intimate details of their lives, the problems they're having with their girl or boy friends, or with alcohol or gambling or philandering – things which most people hide away in their heart's core... But no – out it all comes, and the audience loves it, and now and then somebody stands up and either upbraids or congratulates the person in the hot seat.

And if the show seems to be flagging, there is a lady who keeps it going the way a conductor handles a choir or an orchestra; and the lurid pot begins to bubble again. Everybody – even the man in the hot seat – seems to be enjoying it mightily.

But at last the great moment comes and the young lady who has been wronged in some way or another, is summoned by 'the conductor'. The curtains part, and the injured party appears, to mingled cheers and boos, and she gives her version of the story; and so the lemon gets squeezed dry. More often than not the lovers are reconciled. There are smiles all round, and the programme is sweetly and romantically rounded out, like in a Shakespeare comedy.

But I couldn't watch one of those shows more than once a month, at the most.

Perhaps it might go over big in Shopping Week, at the Town Hall. It's only a suggestion ....

I also watched, reclining on my couch and adding another lump of coal to the fire from time to time, one or other of the many game shows.

Some I wouldn't want to see again. But there is one called *Countdown* which can be quite compelling, because the people who take part in it are intelligent and delightful. It is a game of word-making from a random selection of letters, and of number-building from a few arbitrarily-chosen numbers, to arrive, by addition, multiplication, subtraction and division at a set grand total.

Letters is my trade, and so I ought to be good at the word-making, but my mind goes numb and after a few seconds I give up. It's amazing what words some of the contestants can achieve.

Strangely enough, I can do the numbers better.

That might be tried on a wet night in Shopping Week, but we'd have to have such delightful presenters as Richard Whiteley and Carol Vorderman.

I hope I won't be watching afternoon TV for very much longer.

Snow-times

1 February 1996

I am writing this in the last days of January, and the perpetual winds from the east are like a gang of ruffians with knives in their teeth stampeding up our Hamnavoe piers and closes.

What savage joy they have, especially at high tide, when they send the waves crashing against the pier right below Mayburn, and send dazzling torn sheets of spray across the Museum Pier and Flaws's Pier.

The fine scum of the waves is driven like thin cold mist and lies on our windowpanes, fine encrustations of salt, that will be washed away by the rain when it comes, eventually ... but, I feel, if this relentless wind were to shift a point or two to the north, it would not be rain that cleanses but the snow and ice that smothers and solders every window... One thinks of Christmas Eve, and shudders slightly.

January has turned its quern so fiercely and relentlessly that I have been virtually housebound since Yule, and I half forget what Stromness looks like!

But venture out I must soon: there are things that one can only do oneself – such as, operate the hole-in-the-wall, or cash dispenser; that took me a while to learn, but now I can manage it, just.

I think of January always as the fiercest month of the year – when Winter, knowing that its power is waning in the growing light, behaves as savagely as a cornered lion, and roars and slashes right and left: 'I'll show you all, there's life in the old King yet, though he seems bowed and white-bearded!'

So we pray for this ferocious tyrant to pass away, and for his gentler daughter February to assume her reign. See, she comes, snowdrops and crocuses spilling from her fingers.

But February is the true daughter of her father January, and has inherited many of his ways.

No snow, surely, in February!

Never believe it. A few years ago, in February, I had to see the eye specialist in the hospital in Kirkwall. The taxi had a clear run, going in. Going home again, after a sudden wild blizzard, Mrs Brass said we might make Stromness if we could get to the top of Hatston Brae. We got through, just.

A year or two later, I came home from shopping among a few lazy flakes. I was expecting two publishing friends, who had signed in at The Braes that afternoon. It was the last day of February... Half an hour later, I opened the door to two men who looked as if they had dropped by from the South Pole. My balcony was knee-deep in snow, all of Stromness was covered with a thick white quilt.

But March – by March it is equinox, springtime. Mighty gales, but no snow.

At the delightful cottage of Don – Tam and Gunnie being away on holiday – I got up at 4 or 5am to let the cat in, who was scraping at the window.

The window was frozen in its socket. The fields, all the way to the Black Craig, shone eerie white in the blue darkness ... the poor brae cat had to find what shelter he could.

March, maybe, has a fleeting snow-time. But April surely never... I remember, in Peter Esson's tailor shop, hearing how a bridegroom of a generation earlier, couldn't get through the snowdrifts to Sandwick for the marriage in the lyrical month of April.

The Mystery of Time

8 February 1996

I'm writing this on the last morning of January, having just had breakfast of an egg, toast and marmalade, and tea. (How good the first morning cup of tea is!)

Harry Lauder – who was the Billy Connolly of sixty years ago – used to sing: 'It's fine to get up in the morning / But it's better to lie in your bed...'

It's not fun at all to lie in bed if you're not sleeping, so I heave out of bed – having listened for an hour to politicians argue-barguing on the radio – at 8.30 every morning, and go into the cold kitchen and switch on the fan heater and the kettle and put bread in the toaster.

And soon breakfast is on the table, and the little kitchen is perceptibly warmer. And today is the last day of January, probably the most dreaded month of the calendar.

Children have curious notions of time. I never had difficulty in accepting that February comes at once after January and March after February, in the river of time flowing uninterruptedly through the year. Also that New Year follows Hogmanay on the stroke of midnight.

But, at the age of six or seven, I had great difficulty in accepting that one day flows into another at midnight, in the seamless garment of time.

Perhaps it was because my generation went to bed at 8pm or so, and woke up at 8am the next morning. What had happened meantime? It seemed to me that once Tuesday, say, ended, there was a great whirling chaos of night and darkness before Wednesday began.

I wonder if other children have had this difficulty?

The mystery of Time seems to obsess many writers in the twentieth century, though it is hardly mentioned by the great bards and novelists who preceded them.

T. S. Eliot, Priestley, Yeats, J. W. Dunne, Edwin Muir, Martin Amis are only a few of the writers intrigued by the mystery of Time. It has become one of the great themes of modern literature.

Maybe the scientists, especially Einstein, sparked off the latent curiosity in people's minds – where do we come from? What are we doing here? Where are we going...? The meaning of the mystery of being has been there for a very long time.

We have come to put so much faith in science to explain everything to us – every phenomenon, however difficult – that we swallow in its entirety the 'Big Bang' theory. Everything in the universe, from the pen I'm holding in my hand to the last star in the remotest galaxy, trillions of light-years away, started with this Big Bang.

We are entitled to ask, what was there before the Big Bang? And how did the Big Bang happen?

I have heard one or two bright young scientists on TV trying to enlighten us. I must say, their explanations were too subtle and difficult for me to grasp. The mystery remains, though rationalists for the last five hundred years have done their best to shed the light of common day on what remains utterly inexplicable.

The 'Big Bang' theory does nothing to satisfy the perennial human hunger for what is true and good and beautiful.

Indeed, the magnificent opening chapter of Genesis in the Old Testament does much more in the way of touching the mind and heart (though Bible reading is not in vogue nowadays).

> In the beginning God created the heaven and the earth. And the earth was without form, and void; and darkness was upon the face of the deep... And God said, 'Let there be light'...

This is a very serious vein to be writing about on the last day of January, when the songs of Burns and Up-Helly-Aa are still echoing among the stars in their courses.

Ingratitude Comes with Affluence

22 February 1996

A beautiful late winter morning it is, after the weekend storms.

It's good, to draw back the bedroom curtains and see sun on the gardens and roofs of Hamnavoe, at 8am.

And, downstairs, the sea through the harbour-facing window bright and blue.

It is like a morning near the beginning of time.

Whereas, last Friday and Saturday! – those forty-eight hours were like left-overs of old chaos.

There must have been similar days in my past – many of them – but this particular storm gnawed at my nerves as never before!

I suppose, as one gets older, bad weather becomes an ever-increasing nuisance, like some wild untamed creature feasting off blood and bones and mind.

And yet – such is the sense of ingratitude that comes with an age of affluence – there is a roof over your head and food in your cupboard and fire in your hearth; and we ought to be full of gratitude, thinking of the millions who lack such essentials.

Poor old King Lear, shut out in the storm, learned reality the hard way –

> Poor naked wretches, wheresoe'er you are,
> That bide the pelting of this pitiless storm,
> How shall your houseless heads and unfed sides,
> Your loop'd and window'd raggedness, defend you
> From seasons such as these?...
>
> ...Take physic, pomp;
> Expose thyself to feel what wretches feel,
> That thou mayst shake the superflux to them,
> And show the heavens more just...

I think gratitude is draining away from our civilisation. No wonder, the media are so much given to grousings and complainings. There is hardly a glad or a joyful voice raised from a society whose only concern, it seems, is to own a bigger better car, and fill the house with time-saving gadgets, and wonder about the next holiday in the sun...

And yet, when I was a child, Stromness was a poorer place materially than it is today; but there was more laughter along the street. And the women were happy looking after growing families, and even seeing to the laborious weekly washday in winter.

My mother, for example, sang about her household tasks all day long, like a bee among flowers – and occasionally, if she was moved about anything, she might utter a phrase in Gaelic.

And fancy, they didn't even have wireless or television! But their quality of life was probably, in spite of moderate poverty, higher than it is today.

It may have had something to do with the Ten Commandments and the Sermon on the Mount after all, and the fact that Stromnessians went, family by family, to one or other of the three kirks, on a Sunday.

Stromness is only a tiny microcosm within Western society. But I have seen a great change in our community since my childhood in the twenties and thirties.

How delightful the new Burns stamps are! I think they may be one of the best issues ever put out by GPO. The rose and the mouse are delightful, and the scripts and typeface delightful late-eighteenth-century.

Away back in 1959, there was a Burns issue, but not so striking, I think, as this present issue.

Thomas Hardy, too – I treasure a few of the stamps dedicated to him.

Maybe I've forgotten, but has there been a Shakespeare issue? As April 23 is both his birth-date and his death-date, there ought to be a Shakespeare stamp about that time, especially as the freshness and brightness of Spring came with unrivalled lyricism from his pen.

Young Girl at the Door of Spring

29 February 1996

Today, as you read this, is the 29th of February, a day that only happens every fourth year.

It seems that the earth takes rather more than 365 days to circle the sun, and so we need this quadrennial extra day. (But even so, you would think, there must be a few extra seconds and minutes more or less, every year: and how do they get gathered in?)

There's something good about February, in spite of the pier-tearing gales she has hurled at us this winter... The memory goes back to childhood, to having the first tea at five o'clock without lamplight... That was a wonderful annunciation of spring, to a child.

I'm certain that on the back of our school jotters, along with tables of measurements and weights, was the verse:

> Thirty days hath September,
> April, June, and November.
> All the rest have thirty-one,
> Excepting February alone
> That hath but twenty-eight days clear
> And twenty-nine in each leap-year.

It occurred to me only many years later what a strange little mnemonic verse it was.

Why should the briefest month get half the poem to itself – three lines – and another four months be allotted two lines? But the mighty months of the year – the heavyweights, with thirty-one days in their tally – are not even accorded the courtesy of a mention.

Not flowery July, not icy January, not March of the great gales, not May with its dews and legions of fish, not August of the golden sheaves, not December with its light-out-of-darkness, which mystery even the Maeshowe builders responded to with such joy and eagerness.

So, well done, February, that seems always like a young girl at the door of Spring, with a crocus and a snowdrop in her fingers.

The unspoken wonder of the growing light! We feel it instinctively, as children.

From November to January, the schoolchildren of Outertown (or 'Ootertoon', as it should be – those mapmakers have a lot to answer for) were let out of the classrooms earlier in the afternoons, so that they could be home before dark. But from February on, they kept the same hours as the town children.

The town children (or 'bairns' it should be) never gave a thought to what the country pupils had to endure on a stormy winter day, to get to the school and back again.

Many a drenching they got, many a wind-battering, many a snowstorm.

Whereas, a few wild leaps brought me and my town 'yamils' home to fire and lamplight and tea.

A Weakness for Paper

7 March 1996

Everybody, I think, has a desire for something that he or she doesn't need. A rich man wants more money. A travelled person wants to see Bohemia, say, or the Falklands, and generally he comes back no wiser than he set out. A collector dreams that he (or she) would be utterly happy if he could lay hands on this coin or that set of stamps, or a certain edition of a book (though it is freely available as a paperback).

I have a weakness for paper. Just blank sheets of paper, or writing pads, or spiral notebooks such as reporters use. I don't trust myself in Rae's shop, because there's a good chance I'll buy a notebook or a ream that I don't really need.

(As usual, Freudians would have an explanation for this compulsion, but I've long been tired of Freud and that lot.)

So, over the years, I find myself walled in with entrenchments of paper, enough for Shakespeare or Dickens to have written their complete works on.

I know I'll never get to the end of this multiplicity of paper, for I only use twenty or thirty sheets of varying sizes in a week. Yet the very fact that the paper is there, is a comfort to me – a reassurance – a spur to further effort – a challenge.

I don't know what I'd have done in my great-grandfather's time, when there were no sheets of paper other than in the minister's library, or in the factor's desk or on the lawyer's table.

I'm no good at *telling* stories; words are ineffectual and colourless in my mouth; but set me in front of a few sheets of paper, and images and rhythms jostle for utterance.

I would have been no good in a drinking hall of a thousand years ago, in Iceland or Orkney, when the sagas were being composed: but if some potentate – earl or bishop – said, 'These events should be written on vellum,' then I might have volunteered with ill-concealed eagerness... Ten to one, the real storyteller wouldn't have been able to read or write! (He 'couldn't have told a B from a bull's foot,' as Isaac Newlands said, long ago, to the sheriff in Kirkwall.)

So I'm very glad that, four generations ago, they built that school on the side of Brinkie's Brae; although, from a child's point of view, it was little more than a prison-house. At any rate, I was taught there to read and write.

How pleasant when Brian my neighbour comes back from the South with a huge box, crammed with 'punched' paper... How pleasant to handle a ream of real hand-made watermarked paper, the kind that only poems should be written on...

Sometimes, if there's no paper immediately to hand, I scrawl a few lines on the back of an envelope, or any random scrap that's been lying in my pocket for days or weeks.

The other day I wrote to a company in the South for a supply of a thousand address labels. There, in their leaflet, the company advertised addressed notepaper and envelopes.

As I said, I have enough paper to last well into the twenty-first century; but there – I really couldn't help it – I included writing paper in my order.

And may the green trees forgive me.

Rheumatism, Unwelcome Tenant

14 March 1996

For no reason at all, there was this flash of pain in the left foot! That was two days ago, and whenever I move, the knife goes in again.

Well, I don't worry overmuch about such things. The rheumatics, or gout, or whatever it is, has come irregularly over the past two decades; and after a week or two, has gone as mysteriously as it came.

And if it is not in the foot, it can be in the shoulder, or in the ball of the thumb, or in the lower back.

They say, nearly everybody in Orkney has rheumatism sooner or later: and they put it down to the damp climate, or the east wind, or the fact that we don't take enough fruit in our diet. (How did the Orcadians of two or three centuries ago fare, who never tasted an apple, an orange, or a pear in their lives? We don't read about them hobbling here and there on sticks and crutches.)

Or they say, it's hereditary, it runs in families. And certainly, in the early 1930s, my father was severely assaulted with rheumatism (it was called 'rheumatoid arthritis'), and it struck him first in the heel and the ankle. Being a postman, it must have been like working with a tight, spiked shackle on; but he persevered.

At last the trouble took complete possession of him, and went into his hands so that they became swollen and deformed; and that was no good for his second trade, which was a part-time tailor at Peter Esson's at the foot of the Kirk Road.

I remember the large quantities of aspirins he swallowed.

Men of his generation hated to be idle; in the last year of his life he got a job in Lyness as 'a hut-tender', for there was great activity there. And there he died, quite suddenly, in 1940.

He used to say that in the end, the pain left him entirely, having done its deforming damage...

So, with a little twinge in the foot or the thumb-joint, from time to time, I'm not complaining. Not yet, anyway. I haven't even taken an aspirin. But I whisper in a low voice to the pain in the left foot, 'I know you're there. Nobody invited you. You're not a welcome tenant. I'd be glad if you'd just pack up and clear out, as you've done in the past often. Above all, I don't want you claiming large parts of me, as you did with my father seventy years ago'...

There is a school of belief that there is such an ocean of pain in the world – most of it happening beyond our immediate horizons in places like Rwanda and in the deep rainforests of the Amazon and in the Caucasus and in the cities of Yugoslavia – that it is a kind of privilege to take on some of the burden, 'and show the heavens more just', as old tormented Lear shouted into the storm.

What's a crick in the neck, or a touch of neuralgia, in the world-tempest of suffering? Whether you agree with this pain-sharing philosophy or not, I must say it brings a slight relief, to think that one may be in some kind of unity with a wounded person in Sarajevo or the Caucasus or in Israel/Palestine.

But if the knife in my left foot were to become a tempest of daggers, I'd hobble in double-quick time to the jar of aspirins; and after that to the surgery asking for 'some sweet oblivious antidote'...

Storm and Satellite

21 March 1996

The equinoctial gales have set in early this year, with tumults of rain.

You get wet even walking down the steps to a waiting car.

Listening to Radio 4 yesterday afternoon, the weatherman said there would be storm-force winds over Orkney and Shetland later that night, and he even went further and said the East Mainland and the North Isles would bear the full brunt of it. (You wonder how they can be so precise as that.)

On the radio news there had been word of the Chinese satellite for years out of control, about to crash on to the earth, also tonight. It's as big as a house and is travelling at about a thousand miles an hour, and it has been crossing Britain on its wayward trajectory, like some drunkard of the skies, once or twice a day. Let it not choose to fall on Orkney – not on Stromness either – especially not on

Mayburn Court (or there won't be any 'Under Brinkie's Brae' more, if it does).

Quite apart from such a sensational event, we elderly householders worry about those storms that shake our houses a dozen times a year. (In childhood, a storm was a wonderful thing – you lay in your warm bed and exulted as the waves crashed against the pier below and the gale howled and shrieked in the lum. There was a feeling of total security.) But the same child, grown old, worries about chimney-cans being blown down, and rain seeping under the tightly-closed windows, and rotting the wood, and the cruel prolongation of winter. The daffodils, wiser than us, know how to wait.

Likewise, children would have been delighted about the Chinese rocket on its way back to earth.

About the year 1930, having been well nurtured on *The Wizard* and *The Rover*, we would have expected the sky-wanderer to land close to some big city like London, never in a few sea-washed islands like Orkney. A door would have opened in the side. A small man with a yellow face and slant eyes would have stepped out and announced the takeover of Britain and Europe and the Earth!... The guns brought to bear on this ambassador from some secret laboratory in the Gobi Desert – the defensive bullets would have drifted off him like confetti. Step by step he descends the steps, followed by a hundred or more similarly invincible invaders.

The world is done for! We ten-year-old readers of *The Wizard* understood all that well.

We also understood that somewhere a hero, a saviour, a fearless patriot was waiting; and that he and his intrepid lads would at last confront the invaders fearlessly, and though the odds seemed stacked against them overwhelmingly, the home boys would outwit and outmanoeuvre the aliens all along the line, and so save the British Empire and civilisation in general...

But those glories have vanished, with other outworn myths – and not before time, say many.

I heard on the early morning news that the satellite fell into the South Atlantic, after all.

William and Mareon Clark

4 April 1996

There ought to be a big party, open-air at Graham Place or the Pier Head, some time this year, because – if a date for the birth of Stromness has to be placed in some year – our town is four hundred years old.

Actually, in all fairness, the celebration ought to have been last year, 1995. But, better late than never.

In 1580 a feu charter was granted by Earl Robert Stewart to William Clark and his wife Mareon Chalmer, 'With power of brewing and selling, keiping of ostelrie and bying of al thingis appertening thairto for furnissing of the commounes and utheris resorting thairaway...'

In the Bishopric Rental of 1595 appears the entry, 'William Clairkis house now bigged'.

And so, the town of Stromness might be said to have begun, with William Clark's inn, at the end of the blue tongue of sea that is Stromness harbour. There is not a stone of the inn standing. It stood probably near where the new school is.

An inn is not built for a few fishing families and crofting families. They would have baked their own bread and brewed their own beer, and kept their own pigs and poultry.

Who, then, were going to eat at the Clarks' table and sit round their fine new peat-fire? Sailors, we must presume. And not only Scottish sailors, but the crews of French and Scandinavian and Dutch and Spanish ships seeking shelter from westerly gales.

America had been discovered. Bigger ships with wider spreads of sail were abroad on the oceans of the world. Merchants and skippers reckoned on cargoes and fortunes their fathers had never dreamed of.

Yes, it must have been common knowledge on the high seas that 'the shoreside of Stromness' was a good watering place.

And it was possible to get fresh fish and vegetables, beef and eggs and ale. But it took time to scour the countryside for those commodities, so welcome to men who had been at sea for weeks. Much more convenient to buy those provisions at an inn, a central gathering place.

And oh! the joy of sitting at an open fire drinking good ale, and eating steaks and new-baked bread, to sailors weary of the heave and toss of the sea...

We must think that William and Mareon Clark's venture was a great success. The nearby farms, Garson and Hemmigar and Howe would have been only too willing to stock the larders and cupboards of the new inn. And the fishermen of the growing hamlet of Hamnavoe, would have brought their haddocks and lobsters.

At the time of the lighting of the lamps with the ale-barrel flowing well, Clarks' Inn with all the foreign sailors would have been like a room in Babel...

Let's hope they all got on with one another – though, alas, there must have been a brawl or two.

Little did the good host William Clark imagine that, two and a half centuries later, there would be about forty drinking places in the flourishing town of Stromness...

The First Wash of Spring

11 April 1996

This morning – as I write – is April 3, and the first wash of Spring has gone over the earth.

It is such a beautiful word – April – that even to utter it lightens the heart. It is a little poem in itself. It is full of delightful images. It has its own music – little trembling lamb-cries at the end of a field. The first daring lark lost in light.

You feel, in April, that you have come through another winter, a little bruised maybe, but unbowed.

Those chalices of light, the daffodils, having been sorely battered by the March storms, are shedding, one by one, their green covers and opening their vernal tapers.

Soon all of Orkney will be stitched by golden threads of daffodils, a lovely spread garment for Primavera.

(Goodness, I seem to have got my images all confused there – chalices, tapers, coats – but one may be allowed a little exuberance, tasting now the first wine of Spring. Wine! There's another image to add to the heap!)

So we ought to relish each one of the thirty days of April, the month that tastes of childhood. Easter, too, often falls in April, and April the sixteenth is that wonderful day in the Orkney calendar, the martyrdom of St Magnus in Egilsay.

Most of the months in the calendar have their own beautiful names. May is when the cuithes[1] have their first drink of the floods, and come swarming in to keep their ancient tryst with men (and of course with women, too, I hasten to add, for you can't be too careful nowadays, with all those militant ladies around; and what about the children? – they have their own rites and secrets that are lost to us adults). But still with a word like mankind – who in their senses would want to use 'personkind'?

I have digressed a long way.

The word 'June' is beautiful too, of course, but like May it has a curtness that lacks the lyricism of 'April'. In midsummer there is perhaps too much – what month-name devised by man could hope to contain the light and multitudinous beauties of the season? Best to be simple and brief, to hold the word to the nostrils like a plucked wild clover... Such enchantment, under the light that never leaves the sky – not at midnight even. But, of course, in the name of progress and 'enlightenment' we have sacrificed the ancient ceremonies of midsummer, the fires on every hilltop in every parish and island. (There is a price to be paid for Progress; already the 'tabs' are being shown us, one after the other. But let that be, meantime.)

I had hoped to cut a swathe through all the month-names in the year. But alas I have run out of space – and besides, I'm sure we have been that way before; and if there is one thing a writer must beware of, it is to offer second-hand goods to his readers.

1 older coalfish